Studies in Caribbean Literature

An Introduction to the
French Caribbean Novel

STUDIES IN CARIBBEAN LITERATURE

The Novels of George Lamming
SANDRA POUCHET PAQUET

The West Indian Novel and its Background
KENNETH RAMCHAND

West Indian Poetry
LLOYD W. BROWN

An Introduction to the French Caribbean Novel
BEVERLEY ORMEROD

An Introduction to the French Caribbean Novel

BEVERLEY ORMEROD

*Senior Lecturer, Department of French Studies
University of Western Australia*

LONDON
HEINEMANN
KINGSTON PORT OF SPAIN

Heinemann Educational Books Ltd
22 Bedford Square, London WC1B 3HH
PO Box 1028, Kingston, Jamaica
27 Belmont Circular Road, Port of Spain, Trinidad

IBADAN NAIROBI
EDINBURGH MELBOURNE AUCKLAND
SINGAPORE HONG KONG KUALA LUMPUR NEW DELHI

Heinemann Educational Books Inc.
70 Court Street, Portsmouth, New Hampshire 03801, USA

British Library Cataloguing in Publication Data

Ormerod, Beverley
An introduction to the French Caribbean novel.
—(Studies in Caribbean literature)
1. Caribbean fiction (French)—History and criticism
2. French fiction—20th century
—History and criticism
I. Title   II. Series
843   PQ3944

ISBN 0-435-91839-7

Set in 9/10 pt English Times by Colset Pte Ltd
Printed and bound in Great Britain by
Biddles Ltd, Guildford and King's Lynn

FOR DAVID

Texts studied in this book

Aimé Césaire, *Return to My Native Land (Cahier d'un retour au pays natal)*, trans. John Berger and Anna Bostock, intro. Mazisi Kunene (Harmondsworth: Penguin Books 1969).

Jacques Roumain, *Masters of the Dew*, trans. Langston Hughes and Mercer Cook, intro. J. Michael Dash (London: Heinemann Caribbean Writers Series 12, 1978).

Edouard Glissant, *The Ripening*, trans. Frances Frenaye (New York: George Braziller, 1959). Forthcoming in Heinemann Caribbean Writers Series.

Joseph Zobel, *Black Shack Alley*, trans. and intro. Keith Q. Warner (London: Heinemann Caribbean Writers Series 21, 1980).

Michèle Lacrosil, *Demain Jab-Herma* (Paris: Gallimard, 1967).

Jacques Stephen Alexis, *Compère Général Soleil (Comrade General Sun)* (Paris: Gallimard, 1955).

Simone Schwarz-Bart, The Bridge of Beyond, trans. Barbara Bray, intro. Bridget Jones (London: Heinemann Caribbean Writers Series 27, 1982).

Contents

Acknowledgements   viii

Introduction: Writers in Search of Paradise   1

1   Fall and Redemption in Jacques Roumain's *Masters of the Dew*   17

2   The Freeing of the Waters: Edouard Glissant's *The Ripening*   36

3   The Plantation as Hell: The Novels of Joseph Zobel and Michèle Lacrosil   56

4   Paradise Redefined: The Marxist Vision of Alexis' *Comrade General Sun*   87

5   The Boat and the Tree: Simone Schwarz-Bart's *The Bridge of Beyond*   108

Conclusion   132

Bibliography   140

Index   146

Acknowledgements

Every member of my family, and all of my friends from the many islands of the West Indies, have contributed to my awareness of the fascinating variety and subtlety of West Indian social attitudes. To them all, I owe a debt of gratitude for setting me upon the path of exploration which led to the writing of this book. In particular, I should like to thank Sybil and Frederick Evans, and Vivienne Stedman, who have shared with me their memories and insights into Jamaican history; Kathleen Wilson, who has faithfully kept me in touch with Caribbean events during my years on the other side of the world; Hazel Evans, who instilled in me her love of the French language and so opened my first window on to the Francophone world; and Ivy Wilson, Iris Loeffler, Olive McIntosh and Erma Arnold, who have all given me something precious of the West Indian past.

This study was mainly written thousands of miles away from the islands with which it is concerned. Throughout its composition, my husband provided me with an essential link with the West Indies. I am deeply appreciative of his unfailing interest and support, and of his lucid, generous and constructive comments upon each stage of the manuscript. I dedicate this book to him with my love.

It is a pleasure to record my gratitude to Danielle Morris, for her patience and skill in the typing of my manuscript; to the University of the West Indies, for the research grant which enabled me, in 1968, to make my first visit to the French-speaking islands of the Caribbean; and to the University of Western Australia, for the study leave in 1980 which allowed me to return to the West Indies in order to gather additional material for this book. I am also indebted to Professor J.R. Lawler, Professor C.D. Boak, and the Board of Regents of the University of Wisconsin for granting me permission to use material which previously appeared in sections of the following articles of mine published in journals edited by them: 'Césaire's *Cahier*: An Aesthetic of Commitment', *Dalhousie French Studies* (1, 1979); 'Fall and Salvation Motifs in Césaire's *Cahier* and Theatre', *Essays in French Literature* (19, 1982), and 'Beyond Négritude: Some Aspects of the Work of Edouard Glissant', *Contemporary Literature* (15, 1974).

Introduction

Writers in Search of Paradise

'Islands that are scars upon the water'[1]

The concept of a lost paradise is one of the most plangent and enduring motifs in western literature. For the erudite reader, its associations may be explicitly tied to the Christian concepts of man's Fall and his expulsion from the Garden of Eden, his entry into the harsh realities of daily sweat, sorrow and mortality; or they may recall Ovid's Golden Age and the gentle world of Greek pastoral, bathed in sunlight and sensuous pleasures, a world of eternal innocence and joy. But at a more immediate level of response, every adult human being can identify in his own life a sense of loss as the passing years withdraw from him the delights and hopeful dreams of youth. Time guards the gates of the Eden of childhood as sternly as any angel with drawn sword; there is no returning to that era of simplicity and optimism, with its divine illusion of permanence.

The universal theme of man's loss of Eden takes on a particular poignancy in the literature of the Caribbean islands, where it is inevitably related to the historical experience of slavery. The moment when Africans were captured and sold into slavery: the moment of dispossession and uprooting, which deprived a race of its rightful inheritance, its freedom, its culture and religion, its very language, is felt to be indeed an expulsion from a Golden Age. The very scale of the disaster – an estimated 20 million Africans transported to the New World during the three centuries of the European slave trade, 5 million of them destined to work, and die, in the West Indian canefields[2] – lends it the proportions of the archetypal cosmic myth. The motifs of loss and exile, with their accompanying melancholy, are to be found even in the popular lyrics of the Caribbean, often expressed through the biblical imagery that is now second nature to the descendants of Christianized slaves:

> By the rivers of Babylon
> Where we sat down
> And there we wept
> When we remembered Zion.
> For the wicked carried us away
> Captivity
> Require from us a song
> How can we sing King Alpha song
> In a strange land?[3]

Africa, then, is not so much a geographic entity as a talisman, a symbol of the vanished bliss which preceded enslavement, a time associated with innocence and natural joy, comparable to the pastoral world of childhood. The French Guyanese poet Léon Damas, whose *Pigments* (1937) was a turning-point in militant black literature, implicitly compares Africa before slavery to the

1

privileged state of childhood in demanding that Europe restore to him the dolls from which his ancestors were torn:

> Give me back my black dolls
> let me play with them
> naive, spontaneous games . . .
> become once more myself
> myself renewed
> from what I was Yesterday
> yesterday
>   free of complexes
>   yesterday
> when the time of uprooting came[4].

The ideas of uprooting and separation from self in this poem, which is entitled 'Limbé' (nostalgia), like the phrases 'carried us away' and 'in a strange land' of the popular song, underline another aspect of the catastrophe, felt instinctively even at grassroots level. Slavery was the starting-point of alienation, loss of pride in one's race and of confidence in oneself. The cruelties of the colonial era and the harsh realities of the present have served to perpetuate this state of alienation, mirrored at a literal level by the waves of emigration among West Indians lacking belief in the viability of their islands, or simply faith in the possibility of personal fulfilment in the land of their birth. Emigration, at once an act of escape and of seeking, at its most extreme expresses a perception of the West Indies as 'captivity' and a belief in the existence of a Promised Land through which the state of paradise can be reattained. For many, the Promised Land is America or Europe: V.S. Naipaul has graphically recorded the joy of the island scholar discovering the intellectual pleasures of England and his horror when, lulled to sleep by his electric fire, he dreams he is back in tropical Trinidad.[5] For many others, from the French Caribbean contemporaries of Damas to the Rastafarian cultists of today, it is Africa that promises healing and happiness: an unknown yet trusted Africa, still the 'imaginary continent' which Sartre perceived as the well-spring of the *Négritude* movement.[6]

The title of Aimé Césaire's *Cahier d'un retour au pays natal* (literally, *Notebook of a Return to My Native Land*), the best-known and probably the most influential work in French Caribbean literature, ostensibly refers to a return to the poet's own island of Martinique after years spent in a state of spiritual exile in France. But as the poem unfolds, that state of exile is increasingly identified with the inner experience of alienation, and the 'return' of the title becomes a return to the poet's true self through a rediscovery of his African roots. Like Damas, Césaire portrays the enslavement of his ancestors as a massive injury to which the Caribbean islands themselves still bear mute witness:

> Islands that are scars upon the water
> islands that are evidence of wounds.   (p. 82)

Through the image of scars on the water – which echoes other metaphors of shipwreck and waterlogged debris, suggestive of warped and capsized lives, of defeat and catastrophe (pp. 37, 41, 60, 83) – Césaire seeks to convey his tragic sense that the society which he describes is still crippled, still floundering in a wilderness of racial and cultural deprivation that was triggered by the initial disaster of slavery. In its idiosyncratic reworking of the myth of Eden, the *Cahier*'s treatment of the themes of Fall and Redemption, with its constant fusion of poetic image and social reality, has set the pattern for modern Caribbean writing. Since the *Cahier*'s first appearance in 1939, the major literary works to emerge from the French Caribbean have all accepted Césaire's basic premise of a historic loss and of the need to devise present strategies to overcome the consequences of this loss. West Indian writers, whether novelists, poets or playwrights, are almost never adherents of the doctrine of art for art's sake. The authors to be examined in the present study are all concerned with giving imaginative expression to the psychological and political problems of the islands, all strongly committed to the rehabilitation of an alienated people and the fostering of social change.

Césaire himself, like his close friend and contemporary in Africa, Léopold Sédar Senghor, belongs to a generation which has attempted to combine two methods of healing the wounds inflicted by colonialism: on the one hand, by playing an active political role in the development of their countries; on the other, by writing works destined to promote the concepts of *Négritude*: the affirmation of black pride and dignity, the diffusion of black – sometimes specifically African – cultural values. Césaire's political intentions are clearly announced in the *Cahier*: like Christ, he comes with a sword to reform society and cleanse it of abuses; like the African witch-doctor, he will draw upon magic powers to re-create the quality of life in his native land. With the image of the ship's figurehead ('Make of my head a prow', p. 77) he declares his candidature for the leadership of a new Martinican nation. In the decades that have elapsed since the publication of the *Cahier*, his political stature has grown, but his powers remain limited by the fact that the French Caribbean islands, apart from Haiti, are still owned and ruled by France. Their official status as Departments of France has not greatly altered the realities of political and cultural colonialism: the high school courses, radio and television programmes sent from France, the French officials appointed to key positions, even the weekly Air France arrivals of French fruit and vegetables for consumption by white expatriates and a Europeanized middle class. The government's lack of encouragement for traditional agriculture, the saturation of the information services with news of the most remote provinces of metropolitan France at the expense of news about events in neighbouring West Indian islands, are further aspects of the official policy of assimilation with France and the desire to prevent any popular stirrings towards autonomy or a sense of pan-Caribbean solidarity. This deliberately created cocoon of isolation has not, however, been able to contain the increasing tension of the population, which has expressed itself in sporadic manifestations of violent discontent. Césaire's last play, an adaptation of Shakespeare's *Tempest* for black theatre, protests anew against the social and psychological damage done by colonialism, personified by a Prospero whose mission is to protect civilization from the invasion of the jungle. In *Une tempête* (1969) Caliban adopts the stance of the black reformer whose twin goals are political independence, and freedom from the false self-image which Prospero has imposed upon him. His cry of defiance – 'To take back my island and regain my freedom'[7] – could as easily have come from the passionate pages of the early *Cahier*, and the ongoing French presence in Martinique and Guadeloupe no doubt explains the strong thematic continuity and nationalistic commitment in the literature of these islands over recent decades.

Introduction

The *Cahier* is built upon themes that will be returned to constantly by later writers: the devastating loss of pre-colonial Africa, seen as a paradise of freedom, dignity and physical well-being; the weary centuries of slavery and their heritage of hardship and oppression; the need for salvation from a continuing condition of inferiority and alienation. The author considers the psychological make-up of his fellow West Indians to be still influenced by the memory of slavery, and still affected by an unacknowledged rancour against Africa – 'Africa which is reproached for not having protected her children, or for having handed them over, but which, at the same time, still has the secret savour of a lost paradise'.[8] Césaire was not the first Caribbean writer to portray Africa with nostalgia, nor indeed the first to perceive the profound ambivalence in West Indian attitudes to this distant mother country: a source, perhaps, of intellectual pride, and yet a source of private shame. The writers of the Harlem Renaissance, several of whom were of Caribbean origin, had consciously sought to explore their sense of African identity in the 1920s; in the same era, the Haitian anthropologist Jean Price-Mars had published a study of ancient African civilizations and of African survivals in Haitian folk-ways, which urged a generation of novelists and poets to weave these despised peasant customs into the fabric of their work.[9] Césaire was, however, the first to explore, in sustained poetic and dramatic works, the nature of the West Indian's uneasy relationship with Africa, and to link this relationship with the dynamics of social behaviour in the Caribbean today. He was the first to make poetry out of the deep sense of loss and wrong, the despair and self-contempt of the Caribbean proletariat. Like Milton's angel who tells the fallen Adam that while he can never return to the Garden of Eden, he may find 'a paradise within [him], happier far',[10] Césaire suggests that although Africa can never be regained, a different kind of release and restoration may be sought through the acceptance of racial identity and the possibility of reintegration into society at a new level, with a Caribbean allegiance, and in a context of freedom and harmony.

It is possible to read the *Cahier* solely as a poetic expression of the state of fallen Caribbean man, together with an affirmation of the poet's self-assumed task as Redeemer. Viewed in this light, the work abounds with bitter statements concerning the maimed and desolate condition of the inhabitants of Martinique. The opening sequence of the *Cahier* (pp. 37–42) presents a town which lies prostrate and ignominious. Within the space of a few lines, a profusion of adjectives drives home the themes of defeat and mutilation: 'this town, flat, displayed, brought down . . . inert . . . sullen . . . dumb, thwarted . . . set upon, gnawed, reduced'. An implicit parallel is drawn between the humbled, flattened town and the figure of Christ on his way to the Crucifixion in the phrase 'breathless under its geometric burden of crosses'. Life within the town is characterized by disease and deformity, and by a frightening sense of darkness, immobility and menace; the music of the stars is as dead as a smashed *balafong* – the image of this broken African xylophone suggesting a brutal disruption of former black harmony. The leitmotif of a fall from grace recurs when the poet describes the Martinicans' eager anticipation of joy at Christmas. Their hopes, based on illusions, rise dizzily upwards, only to fall back to earth as a fruit drops and splatters. This downward plunge bursts open the life inside the huts 'like an over-ripe pomegranate' (p. 43) – and the image of the pomegranate recalls the legend of Proserpina, who by tasting this fruit destroyed her own hope of returning from the Underworld to be reunited with her mother in the light of the upper air. The motif is repeated in a later modulation where the false, rum-induced ecstasy of the Christmas singers soars and then plummets back into fear, anguish and the dread of hell-fire. These illusory hopes, these desperate and futile gestures, are aspects of a spasmodic and instinctive striving after what has been forever lost. 'Trying to bring back the golden shower of privileged moments, the umbilical cord redrawn in its frail splendour' (p. 42): by evoking the links between childhood, Eden and joy, such phrases suggest the tragic sense of being fallen which haunts the descendants of the transported African slaves. The poet's desire to return to his native land is also a desire to find that land somehow miraculously transformed into the paradise of the West Indian communal dream: 'always at the distance of a mirage, an earth – a thousand times more native, golden with a sun no prism has sampled – a fraternal earth where all is freed, my earth' (p. 50). In ironic defiance of the Christian – European – angels who, like customs officers (p. 57), bar the entrance to Eden, the poet seeks to create his own paradise by means of pagan incantation destined to suggest a return to his African roots:

> voom roh oh to let my own skies
> open . . .

> Voom roh
> fly away
> . . . higher
> than witches towards other stars . . .

> voom roh oh
> let the promised time come again.   (pp. 58–9)

But all the time, the reality before his eyes is no more than an empty simulacrum of real life (p. 51), and his compatriots – these few thousand death-bearers who turn round and round within the hollow calabash of the island (p. 52) – carry within themselves, like Adam's doomed descendants, the seeds of their own destruction. Images of deprivation and bondage ('I am cut off from the fresh oases of fraternity', p. 51; 'This horizon is too sure/and nervous as a gaoler', p. 52) link the poet with the fallen state he observes in those around him.

This critical and pessimistic view of present-day life in the West Indies reappears, and is indeed taken for granted, in all the important works published by French Caribbean writers since the appearance of the *Cahier*. At the same time, no writer is content simply to offer an objective portrayal of grim reality. Each attempts to suggest a solution, a path towards salvation. In the *Cahier* itself, Césaire sets against the image of fallen Caribbean man the figure of a future Redeemer. He seeks to be the steward, the trustee, of his race, sowing the seeds of change, bringing his island to a time of harvest and rejoicing (p. 77). At one level, this desire is expressed in terms of African healing: the poet implicitly assumes the role of the witch-doctor whose lips know how to suck the poison from wounds, whose hands can unfasten the iron rings that bind the ankles of slaves (p. 82). At another level, by deliberate verbal echoes of biblical imagery, expressions and rhythms, Césaire transposes the traditional gestures of Christ to a secular and specifically Caribbean context. In such passages he himself takes on the role of the Messiah come from afar to save his people:

> I would arrive sleek and young in that country, my country, and I would
> say to that country whose clay is part of my flesh: 'I have wandered far
> and I am coming back to the lonely ugliness of your wounds' . . .
> And I would say to it:
> 'My mouth shall be the mouth of misfortunes which have no mouth,
> my voice the freedom of those freedoms which break down in the prison-
> cell of despair.'   (p. 50)

Christ's identification of himself with the poor and oppressed makes him not only the Saviour, but the ally and symbol of the fallen. As he suffered, was mocked and defiled by the authorities of his day, so did the slave ancestors of Césaire experience torment and degradation. This analogy is suggested in a section of the *Cahier* whose starting-point is a mention of sugar-cane, symbol of Europe's greed for a profitable trade which depended upon the exploitation of African slaves. For this historical reason, cane is associated in the *Cahier* with abjection: 'For centuries this country repeated . . . that we are walking manure hideously proffering the promise of tender cane' (p. 67). In the follow-ing passage, the mention of the plant leads immediately to the ancestral memory of captivity and then, directly, to the evocation of the Christ-slave's victimization and martyrdom, the biblical crown of thorns being replaced by the prickly *datura* or thorn-apple. At each stage the poet is present in a dif-ferent guise, first as the child born into slavery, then as the harried African ancestor, and finally as the Christ-figure, dignified and defiant, paraded like an animal within the circle of his captors:

> – On a road I am a child chewing
> a sugar-cane root.
> – On a bloody road being dragged
> I am a man with a rope round my neck.
> – Upright in the middle of an immense circus
> on my black forehead is a crown of thorn-apple.   (p. 58)

The role of this black Messiah is clearly defined as a revolutionary one: he is to begin the End of the World (p. 60). The implications here are twofold. At one level, he prophesies immediate upheaval, reversal of the existing social order which outrages him by the injustices and indignities which it heaps upon the black in particular, and upon the proletariat in general. While the poet speaks above all for his own race, desiring to be the father, brother, son and lover of a unique people (p. 77), the *Cahier* implicitly accepts the Marxist doctrine of the brotherhood of all the exploited, all the victims of capitalism. Césaire, who was to resign from the French Communist Party in protest at the Soviet Union's invasion of Hungary in 1956, previously believed for many years that Marxism was free of paternalism, and genuinely in sympathy with nationalistic aspirations, with *Négritude* and with the goal of black self-determination.[11] By identifying the problem of the proletariat with the colonial problem (as Césaire himself did in his *Discours sur le colonialisme* of 1955), Marxism promised to transcend the barriers of race throughout the world. This political sense of unity in a common cause is evident in the *Cahier*, which links the West Indian proletarian with the Jew, the Kaffir, the Calcutta Hindu, the voteless man in Harlem: every underdog is the 'famine man, curse man, torture man' (p. 48), who may be seized at any moment, beaten or even killed with no need for excuse or future accounting to anyone. The vision of social justice, so ironically similar in the Gospels and in the Marxist creed, is reiterated by the *Cahier*'s Redeemer-figure who strives to satisfy a universal hunger, to quench a universal thirst (p. 78). Communism's promise of a revolutionary change in class structure was to retain a strong intellectual and emotional appeal for future Caribbean writers confronted by glaring and unacceptable inequalities in the existing social order of their islands.

At the same time, the notion of the End of the World has clear apocalyptic associations, suggesting both the judgement and punishment of the wicked (the exploiters), and the resurrection of the innocent (the descendants of the enslaved), to be restored to union with the Redeemer and a place in paradise. Several key passages of the *Cahier* have an apocalyptic theme. In the first, the dormant Martinican volcano – symbol of apathy and a timorous absence of protest among the inhabitants – is seen as suddenly erupting at some future hour when naked waters will sweep away the stains of the present (p. 38). The second is again a prediction of the future volcanic eruption, but this time the natural catastrophe is presented on a still more grandiose scale, with continents breaking their moorings and lands cracking apart before the pressure of exploding rivers, while the resurgent courage of the oppressed wins them a new life springing from the dungheap of the old (pp. 70–1) – just as the slaves who were the 'walking manure' of the canefields will eventually rise up with the slender, sturdy grace of the *filao* or casuarina (p. 92), symbol of resistance and evergreen fidelity. The third passage prophesies the future alliance of the poet and his native land, no longer flat, inert, sprawling in degradation, but upright like the Christ-figure with his thorn-apple crown, listening to a voice from above that bores through the night 'like the sting of an apocalyptic wasp' (pp. 84–5), proclaiming that no race holds a monopoly of beauty, intelligence and strength, that it is up to man to conquer all rigid prohibitions and assume his rightful place among his peers.

Future fertility and spiritual renewal are also suggested by surrealistic images, such as that of the pearly revolt of the dolphins breaking the shell of the sea (p. 73). The dolphin is a traditional Christian symbol of resurrection and salvation; the shell, an ancient womb symbol and prophylaxis against sterility, is also an emblem of hope, resurrection and regeneration.[12] As the images of volcanic eruption and tidal waves express the poet's vision of a future revolution, so do metaphors of flowing blood, explosive rhetoric and sexual energy – rape and violent birth, or rebirth – mirror the assumption by the black man of an independent destiny:

> I break open the yolk-bag
> that separates me from myself
> I force the great waters that gird me with blood.   (p. 62)

> Words? We are handling
> quarters of the world, we are marrying
> delirious continents, we are breaking down
> steaming doors,
> words, ah yes, words! but
> words of fresh blood, words which are
> tidal waves . . . and lavas and bush-fires.   (pp. 61–2)

Introduction

In gentler, but still prophetic, passages, the poet uses the image of a ship to suggest a positive forging ahead towards new and ardently desired freedoms. Yet the voyage suggested is not one of escape, but rather one of return to a known and long-lost Eden. The scarred islands in the encircling water take on the appearance of a beautiful hull which the poet caresses with his ocean hands, steering it back to its true path (p. 83). The slave-ship of the past is transformed into a vigorous canoe which moves stubbornly through the assaults of the waves to dance a triumphant dance as it enters the safety of the harbour (p. 79), greeted by the *lambi*, the Caribbean conch-shell, blown to announce good tidings. The happy landfall brings the poet and his race to 'future orchards', 'heady sweet blossoms', 'the succulence of fruit' (p. 78). So the revolutionary images and the sea voyage lead us back to the essential notion of the lost garden of paradise. The primal associations of paradise and childhood are reasserted at the cosmic level in the concluding lines of the *Cahier*: 'bind my black resonance to the very navel of the world' (p. 92). Here, too, the image of the rising dove offers a joyous counterpoint to the earlier melancholy leitmotif of the Fall. Attribute of Venus and emblem of lovers' caresses, but also the enduring symbol of peace and harmony, the dove soars through the sky in a vertical flight which suggests both sexual energy and a movement of purification.

The *Cahier* is a poem, not a political manual, and it is poetically vague about the precise means whereby the Redeemer-figure will save his race. But alongside its message of the need for social and political reform, there is also an urgent attempt to convince the individual West Indian reader that if he accepts European values passively, he is opting for shame, bitterness and self-destruction, joining those 'who never get over being made in the likeness of the devil and not in the likeness of God' (p. 86), those who have capitulated to the traditional European estimate of blacks as inferior, unworthy, second-rate. The path away from such a state of alienation is, for Césaire, the path of *Négritude*. At the heart of Caribbean alienation is the shame of being descended from African slaves. The cure proposed is to revise the Caribbean conception of Africa – borrowed from European slave-owners – as a backward, savage and contemptible country. In the decades before the *Cahier* was composed, the European surrealist movement had brought primitive art forms into fashion; African sculpture was being seen as valid and beautiful in its own right, no longer as a mere deviation from a European aesthetic norm. Along with the primitive, the irrational and the instinctive had come into vogue. For Césaire, these surrealist notions had far more to offer to blacks than to Europeans; in a 1977 radio interview[13] he made the point that they enabled him to free himself from the French cult of logic, and showed him the way to present Africa to his compatriots as a source of legitimate pride, praising it for the very qualities which had formerly attracted European derision. Africa was not reason, but emotion, instinct, spontaneity, an intuitive art of living. To be born black was to share a birthright of mystical union with all the forces of nature. *Négritude* 'plunges into the red flesh of the soil [and] the blazing flesh of the sky'; it is the silo that stores and ripens 'all of the earth that belongs most to the earth' (pp. 74–5). This cluster of images linking human sexuality with the vigour and fruitfulness of nature, which forms one of the climactic moments of the *Cahier*, is an ecstatic expression of Césaire's belief that he had found the key to a new, positive, healing self-image for every member of his race.

If later black writers have not quarrelled with Césaire's indictment of colonialism, or denied his vision of the Caribbean islands as alienated and fallen, few, however, have been willing to accept Césairean *Négritude* as a solution to the identity crisis of the West Indian. The rediscovery of African roots is now an accepted enterprise at both the personal and the political level in some of the independent islands, but the *Cahier*'s perception of emotion and intuition as exclusively black qualities, with its concomitant – if implicit – acceptance of intellectual excellence as an exclusively white property, is rejected by contemporary black intellectuals as a romantic, and insulting, fallacy. The *Cahier*'s celebrated praise of the irrational is understandable in its historical context, that of French surrealism in the 1920s and 1930s, when instinct was glorified and reason became a dirty word. On those terms, Césaire's mystical vision of Africa as a pre-Cartesian paradise could not be mistaken for an insult; it was, on the contrary, a paean of the most hyperbolic order:

> Heia for those who have never invented anything
> those who never explored anything
> those who never tamed anything
>
> those who give themselves up to the essence of all things
> ignorant of surfaces but struck by the movement of all things
> free of the desire to tame but familiar with the play of the world
>
> truly the eldest sons of the world
> open to all the breaths of the world
> fraternal territory of all breaths
> undrained bed of the waters of the world
> spark of the sacred fire of the world
> flesh of the flesh of the world pumping with the very movement
>   of the world. (p. 75)

Essence, movement, breath, water, fire and throbbing flesh: the passage is bent on evoking the physical, the domain of the senses, of self-abandonment to play and gesture: of fruitful reality, one might say, as opposed to vain abstraction. Viewed in a less sympathetic light, however, the lines are also suggestive of a passive acceptance of – almost a willing subjection to – the experience of invasion: being porous to the penetration of the winds, lying prone beneath the weight of the waters, pulsating only when set into motion by the outer motion of the world itself. These, according to the *Cahier*, are the ancestral virtues of Africa; and confronting them are the dynamic attributes of Europe: invention, exploration, conquest. There is little here to comfort those descended from slaves upon whom passivity was forcibly imposed: whose subjection was the direct outcome of the energetic and dominating thrust of Europe.

Moreover, in the terms of the *Cahier*, to embrace rhythm, intuition and emotion was to reject Europe's cult of reason in favour of a divine and savage insanity, a 'flaming madness' (p. 55). This divorce between white reason and black instinct, sensuousness, un-reason, is the most controversial aspect of the *Cahier*. Frantz Fanon, the Martinican psychiatrist and political militant, sardonically recalls in *Peau noire, masques blancs (Black Skin, White Masks)* his initial enthusiasm for Césaire's promise of salvation through the irrational, and his progressive disillusionment with a concept which ultimately served to reinforce popular prejudices against the 'backward' and 'primitive' nature of the black man – the simple (rather than noble) savage.[14] In more recent years, Wole Soyinka has lucidly criticized the way in which *Négritude*, although eager to defend the black race against the charge of being inferior, apparently saw no need to question, much less refute, the European premise that the black man is incapable of analytical thought and scientific inventiveness. It preferred to assert that while he *is* different from the white man, he is *equally* worthy of admiration for his intuitive sensibility.[15] To say that instinctive understanding (equated by, for example, Senghor[16] with African dance, rhythm, capacity for sexual pleasure) is a sign of human development equal to European abstract reasoning may be a valid metaphoric statement, but it has little to do with the social and political dilemmas of the Caribbean today, and would seem, moreover, to propose a truncated form of experience as an ideal way of life. It is noticeable that in the 1977 radio interview already mentioned, while Césaire defends *Négritude* as still being a valid and important concept, he now does so on the grounds that its stress on emotion and humanity is a useful corrective to the priorities of white technology, which has put men on the moon but has not eradicated the world-wide problem of hunger. He has moved away from surrealistic metaphor to straightforward political statement.

Yet the *Cahier* is by no means a passive or abstract text: it forces upon the reader the poet's own sense of outrage, and obliges him to recognize the intolerable nature of living conditions – both moral and material – which for too long were taken for granted as inevitable and unchangeable. It mercilessly depicts the prevalence, and the dangers, of apathy, widespread even among those who should be most vitally concerned with the need for reform. The clamouring crowds in the streets of Fort-de-France are accused of disowning the true cry of protest that they should utter, of being strangely blind to their own hunger and misery: lacking solidarity, unwilling to affirm the need for freedom, paradoxically 'garrulous and dumb' (p. 39). But there is compassion in the accusation: the present-day silence and inertia are seen as symptoms of an alienation which has its roots in the past, when the slave could make no effective protest against the brutality of his owner, when his choice lay between the false, ingratiating smile of acceptance or the abortive revolt, and the only sounds were those made by his tormentors:

> O quiet years of God on this clod of an earth
> and the whip argued with the swarming flies over the
> sweet dew of our wounds.   (p. 87)

Passivity and resignation, suggested not only by the metaphor of the dormant volcano but by other images of throats blocked or impaled (pp. 59, 65) and trumpets absurdly muted (pp. 53, 64), are associated with sexual emasculation (of which the town itself is a symbol, unable to 'stand up and pierce the sky with its protest', p. 45) and the stagnancy of swamps and lagoons choked with the blood of doomed rebellions (pp. 53, 64). In opposition to these despairing motifs, the poem sets up a network of positive, optimistic images of action, forcefulness and successful revolt. They are largely inspired by the poet's very real sense of a sexual vigour already present in the Caribbean landscape, and forming the backdrop to the *Cahier*: the plump breasts of the hills, the upright palm-trees, the rushing waterfalls, the wild sucking of the sea along the windward shores. At the metaphorical level, the physical presence of the land ('stretched earth/drunken earth/earth great sex raised in the sun', p. 49) corresponds to the phallic energy of *Négritude* with its mystical simultaneous penetration of earth and sky (p. 75). The same vertical movement is linked with Toussaint Louverture's defiance of the French and his liberation of the Haitian slaves at the end of the eighteenth century:

> a man alone defying the white
> cries of a white death . . .
> an old nigger standing upright against
> the waters of the sky   (pp. 53-4)

and it is echoed in Césaire's vision of the day when the prostrate blacks in the hold of the slave-ship will rise to their feet, metamorphosed into captain and crew of their own destiny, upright at the helm and the compass, fearlessly advancing in the wind and the sun (pp. 88-9). The apocalyptic eruption of the volcano is the ultimate phallic symbol of revolutionary protest and fruitful change.

The *Cahier*, then, contrasts its perceptions of self-defeating apathy and resignation with a dynamic projection into a radically altered future, and further creates a heroic protagonist who is not only the saviour but also the lover of his race, borrowing the energies of sea and wind to lick, to caress, to shape, move and control (p. 83). Its major themes and images acknowledge contemporary disaster, yet fire the imagination of all those who ardently desire reform. Although some of the key premises of Césaire's *Négritude* have been ignored or rejected by later Caribbean writers, most of their work may be seen as a series of variations upon the central themes of the *Cahier*: the mourning of a past loss and a fallen state; the search for escape from present wretchedness; the vision of future release, of salvation through a personal spiritual renaissance or through some magical redemption and restoration at the national level.

The Césairean motifs of Fall and alienation are strongly reiterated in each of the six major novels to be discussed in the present study. The earliest of these, Jacques Roumain's *Gouverneurs de la rosée (Masters of the Dew)*, written in 1944, opens upon a classic Old Testament figure of suffering humanity: an old woman plunging her hands into the dust and bewailing her own mortality.[17] Her terrified sense of being cut off from God is suggested by her despairing repetition of the phrase 'We're all going to die', and by the barren landscape which surrounds her: the gnawed fingers of cactus, the blighted thorn acacias and the ruined millet fields beneath the searing wind. The novelist's ironic interjection – so many humans are calling on the Lord all the time that he stops up his ears in irritation, leaving them to fend for themselves – recalls the biblical notion of God's withdrawing his favour from Adam's descendants. But at once, the idea of the biblical outcast is transposed to a West Indian setting by the response of the old woman's husband: 'Yes . . . a black man's really bad off'. Thus, by these few words placed in the mouth of a sententious old man, the swirling clouds of dust and the endless, devastating drought become symbolic not merely of man's expulsion from Eden but, specifically, of God's having abandoned the black race. Through the syncretic nature of Haitian religious worship, in which Christian saints are assimilated to voodoo divinities, the themes of metaphysical isolation and rejection by God are enlarged so as to embrace a whole pantheon of arbitrarily unhelpful supernatural beings, 'all the saints and . . . those deaf and blind African deities who did not hear her, who had turned away from her sorrow and her tribulations' (p. 33). As in Césaire's *Cahier*, the symptom of inner alienation is outer passivity: Roumain's peasants fatalistically accept what they interpret as the displeasure of the gods, making no attempt to overcome the drought conditions by seeking new sources of water. Their attitude of resignation is not merely a textbook illustration of the concept of alienation, however; it is an important element in the structure of the book, whose inner tension depends upon the conflict between the passive forces of conservatism in the village, and the energetic drive of the hero towards personal freedom and the salvation of the community. The drought-ridden Haitian valley becomes a microcosm of the human condition after Adam's Fall, and at the same time a symbol of the particular ills which have afflicted the black West Indian since slavery.

There is a similar use of landscape to echo the black human condition in Edouard Glissant's *La Lézarde* (1958: translated as *The Ripening*), where the main protagonist descends from the splendid mountain beauty of his home towards the muddy town below, which is itself the antechamber to the flat, monotonous canefields with their sweet sickly smell of death.[18] The hero's path follows that of the river Lézarde itself, which rises in the mountains, the traditional place of refuge for runaway slaves in past centuries, and flows through the poverty-stricken flatlands to reach its muddy delta. The river's course from mountain to sea is used poetically by the author to represent the situation of Martinique, moving from the old unhappy history of slavery to a state of freedom – not yet fully achieved – which is embodied in the image of the unenslaveable sea. Like Césaire, Glissant uses the presence of the canefields, with their oppressive combination of fierce heat, desiccating winds and harsh prickly vegetation, as a constant reminder of slavery and a symbol of present-day Caribbean suffering; in *The Ripening* the stiff tall rows of cane hissing in the breeze create the illusion of a sinister prison (p. 70). This symbolic value attributed to the canefields is present in all the non-Haitian novels, perhaps because of the greater duration of slavery in the French-owned islands. The child narrator of Joseph Zobel's Martinican novel of 1950, *La Rue Cases-Nègres (Black Shack Alley)*, believes in the existence of invisible executioners who condemn blacks to work in the canefields, through sun and storm, from the age of eight until they finally drop dead.[19] In *Demain Jab-Herma (Tomorrow Jab-Herma)*, Michèle Lacrosil depicts the Guadeloupean canecutters of the late 1960s as utterly depersonalized by the nature of their work: faces and hands invisible beneath the rags which they must wear to protect themselves against the sharp-edged leaves, they seem no more than shapeless bundles of cloth moving like automata through the stalks as they and their forefathers have moved for three centuries.[20] In the more recent Guadeloupean novel of Simone Schwarz-Bart, *Pluie et vent sur Télumée Miracle* (1972; literally *Rain and Wind on Telumee Miracle*, and translated under the title *The Bridge of Beyond*), life in the cane valleys is one of anguish and degradation, symbolic both of the curse on Adam's seed – 'in the sweat of thy face shalt thou eat bread, till thou return unto the ground' (Genesis 3:19) – and of the despotic exercise of power on the part of the white management over the descendants of black slaves: 'A foreman told me what my job was, and I found myself plunged at a blow into the heart of malediction. The machetes skimmed low, the stems fell, and the prickles flew everywhere, like splinters of glass, into my back, my nose, my legs . . . And I understood at last what a Negro is . . . And I thought, it's here, in the midst of the cane prickles, that a Negro ought to be.'[21]

The social hierarchies of the Caribbean, for centuries inseparably linked with race and colour, are another important factor in the sense of Fall and the inability to accept racial identity. Césaire's *Cahier* (p. 86) suggests the links between race and social class in its portrait of 'those who think that to be a Negro is like being a second-grade clerk', and dramatizes the conflict between racial solidarity and social ambition in its unforgettable vignette of a tramcar encounter between the young poet and a battered, smelly, starving ex-boxer (pp. 68–9). As the women in the tram sneer at the down-and-out, the poet sneers with them, overcome simultaneously by cowardice and by the humiliation of being let down in public by this member of his own race. The prevalence of racial shame is the heritage of slavery, of white indoctrination of the obedient 'good nigger' with the idea 'that he could never trick his own oppressive fate, that he had no power over his own destiny; that an unkind Lord had for all eternity written prohibitions into the nature of his pelvis' (p. 87). These white-originated prejudices, designed to maintain an attitude of subjection among the slaves, were eventually accepted and internalized by many of their descendants, like the old woman in *The Bridge of Beyond* who brings up her grandson in the belief that 'a Negro is a well of sins, a creature of the devil' (p. 149).

The problem of racial identity is, however, much more complex than the simple black/white division of the earliest days of slavery. In Haiti, for example, due to the slave-owners' habit of taking black mistresses, by the eighteenth century there was an elaborate system of colour stratification based on the individual's genetic composition of 128 theoretical parts. The following account gives some idea of the fanatical zeal of the classifiers:

> The true Mulatto was the child of the pure black and the pure white. The child of the white and the Mulatto woman was a quarteron with 96 parts white and 32 parts black. But the quarteron could be produced by the white and the marabou in the proportion of 88 to 40, or by the white and the sacatra, in the proportion of 72 to 56 and so on all through the 128 varieties. But the sang-mêlé with 127 white parts and 1 black part was still a man of colour.[22]

(The marabou was the offspring of a quarteron and a white woman; the sacatra, that of a Negro and a griffonne; the griffe, that of a mulatto and a Negress.)[23] Until very recent times, social mobility in the Caribbean was determined in large measure by lightness of complexion, although other factors such as parentage, education and economic situation also played their part. Michèle Lacrosil, whose novels deal at some length with the subtle forms of discrimination among those of varying skin shades, uses neurosis about colour as the principal motivation of the young mulatto, Cragget, of *Tomorrow Jab-Herma*, whose tragic sense of alienation both from white society and from his black fellow labourers ultimately leads him to murder and suicide. Yet another variation on this theme is to be found in Jacques Stéphen Alexis' *Compère Général Soleil* (*Comrade General Sun*, 1955),[24] set in Haiti, where, since a revolutionary coalition of blacks and mulattos expelled the slave-owners in 1804, mulattos have occupied the élite social positions once held by the white plantocracy. The central character, a black slum-dweller, remembers his earliest childhood as a sort of pastoral dream which came to an abrupt end when his widowed mother, too poor to feed him in the countryside, sent him at the age of eight to become the servant – the slave, in all but name – of a cruelly exploitative brown middle-class family in the city. This practice, which still continues in Haiti today, makes the child the property of his new masters, totally dependent upon their will and with no redress against any abuses they may inflict upon him. 'I was the child with no childhood,' says Hilarion, 'the one who can't feel suffering, the one fed on scraps and garbage, the emptier of hateful chamber-pots, the monkey, the clown . . . That's where I learnt to know life' (p. 346).

Throughout a career of odd jobs, petty crime, attempts at self-education, profitless emigration to the neighbouring Dominican Republic, and final adoption of Communist ideals, the hero is seeking to understand why blacks seem predestined to draw the losing straws in life. In Alexis' view, a century and a half after Haitian independence, its black proletariat seems to have drawn no nearer to prosperity or individual freedom, and is still the victim of racial and social prejudices which perpetuate the memory of the original Fall of the Africans into slavery.

Each of these novels, then, projects a Césairean vision of the West Indian islands as 'scars upon the water', flawed by an unjust social structure, inherited from the colonial era, which keeps the various sections of the community in a state of mutual estrangement and militates against the acceptance of racial or national identity. Many of the characters presented have little insight into the causes of their own alienation, and not all are fully aware of their situation as degrading or untenable; but even the most passive and resigned among them dream of escape from an impoverished and restrictive environment. At the realistic level, the unlikelihood of realizing such an ambition is epitomized by the self-delusions of the cane workers in *Tomorrow Jab-Herma*, who hope to find a legendary buried treasure on a mysterious island adjoining the sugar estate, and for whom the talismanic word 'gold' can charm away, if only temporarily, the monotonous drudgery of their lives. But in most of these novels, the perceived need for social reform impels the author to offer some vision of future release, expressed at a level where realism and symbolism are fused.

The present study will examine each of the six novels in terms of their transposition to a secular plane of the biblical themes of the Fall from Paradise and the return to the Promised Land. The first two novels to be discussed, Roumain's *Masters of the Dew* and Glissant's *The Ripening*, draw on the age-old solution of the Redeemer who comes from afar to save his people. In the first case, the Messiah figure is also used to preach a Marxist message, proposing a form of social revolution adapted to the situation of an illiterate and superstitious rural community. In the second, a dreamy, poetic evocation of the politicizing of the shepherd boy from the mountains is made to suggest the possibility of radical alterations in the ways of thinking and the behaviour of Caribbean society. The next two novels, Lacrosil's *Tomorrow Jab-Herma* and Zobel's *Black Shack Alley*, are both set on sugar estates whose living conditions, as we have seen, are associated with the situation of fallen man. Here there is no introduction of an external Redeemer figure: change comes from within. In Lacrosil's novel, the formal and apparently fixed pattern of relationships on the estate begins to dissolve and regroup itself under the pressures of economic and racial stress, and the final glimpse through the kaleidoscope shows an intriguing shift in the balance of power. The social hierarchy in Zobel's novel remains, on the contrary, unaltered: it is the hero – but he alone – who manages to get away, to move towards the better future which, for his grandmother, was only a mirage perpetually deferred. The last two novels to be considered, Alexis' *Comrade General Sun* and

Schwarz-Bart's *The Bridge of Beyond*, are superficially alike in that each is centred upon a protagonist who never succeeds in escaping from the condition of abject poverty, caught either in urban squalor or in the desperate physical hardships of the West Indian countryside.

Yet the first remains profoundly tragic, despite the hero's dying prophecy of a Communist miracle symbolized by the red sun which will banish the unbearable night of the present, like Césaire's apocalyptic tidal waves and volcanic eruptions; while the second, for all its pathos, moves buoyantly towards a solution based on an almost mystical faith in the resilience of human nature and the ability of the black race to endure and survive, to make, of the humblest of gardens, its own paradise.

Notes

1 Aimé Césaire, *Return to My Native Land (Cahier d'un retour au pays natal)*, trans. John Berger and Anna Bostock, intro. Mazisi Kunene (Harmondsworth: Penguin Books, 1969), p. 82. All subsequent quotations from Césaire's *Cahier* are taken from this translation.

2 See F.R. Augier, S.C. Gordon, D.G. Hall and M. Reckord, *The Making of the West Indies* (London: Longman, 1960), p. 67. This is a conservative estimate: totals of 50 million or more are suggested by Basil Davidson in *The African Slave Trade: Precolonial History 1450-1850* (originally published as *Black Mother*; Boston: Atlantic-Little, Brown, 1961), p. 80, and Joseph Ki-Zerbo in *Histoire de l'Afrique noire* (Paris: Hatier, 1978), p. 218.

3 'Rivers of Babylon' (The Melodians), from the soundtrack of the Jamaican film *The Harder They Come*, Island Records, C34684 (1972).

4 L.-G. Damas, *Pigments* (Paris: Présence Africaine, 1937), p. 42 (my translation).

5 V.S. Naipaul, *The Middle Passage* (London: Andre Deutsch, 1962), p. 41.

6 Jean-Paul Sartre, 'Orphée noir', introduction to Léopold Sédar Senghor's *Anthologie de la nouvelle poésie nègre et malgache* (1948; rpt. Paris: Presses Universitaires de France, 1969), p. xvi.

7 Aimé Césaire, *Une tempête* (Paris: Éditions du Seuil, 1969), p. 87 (my translation).

8 Aimé Césaire, introduction to Daniel Guérin's *Les Antilles décolonisées* (Paris: Présence Africaine, 1956), pp. 15-16 (my translation).

9 On the Harlem Renaissance, see Jean Wagner, *Black Poets of the United States*, trans. Kenneth Douglas (Urbana: University of Illinois Press, 1973); on Haiti, see Jean Price-Mars, *Ainsi parla l'oncle* (1928; new ed. Ottawa: Leméac, 1973), and for the theme of nostalgia for Africa, see Maurice A. Lubin's anthology, *L'Afrique dans la poésie haïtienne* (Port-au-Prince: Éditions Panorama, 1965).

10 John Milton, *Paradise Lost*, XII, 587.

11 On Césaire's relations with the Communist Party, see M. a M. Ngal, *Aimé Césaire: un homme à la recherche d'une patrie* (Dakar: Les Nouvelles Éditions Africaines, 1975), pp. 210-13.

12 See James Hall, *Dictionary of Subjects and Symbols in Art* (London: John Murray, 1974), p. 105, and Jana Garai, *The Book of Symbols* (London: Lorrimer, 1973), pp. 88 and 140.

13 Interview with Édouard Maunick on *France-Culture*, 1977.

14 Frantz Fanon, *Black Skin, White Masks*, trans. Charles Lam Markmann (New York: Grove Press, 1967), pp. 122-32.

15 Wole Soyinka, *Myth, Literature and the African World* (Cambridge: Cambridge University Press, 1976), pp. 126-30.

16 See, for example, the article on 'The African apprehension of reality' in Senghor, *Prose and Poetry*, trans. John Reed and Clive Wake (London: Oxford University Press, 1965; Heinemann, 1976), pp. 29-34.

17 Jacques Roumain, *Masters of the Dew*, trans. Langston Hughes and Mercer Cook, intro. J. Michael Dash (London: Heinemann, 1978), p. 23. All quotations are taken from this translation.

Introduction

18 Edouard Glissant, *The Ripening*, trans. Frances Frenaye (New York: George Braziller, 1959), p. 69. All quotations are taken from this translation.

19 Joseph Zobel, *Black Shack Alley*, trans. and intro. Keith Q. Warner (London: Heinemann, 1980), p. 122. All quotations are taken from this translation.

20 Michèle Lacrosil, *Demain Jab-Herma* (Paris: Gallimard, 1967), p. 72. All page references are to this edition; translations are my own.

21 Simone Schwarz-Bart, *The Bridge of Beyond*, trans. Barbara Bray, intro. Bridget Jones (London: Heinemann, 1982), pp. 136–7. All quotations are taken from this translation.

22 C.L.R. James, *The Black Jacobins* (1938; rev. ed. New York: Vintage Books, 1963), p. 38. For an account of a similar (but less detailed) system of colour distinctions in the British islands, see B.W. Higman, *Slave Population and Economy in Jamaica, 1807–1834* (Cambridge: Cambridge University Press, 1976), pp. 139–40.

23 Aimé Césaire, *Toussaint Louverture* (Paris: Présence Africaine, 1961), p. 31.

24 Jacques Stéphen Alexis, *Compère Général Soleil* (Paris: Gallimard, 1955). All page references are to this edition; translations are my own.

1

Fall and Redemption in
Jacques Roumain's *Masters of the Dew*

'These future orchards'
(*Cahier*, p. 78).

It is indeed ironic that Haiti, which once boasted proudly of being the first black republic in the world, should now be portrayed as in need of a saviour. Yet the violence, terror and bitterness of the thirteen years preceding independence – from the slave insurrection led by Boukman and inaugurated by a secret voodoo sacrifice in 1791, through the success, betrayal and death of Toussaint, to the wholesale massacres executed by Dessalines and Christophe – seem to have set a self-destructive pattern from which the island has never emerged.[1] Independence was proclaimed on the first day of 1804, and the mood of Haiti was confident and optimistic for some years afterwards, its citizens rejoicing in their liberation from a white colonial regime notorious for its cruelty towards slaves and obstinate in its discrimination against free coloureds. A series of Hymns to Independence reflected the euphoria of the initial period.[2] But by the 1870s a sympathetic foreign visitor was reluctantly declaring himself 'utterly disappointed' in the people and government of Haiti, which had become 'simply . . . a country of revolutions',[3] while Haiti's own poets in the second half of the nineteenth century were mourning the 'lost times of prosperity' and using blight-stricken coconut trees as a symbol of their fears for the future of their native land.[4] There were repeated struggles for power between the coloured élite, economically in the ascendant after the departure of the plantocracy, and the black-controlled army. Black and brown presidents came and went, in an atmosphere of political corruption, social instability and increasing economic stagnation. Between 1843 and 1915, the year when United States Marines began a long occupation of Haiti, there were twenty-two heads of state of whom only one completed his prescribed term. Jacques Roumain's own grandfather, President Tancrède Auguste, was poisoned when Roumain was a child of six – and was subsequently accused of responsibility for the explosion which had blown up his predecessor in office, along with his palace.[5]

These political dramas, unfolding in the towns, remained, however, remote from the lives of the peasant masses who comprise about 90 per cent of the population of Haiti. Although there are many reasons for Roumain's choice of the peasantry as the milieu from which his Redeemer-hero was to emerge, it is not unlikely that his intense disenchantment with the wealthy élite into which he was born may have been partly inspired by the sorry spectacle of public life in Port-au-Prince during his earliest years. The protagonists of his first short stories, published in 1930 – mainly young middle-class intellectuals like himself – are heartsick and disgusted by the materialism and the race and class prejudices of their families and associates, 'filled with sadness, feeling as abandoned and useless as the smashed boxes and the bits of broken pottery' which litter the city's wharves.[6] This mood of disillusionment with the bourgeoisie goes hand in hand with an idealization of the Haitian peasantry that anticipates the terms of Césairean *Négritude*. Roumain perceives qualities of rhythm and harmony in a mountain girl's way of walking and even in a countryman's drummer-like method of beating his wife, while he describes the powerful bodies, 'naive souls' and beautifully controlled movements of a pair of black acrobats as 'a magnificent, insolent psalm to life'.[7] His sense of solidarity with the black peasantry, traditionally despised by the brown urban élite, may be linked not only to his lack of admiration for the élite, but also to three less negative factors. Like all his literary circle, he was influenced by Dr Price-Mars's strong plea for a revaluation of peasant culture in *Ainsi parla l'oncle*, which appeared in 1928, the year after Roumain returned to Haiti as a young man of 20, after studies in Europe. His own Marxist beliefs led him towards an emotional identification with the proletariat of his country. And lastly, there was his militant nationalism, his anger at the American military presence which had dictated the politics and economics of Haiti since 1915, and was not to be withdrawn until 1934: a presence which, in his view, perpetuated the very materialism and racial prejudice which he saw as already endemic in the Haitian bourgeoisie.

The American occupation had brought many unpleasant reminders of the hated conditions of the colonial era. To the existing antagonism between mulattos and blacks was now added a white American prejudice against all persons of coloured blood. The two-tiered social system reverted to being a three-tiered one, which Roumain himself compared to the class structure of the former Saint-Domingue, French colonists now being replaced by American imperialists, the free coloureds by the present-day local élite, the slaves by the Haitian proletariat.[8] If the urban middle class was indignant at being made to feel inferior by the white foreigners who had taken over their country, the peasantry was equally resentful of authoritarian policies imposed by a group which physically resembled the slave-owners of the past. In the early years of the occupation a guerrilla war was fought by peasants against the Marines. When, in 1929, there was another peasant uprising, it was backed by a student strike which developed into a general one; Roumain played an active part in these events, which forced the introduction of a five-year plan for the withdrawal of the Marines, and it was soon afterwards that he was arrested for the first time.[9] In 1933, he spent three months in prison for writings considered politically subversive; in 1934, his founding of the Haitian Communist Party and his publication of the manifesto *Analyse schématique 1932-1934*, criticizing the regime from a Marxist point of view, led to a further two years in prison followed by over five years of exile abroad.[10] Roumain remained faithful to Communism, extending his concern for the peasantry of his own country to all disadvantaged social groups; seeing behind the 'inexorable dissimilarity' created by the externals of race and colour, clan and tribe, nation and religion, a proletarian 'unity of suffering and revolt'.[11] An important aspect of *Masters of the Dew*, completed in 1944 and published posthumously in 1946, is its attempt to transpose Marxist doctrine to a rural Caribbean setting and to equate the Haitian peasantry with Marx's proletariat. Its hero, Manuel, peasant son and lover, Christ-figure, sacrificial king and modern fertility god, is also a Marxist visionary who dreams of a black peasant revolution that will lead to 'a General Assembly of the Masters of the Dew' (p. 75).

Jacques Roumain's *Masters of the Dew*

The Haitian peasant class is probably the poorest in the West Indies, and the one whose material living conditions have changed least since colonial days. In the early period of the Republic, Dessalines, the first black head of state, had instituted a *corvée*, a system of forced labour (first used under slavery to maintain roads and fortifications), which kept the ex-slaves bound to heavy manual, mainly agricultural, work, and limited their freedom as effectively – though not as cruelly – as slavery had done. After Dessalines was assassinated, this feudal system was continued in the northern half of Haiti, ruled by Christophe, where slowly growing economic recovery was dependent upon heavy taxes on agricultural produce, and upon the manual toil of a mass of illiterate serfs. But it was abandoned in the south under the milder regime of Pétion, where state-appropriated lands were gradually divided up and distributed as rewards to ex-soldiers, sold very cheaply, or simply taken over by squatters. When, after Christophe's suicide, the whole of Haiti was reunited, the southern way of life, with its individualistic, haphazard and uneconomical farming methods, became the norm throughout the island, and the brief moment of national prosperity was over. Attempts to re-create a state-directed labour force failed in the 1820s; when the Marines reintroduced the *corvée* in 1919, bitter resentment flared up in a peasant revolt. Forced manual work was indelibly associated with slavery, and unacceptable to a population which had never shared in the benefits of past prosperity gained at the expense of its own labour. Furthermore, lacking education and knowledge of the outside world, the peasantry had no standards of comparison to set beside its own lack of material progress, and in any case preferred living at subsistence level to being compelled into work for the ruling class, which has traditionally exploited the countryside. This exploitation is still symbolized by the inescapable figure of the village *chef de section*, who collects taxes (and may abuse this power by extortion), who represents the authorities in every respect, and is not uncommonly a petty tyrant, like Hilarion, the rural policeman in *Masters of the Dew*. In addition to such human adversaries, the peasants are faced with a constant battle against recurrent droughts and the consequences of long-term, unheeded erosion of the topsoil. Water, even for drinking, is perennially scarce; life expectancy short; the land increasingly infertile. Agricultural methods are primitive and the spectre of starvation is never far away. Roumain's earlier peasant novel, *La Montagne ensorcelée* (*The Bewitched Mountain*, 1931), depicts the rural way of life in sombre accents that recall those of God in Genesis, sentencing Adam to perpetual labour: 'For the man of the soil, each day that dawns brings only the certainty of long painful hours, of a bitter struggle, in the torrid heat, with the rebellious earth.'[12]

Masters of the Dew is set in a remote Haitian village surrounded by mountains, and the bare bones of the story are simple and relatively undramatic. The village is suffering from a crippling drought; a resourceful man, returning from abroad, finds a distant spring and organizes an irrigation scheme, attempting to heal a local feud in the process; he falls in love with a girl of the opposite clan, is attacked by her jealous cousin and subsequently dies of his wounds. The drought is typical of the region, and the manner of the protagonist's death is not unusual in the Caribbean. It is a measure of the novel's strongly symbolic tone that the reader does not think of it in these practical, low-key terms, but in terms of passion, heroism and sacrifice. The great dignity of the narrative, and its ritual, fatalistic quality, are achieved in the first place by the sense of a firm and inevitable time-scheme in which all the characters and events have their appointed place. One of the first critics to comment on Roumain's use of religious symbolism saw the novel as a passage through three periods of time: the lost Eden, the parched and weary waiting, and finally the arrival and death of the Redeemer.[13] In fact, Eden exists here both in the past and in the future, since Roumain's entire emphasis is placed upon one particular aspect of the scriptural tradition: the lushness of the garden. This is, after all, the biblical feature most directly appropriate to a story about peasant farmers whose lives depend utterly upon the co-operation of the earth and the kindness of the elements. Before the drought there was fruitfulness; after the digging of the irrigation canal, there will be fruitfulness once more. Thus, unlike the biblical Adam, Roumain's secular villagers will be able to re-enter the paradise they have lost.

Any narrative concerned with a fall from a privileged status will also focus upon the question of guilt. Different explanations are invoked for the village's distressed situation, according to the world-view of the character involved and according to the symbolic importance of the 'garden' concept at various moments in the book. As we saw in the Introduction, the first page of the novel associates the dusty, barren landscape – the antithesis of the garden – with arbitrary punishment by God and, more specifically, with God's washing his hands of the black race. It is the hero's father, ironically named Bienaimé ('well-beloved'), who attributes to the Lord a particular animosity against the poor and the black: 'a black man's really bad off . . . the Lord created suffering' (pp. 23–4). It is through Bienaimé, too, and still in the opening chapter, that Roumain first relates the idea of the vanished garden to the slaves' loss of Africa, through the talismanic word *Guinée*. Bienaimé, looking at the ruined fields and the dry, cracked bed of the watercourse, is turning over in his mind old memories of prosperity, of the days when water was plentiful, the land fertile, and the inhabitants at peace with one another. The countryside then was a place of shady trees and arching bamboos, luxuriant creepers with mauve and white blossoms, bushes on which the fruit hung in golden shells. The sunlight used to sparkle on dewy fields, the red poinciana bloomed against the clear tropical sky. In this idyllic setting there were comradeship and laughter, the willing sharing of labour in the fields, and then the reward and pleasure of a lavish communal meal made from the rich produce of the land. The happiness and prosperity of the peasants depended not only on the benevolence of nature but also on their own *coumbite*, the co-operative work team which ensured that each man had the support of all for the tasks of clearing or harvesting. The *coumbite* used to begin at dawn, and Bienaimé's recollection of those early mornings is lyrical: 'Into the field of wild grass they went, bare feet in the dew. Pale sky, cool, the chant of wild guinea hens in the distance . . .' (p. 25). In the original French text, it is the grass that is associated with Guinea: 'On entrait dans l'herbe de Guinée'. The key motifs of this scene are closely repeated in a later chapter where Bienaimé's son Manuel is talking to Annaïse, with whom he has just fallen in love. Like Bienaimé, they are looking at the drought-ravaged plain with its blighted cactus and sinister, circling crows. Manuel sees it as it could be once more, if he can find a new source of water: no longer straw-coloured but lush and green, the corn and millet thick in the fields, the banana trees bent under the weight of their bunches. And in words as lyrical as those of his father, he associates the wild Guinea grass with the return of water and fruitfulness, visualizing it growing again on the savanna as 'high as a swollen river' (p. 88).

It is the mention of Guinea which transforms the landscapes of these passages into paradise gardens of the past and the future. For the Haitian peasant, Guinea symbolizes Africa, the land of his racial origin. It is a legendary, rather than a geographic, place, to which the souls of the dead are believed to return; it is incorporated within voodoo ritual[14] and even within the gestures of everyday life, as when old Délira, Manuel's mother, prepares to sow corn by turning formally in the four sacred directions and addressing Christ in the east, the angels of Guinea in the south, the spirits of the dead in the west, and the saints in the north (p. 60). It is the place from which the *houngan*, the voodoo priest, summons the god Legba, guardian of the crossroads between life and death, between the world of man and the immortal world of the *loas*, the voodoo divinities (pp. 66, 71). The concept of Guinea underpins the whole temporal structure of the novel. In the beginning, when the hero returns to his village after years as a canecutter in Cuba, his thoughts in that first hour are of other homecomings and of a form of return that, unknown to him, foreshadows the sacrifice he will make for the future of his people: 'Life is a continual coming back. The dead, they say, come back to Guinea, and even death is only another name for life. The fruit that rots in the ground nourishes a new tree' (p. 42). In the end, when the sacrifice is made and Manuel lies in his coffin, his mother watches the flickering candlelight on his brow and remembers the moment of his homecoming: 'There was a light on your forehead the day you came back from Cuba, and not even death can take it away . . . May this light in your soul guide you through everlasting night, so that you can find the road to that country of Guinea where you'll rest in peace with the wise men of our people' (p. 174).

By a logical extension, Guinea, the land of the ancestors, is associated with peace, power and felicity – the conditions attributed to the paradise of precolonial Africa, to the time before slavery began. When Manuel dies, already a 'Chief' in the eyes of those around him (pp. 159, 166), the crushing blow of his death brings back folk memories of the disaster of slavery that befell the race, and these are linked with the notion originally introduced by Bienaimé and now carried to its extreme: that God is bent upon destroying the black man. Manuel's mistress Annaïse bitterly renounces her former piety: 'It's useless for poor Negroes to cry for grace and forgiveness. You crush us like millet under a mallet! You grind us up like dust! You bring us low! You knock us down! You destroy us!' And in reply his friend Antoine implicitly relates the particular loss of Manuel to the greater loss of the mother country and the defeat of Africa at the hands of the European colonizers: 'From Guinea to today the Negro's walked in storm and tempest and turmoil. "The Good Lord's good," they say. "The Good Lord's white," they *ought* to say" (p. 162).

The fertile landscape of the past is thus doubly symbolic: of the distant African paradise, and of the contentment of the more immediate Haitian past which has been swept away by the prolonged drought. The drought itself is viewed by the majority of the peasants as an inexplicable calamity against which their only recourse is to multiply prayers and offerings to the *loas*. God and the *loas* are interchangeable in this context, and equally remote and unhelpful; there is no essential difference between Délira's calling on the Lord as she crouches in the dust at the start of the novel, and her cousin Destine's reproach to the voodoo divinities: 'Oh, *loas*, my *loas* of Guinea, you don't weigh the work of our hands according to our share of misery. Your scales are false. That's why we're dying with no help and with no hope. Is it fair? Answer me! No, truly it's not fair!' (p. 112). But their sense of injustice is not a dynamic one; it leads to no positive attempts to alter their fate. And the *loas* are elusive; they are involved yet not involved; they promise help but do not actually accept blame. It is the villagers who feel guilt, though not for logical reasons; who, in addressing the gods, regard their own suffering as a form of expiation for some sin as yet unidentified. When Legba speaks to his worshippers through the medium of the man he has possessed, his politeness detaches him from all responsibility for the villagers' current plight: 'I see that your affairs are going badly with this drought. But that will change, that will pass. The good and the bad make a cross. I, Legba, I'm the master of this crossroad. I'll help my Creole children find the right road. They will leave behind this road of misery' (p. 66). And the chorus of entreaties, the pleas for forgiveness which this promise provokes, the use of words like 'penance', 'helpless', 'mercy', all serve to underline the passivity, humility and fatalism of the peasants, their habit of yielding to any powerful external force, and perhaps, indeed, their profound need to set the unbearable harshness of their existence, the apparent futility of their efforts, within the framework of a supernatural system which somehow makes sense of it all. Their emotional dependence on voodoo ritual is suggested by the comparison with an anaesthetic (p. 71) which blurs their awareness of their troubles and sweeps their souls on to a different plane, one dominated by unreality, by the 'déraison farouche' – the fierce unreason – of the African gods.

Manuel is the only character who sees the stricken fields not as a divine punishment but as the direct consequence of human error. The villagers have cut down too many trees for charcoal, huts and fences, have cleared the mountain woods so as to plant over every inch of land, and the result is erosion which has exposed the naked rock strata, rendered hillside cultivation impossible and deprived the plain of water. For there are no trees any longer to attract the rain, and no tree roots to hold the soil in place beneath its onslaught. Constantly, persuasively, Manuel tries to get his family and friends to accept active responsibility for their land: 'It's not God who betrays us. We betray the soil and receive [our] punishment: drought and poverty and desolation' (p. 45). But the idea of human intervention is alien to the peasants, accustomed to believe, like old Délira (pp. 54–5), that the elements are in the hands of God and the appropriate *loas*: Agoué, god of water and the sea, and Loko-atisou, the ancestral *loa* whose name means 'he of the trees'.[15] Manuel, like his creator Roumain, does not believe in the power of the voodoo gods;[16] but in a bold artistic stroke which highlights both the interpersonal conflicts and the metaphysical dimensions of the novel, Roumain uses the *loa* Ogoun to express a divine warning against Manuel's interference in the course of natural events. Ogoun, the god of fire and warfare, erupts uninvited into the ceremony which Manuel's parents are offering in thanksgiving to Legba for his safe return. The opposition between the two gods is sharp. The benevolent Legba always appears as an old peasant with crippled, twisted limbs, leaning on a stick, while Ogoun is virile, hot-tempered, authoritative, and at the height of his powers. His melodramatic entry and menacing manner are in the best tradition of the wicked fairies of folk-tales, but are also, incidentally, recognized behaviour-patterns of several gods in the voodoo pantheon. In the form of the human worshipper he has possessed, Ogoun refuses to withdraw and demands his customary sacred symbols: the red handkerchiefs and the sabre. With hindsight, the reader later associates these objects with the eventual stabbing of

Manuel and the bleeding trail he leaves as he drags his body back to his parents' hut. Ogoun's song warns Manuel – long before the latter's project has been imparted to anyone in the village – that if he digs the canal, he must beware: 'The vein is open, the blood flows' (p. 70). The tone of the song suggests that Manuel is trespassing in forbidden territory, and introduces the archetypal folk-tale motif of the breaking of an interdiction. Although Roumain describes this incident without further explanation or commentary, it is interesting to recall that in voodoo legend Ogoun is connected with the water *loas*, being the lover of Erzulie, consort of Agoué, and herself known as La Sirène (the mermaid) in her sea-aspect. Furthermore, there are interesting points of resemblance between Erzulie, the light-skinned goddess of love who is known in her land-aspect as La Maîtresse, and the 'Maîtresse de l'Eau' of the novel, the mulatto Mistress of the Water who emerges from her spring at midnight, combing her long hair in a gesture considered typical of Erzulie, to sing the passer-by down to a watery grave (p. 144); although the title of Mistress of the Water would more commonly suggest the goddess Aïda Ouédo and her sacred pools.[17] When Manuel's sudden death is announced, some of the villagers are ready to believe that it is the vengeance of the Mistress of the Water (p. 160), whom he has offended by locating her secret spring. The *loas*, with their mysterious powers, are the vital moral force in rural communities, the source of protection, healing and consolation, the most influential factor in the lives of Haitian peasants. Thus the melodramatic device of Ogoun's warning is, in fact, a fitting symbolic expression of the villagers' initial suspicion of Manuel's revolutionary plans for irrigation, and their resistance to his belief that man can control his own destiny. A further small detail suggests the role of voodoo in the novel as a force opposed to progress. Although the thanksgiving ceremony for Manuel's return is being offered to Legba, whose sacred colour is white, the cock sacrificed by the *houngan* is the 'colour of flame' (p. 67) – the colour of Manuel's enemy Ogoun, the god of fire.

In voodoo belief, with its strange blend of the practical and the apparently incredible, there is a particular manifestation of Ogoun in which the god concerns himself with power politics and economic affairs. This is Ogoun St Jacques, Ogoun as St James, his warlike supremacy transformed into the wielding of civic authority. He is the divinity whose influence is sought for political advancement and financial prosperity, as well as for the more humble skills of survival. It is his portrait that Délira keeps in her hut, burning an eternal lamp before it, and the red clothing of the god, resembling fresh blood in the light of the flame, perpetuates the atmosphere of menace introduced by the warning at the voodoo ceremony and kept alive by the old woman's recurrent bad dreams during the period in which her son is out searching the mountains for water. Manuel is aware of the picture's sinister aspect (p. 146) on the night he makes ready to go out to Larivoire's, to persuade the opposing faction in the village feud to forsake the vendetta for the imperative task of forming a *coumbite* to dig the irrigation canal; and in the early hours of the following morning, as he lies mortally wounded, the god seems to brandish his sabre triumphantly above the bed, his crimson cloak wrapping him in a cloud of blood (p. 155). On the human level, Ogoun St Jacques's counterpart is Hilarion, the village policeman who exercises a brutal authority, who warns Manuel against stirring up the peasants to any independent action (pp. 80–1) and plans to torture him into revealing the location of the spring (p. 140). When Hilarion looks through the window of Délira's hut at the dying Manuel, his 'evil head' is framed in the window (p. 158) like a visual echo of the *loa*'s portrait. This intermingling of the realistic and the symbolic is typical of the novel, which is characterized by the subtle interplay of various narrative modes. The function of Ogoun here is to underline the fact that the peasants are at the mercy of all the figures of authority that surround them: the *houngan* whose charges are high for a thanksgiving ceremony (p. 73) and who profits by their ignorance of the causes of illness to ask for large sums of money to rid them of evil spells (p. 132); the bush priest whose funeral services cost less than those of the church (which 'extends no credit to the poor', p. 165), but who also shows his contempt for the small fee he is paid by gabbling the ritual words at an unintelligible speed; Hilarion's shopkeeper wife who exploits the peasants' poverty by extending them credit at exorbitant rates of interest and seeking to impound their property when they fail to pay on time; the market inspectors who abuse their position in order to fleece the countrywomen coming to sell their produce; the crooked justice of the peace, rural police, surveyors and food speculators who live on the peasants 'like fleas' (p. 74), and against whom they have no rights of redress whatsoever. A sense of collaboration, and even of cordial relationships, between the various petty authorities is suggested by the fact that the bush priest hurries off to have a drink with Hilarion after Manuel's funeral (p. 175), and that the *houngan*'s greed is linked in some villagers' minds with that of Hilarion and his wife Florentine (p. 132).

Conversely, it is the peasants' lack of unity that keeps them vulnerable in the face of exploitation. Manuel tries to explain this, in talking to Annaïse and to his friend and disciple, Laurélien, by drawing an analogy with the situation he has lived through in Cuba. His Cuban experience has a dual importance in the narrative. At the literal level, it represents the moment when his political awareness was crystallized in the form of Marxism. Symbolically, it corresponds to an essential phase in an archetypal pattern which has been termed the monomyth, in which the hero, separated from the world into which he was born, undergoes a process of mystical initiation which enables him to return in triumph to his people, bearing a divine reward.[18] The collective crisis of the strike in Cuba is Manuel's initiation into the world of class struggle and social revolution. The canecutters there were divided by skin shades and racial misunderstandings, 'scattered like grains of sand, and the bosses walked on that sand' (p. 90). When they realized that they had a common cause and managed to maintain their strike despite employer resistance and police harassment, they learned the value of solidarity: the grains of sand acquired 'the force of a boulder' and the labourers gained a just wage. Manuel reverts constantly to this experience of militant comradeship in expounding a kind of simplified Marxism. All men are brothers; it is wrong for the workers to possess nothing while the idle boss class enjoys fine houses and gardens; those who plant, water and harvest the land should have the rights and profits of ownership. A massive education programme must be introduced to help the poor to understand and cope with life. When the peasants of Haiti realize at last that they constitute a single force, they will rise up in unity from one end of the country to another in 'a General Assembly of the Masters of the Dew, a great big *coumbite* of farmers [to] clear out poverty and plant a new life' (p. 75). This last statement is not just a Marxist one. It draws upon an elaborate system of thematic cross-references within the novel which link Communist ideals with the immediate realities of rural life, as well as with a plane of symbolic action which, as we shall see, echoes both the Christian tradition and that of older

Jacques Roumain's *Masters of the Dew*

vegetation cults. At the realistic level of the narrative, however, Manuel's words are clearly identified by Hilarion as 'words of rebellion' (pp. 80, 140) displeasing to the authorities, and Manuel himself as a danger. Hilarion has no desire for the villagers to gain a sense of independence and change their present status as serfs. He fears the irrigation project because he understands clearly that the acquisition of water will free the villagers from his exploitative money-lending operations. The possession of water symbolizes, among other things, the control of one's destiny; Manuel expresses this concept elliptically when he says that the Cuban canecutters owned no water save their own sweat (p. 50). The digging of the canal thus assumes the quality of a political act. Manuel, who has already suffered at the hands of the police in Cuba and whom Hilarion attempts to intimidate by sinister threats, is plainly meant to represent the victimized revolutionary hero. In this, curiously, he anticipates the destiny of his creator. The political persecution of Roumain made him an object of worship to his friends. He was to serve as the model for the heroic imprisoned Communist Roumel in Alexis' *Comrade General Sun*, and his life and ideals were to evoke the tribute of a collection of poems by another Haitian writer, Jean Brierre, entitled *Nous garderons le dieu (We will keep the god with us).* [19] Roumain himself fulfilled the classic role of the bourgeois renegade who brings the revolutionary message to the proletariat, which, according to Marxist doctrine, cannot achieve revolutionary consciousness unaided. Although born of the proletariat, not of the bourgeoisie, Manuel is depicted as a superior being by virtue of his intelligence and his years away from the village, and he becomes, like Roumain, the type of the Marxist redeemer.

It is significant that alongside the sweating Cuban proletariat Manuel evokes the figure of their foreign exploiter sitting in the shade of his garden: as well as being political symbols, they are opposing types suggesting fallen man and a hostile god in Eden. In a similar manner, through his use of imagery, Roumain makes a direct link between Manuel's Marxism and the paradise garden of his father's memories, while at the same time connecting it with the symbolic centre of those memories – the rural *coumbite* of the past. Old Bienaimé remembers the days of the *coumbite* as an era of joyful co-operation, 'when they all had lived in harmony, united as the fingers of the hand' (p. 25). When Manuel seeks to explain the need for solidarity to Annaïse, he uses the same image, showing her the weakness of his individual fingers and the firmness of his clenched fist (p. 90) as a graphic demonstration of the meaning of unanimous strike action. At present the villagers' strength lies dormant because of the divisive bitterness of the vendetta; this dormant potential is glimpsed when Manuel clasps the hand of Nérestan, an enemy of his clan, and reflects that 'terrific strength [sleeps] in those thick fingers, rough as bark' (p. 152). It can be realized only if the villagers return to the ways of the past with its fruitful comradeship, for the lesson of the fingers is the same as that of the *coumbite*: 'One needs the other. One perishes without the other's help' (p. 149).

The *coumbite* itself is a kind of literary crossroads where many of the novel's themes converge. It is a bond with Guinea and the lost Eden of Africa, a miraculous survival of Dahomean co-operative work in which a team of labourers, led by a drummer, traditionally cultivated the fields for the benefit of all their village. [20] Without it, the drummer Antoine feels he has lost not only his title of Simidor but his very identity: his life is useless, his role ended (p. 103). In the same way, the villagers' listless resignation in the face of the drought is in strong contrast with the vigour and rhythmic ease which the drumbeats of the Simidor used to inspire within them. The unity of movement induced by the drum symbolizes an emotional unity which existed in the prosperous past, and has now disappeared. Tradition has broken down between the warring factions: the inhabitants no longer exchange the time-honoured greetings, the young and strong no longer help the old and weak. Just as the *coumbite* is associated with a paradise garden in the first chapter of the novel, so its violent disruption is associated with the moment of the Fall, which introduced death into the world. The last *coumbite* to be held was the one at which Bienaimé's brother Sauveur, provoked into rage by a quarrel over land inheritance with his cousin Dorisca, killed the latter 'in the very middle of the *coumbite*' (p. 62). Sauveur subsequently died in prison, and from that time the spirit of harmony and fraternity has been dead in the village. The absence of the *coumbite* is synonymous with dust, poverty and mortality; the villagers are described as 'already dead beneath this dust, in these warm ashes' (p. 32). Although there is no logical connection between the murder and vendetta on the one hand, and the devastating inroads of the drought on the other, a causal link which transcends logic is suggested by the attribution to the dead men of the qualities of the drought – 'Dorisca and Sauveur are already ashes and dust' (p. 125) – and by the attribution to the drought of a moral quality capable of destroying the inhabitants: when Délira describes its effects to Manuel (p. 44), the words of the French text mean literally 'Dryness has invaded us'. The stagnant green water which is all they have left to drink (p. 32) corresponds to a spiritual stagnancy brought on by the vendetta: 'Hate poisons a person's breath. It's like a stagnant pool of green mud, of cooked bile, of spoiled, rancid, mortifying souls' (p. 126). Manuel's words about the brotherhood of all peasants, on the other hand, flow 'clear as water running in the sunlight' (p. 75), bringing new hope to the disheartened Laurélien. Such passages anticipate the symbolic function of the spring of fresh water which Manuel finds, and which will banish the physical and moral aridity of the village. Again, while Roumain offers, through his mouthpiece Manuel, a literal explanation for the disappearance of the rain (the heedless deforestation of the mountain slopes), the symbolic plane of the novel seems to propose that guilt lies elsewhere, by making the arrival of the water dependent upon the laying aside of the vendetta and the renewal of the *coumbite*. This renewal, which is necessary for practical reasons (neither of the feuding clans is numerous enough to dig the irrigation canal alone), thus becomes an act of expiation and healing.

Another important aspect of the *coumbite* is the harmony which it represents between man and earth, a harmony which allows man the mastery of his life and destiny. This is suggested by images of human sexuality and fruitfulness. Old Bienaimé remembers his past farming in terms of love-play: 'after struggling with the earth, after opening it, turning it over and over, moistening it with sweat, sowing it with seed as one does a woman, then came satisfaction: plants, fruit, many ears of corn' (p. 32). When Manuel criticizes the villagers for having abused this privileged contract between man and the land, he uses similar imagery, speaking of the earth as a woman who revolts against mistreatment, but who, well tended, will spread her ripe fields out under the dew (p. 45). With the loss of the *coumbite* man has been alienated from his environment, adversely affected by the breakdown of the material conditions of his existence. Every chapter brings a reminder of the charred fields, the starving animals, the parched and fissured watercourses, the searing heat, the choking dust in the air. The earth is no longer a smiling mistress, but a tortured and skeletal being, 'bled . . . to the bone' (p. 24), her flanks bared by erosion (p. 36), bones of rock piercing her thin layer of skin (p. 57), her scorched back raked by the fingernails of the sun (p. 58). One of Manuel's roles is to restore the harmony between man and the land he tills. His symbolic function as lover of the earth is stressed from the outset, in a passage near the start of Chapter 2 which is not present in the translation of the novel. It is a paragraph of interior monologue which conveys Manuel's exhilaration at finding himself once more on the path to his village, after his fifteen-year absence:

> If you come from a country, if you were born there, born and bred as you might say, well then, you have it in your eyes, your skin, your hands, with its waving tree-tops, the flesh of its soil, the bones of its stones, the blood of its rivers, its sky, its savour, its men and women: it's a presence in your heart that can never be erased, like a girl you love: you know the depths of her gaze, the fruit of her mouth, the hills of her breasts, her hands which fend you off and yet surrender, her knees which have yielded their mysteries, her strength and her weakness, her voice and her silence.

Picking up the theme of the quasi-sexual bond between the labourer and his land, the passage is a poetic statement of a practical rural necessity. The peasant cannot afford to desert or divorce the soil (p. 107), for in it lies his only hope of autonomy. Each man is entitled to own and enjoy his plot of earth, if he remains faithful to it; and the *coumbite*, which requires the fidelity of all, is not only a practical and a symbolic phenomenon, but also a political one: in Marxist terms, it is an act of solidarity accomplished by the proletariat. Once again, we observe the intersecting of themes through the focal point of the *coumbite*.

In order to elaborate the special relationship between Manuel and the land, Roumain makes use of vegetal imagery, and particularly of the image of the tree. The physical deterioration of the land has come about through the betrayal of her forests. Already, in the first chapter of the novel, a tree felled by a charcoal-burner is described in emotive terms as 'mutilated', its branches reduced to 'charred skeletons' (p. 28); while the man bending over the smoking remains, regretting his inability to answer the beguiling call of the *coumbite* work-song, is portrayed as being physically oppressed by his work, his eyes reddened, his throat dry and his mouth filled with a bitter taste. 'Rummaging in his pile of earth and ashes', he is thematically linked with the ashes and dust of the drought and the vendetta's dead. In opposition to this semi-biblical type of mortality is Manuel himself, who identifies with the plants around him, loving them not merely for their usefulness but for their beauty (p. 93), and who compares himself to a living tree: 'I am planted in this soil. I am rooted in this earth. To all that grows, I say, "Honour" ' (p. 56). The contrast between the dead tree and the living one inevitably recalls the opposing types of tree in the Bible: the Tree of the Knowledge of Good and Evil, which is associated with Adam's sin, and the fruit of which brings death into the world; and the Cross of Christ which is its redemptive counterpart, representing the salvation of man and his accession to eternal life. The underlying biblical symbolism in the novel is reinforced by the fact that the passage in which Manuel, the living tree, declares his love and respect for all growing things is set in the context of his first encounter with Gervilen, son of the mulish Dorisca whose greed to acquire more land provoked the village feud and led to his own death at the hands of

Manuel's uncle. Gervilen's hatred of all Manuel's clan is redoubled by his jealously over his cousin Annaïse's love for Manuel. He is destined to be the villain of the story, a role in which he is already cast by Annaïse when she calls him a Judas for spying on her meetings with her lover (p. 95). When Manuel first meets him, bending over his charcoal pit, he appears as a kind of grotesque, deformed version of the charcoal-burner of Chapter 1. 'He was black, thick-set and as short as if he had been hammered down by a rammer. His enormous hands dangled at the ends of his arms like bundles of roots. His hair grew low on his stubborn brow . . . Under protruding eyebrows, his glance shifted like that of a distrustful animal in a bushy hole' (p. 56). His gaze is compared to 'a burning cinder', prolonging the destructive associations of his occupation; his action in rudely turning his back on Manuel to stoop once more over his pit highlights the symbolic differences between the tall, graceful hero who has come through the woods singing a hymn of greeting to the lovely plants around him, and the short, misshapen villain bent upon the ruin of the physical environment. These opposing types of salvation and destruction reinforce the many biblical echoes of the narrative, and in particular the function of Manuel pointed out by Serres, as a black Christ (Manuel = Emmanuel), born of a humble local inhabitant yet with all the prestige of the Messiah come from afar: for the village children he is 'the man who has crossed the sea . . . crowned with a halo of mysteries and legends' (p. 81).

The tree is, of course, an ancient and universal symbol of the entire cosmos, its genesis and its growth.[21] The garden of Eden contained a Tree of Life as well as the tree of Adam's downfall, and it parallels the cosmic trees of many other mythologies. At the level of man, the microcosm, the tree symbolizes the richness and diversity of the human body, while its vertical quality lends further associations of resurrection and triumph. Roumain, who during his years of political exile had studied ethnology at the Musée de l'Homme in Paris and then at Columbia University, would have been well acquainted with this archetypal tradition, upon which he draws for his description of the giant fig tree that rises above the hidden spring which Manuel discovers. Ancient, proud and powerful, it covers the spot with 'venerable shade', and its 'monstrous roots [extend] an authoritative hand over the ownership and secret of this corner of the earth' (p. 108). When Manuel takes Annaïse to see the spring, he compares himself and his beloved to the first man and the first woman as they walk into the 'mysterious shade' of the giant tree (p. 117); Annaïse calls the tree 'the keeper of the water', and water is the key to the resurrection of the dying village; it is beneath this tree, on the ground above the precious water, that she conceives the child who will represent Manuel's survival in human form, as the irrigation canal with its life-bearing water will represent his spiritual resurrection.

In the particular context of Haiti, the tree image takes on additional resonances. At the most literal level, the tree is intimately connected with the business of everyday survival. In a land divorced from the urban mores of supermarkets and doctors, the tree, by virtue of its fruit and leaves, is the source of both food and healing. At the metaphysical level, the tree is the vertical highway of communication between the earth and the Grand Bois d'Ilet, the island below the sea where the voodoo *loas* have their primal location, and which is associated with Guinea. The most ancient of the *loas* are known as *loas racines* ('root *loas*'), and the tree as the avenue of divine approach is represented in stylized form by the *poteau-mitan* or centre-post around which take place the ritual movements and dance of the voodoo ceremony. The stylized tree with branches and roots symmetrically extended to both sides of a horizon is a recurrent motif in the *vêvê*, the ritual symbol drawn on the ground which consecrates to the *loa* which it represents the area which it covers.[22] And in a land plagued by deforestation, the sacred tree of Legba still stands obligatorily at the gate of each voodoo temple, representing not merely an avenue for Legba, but all avenues as well. Moving beyond the immediate Haitian associations to the wider Caribbean context, we find the tree as a frequent metaphoric presence in poetry from Césaire onwards. Georges Ngal has related this importance of vegetal imagery to the historic circumstances of the West Indian's existence. According to Ngal, the notion of the tree's deep, firm roots provides an element of compensation for the slave's own uprooting from Africa and his consequent loss of identity and stability, while its dynamic vertical movement and spreading branches suggest upward growth, expansion and equilibrium.[23] We may compare this with Roumain's use of the image of an uprooted tree adrift in the current of a river to suggest Manuel's feelings of unhappiness and alienation during his canecutting years away from his own country (p. 44). Ngal cites a remark of Césaire's which indicates that for the poet, the tree represents an ideal, integrated personality and also a means of bridging the separation from Africa: 'The tree profoundly rooted in the soil is for me the symbol of man bound to his own nature, and means nostalgia for a lost paradise.'

The rooted tree is therefore the antithesis of alienation and, as such, is harmoniously woven into the moral texture of the novel, since Manuel's message to the afflicted peasants is one of honour and respect for all growing things, and since he himself, the living tree, is to be the instrument of their salvation. Just as the *coumbite* is at the centre of a symbolic complex recalling the lost Eden of Africa, the fruitful work-patterns of the Haitian past, the joys of fraternity and harmony, and the Marxist value of co-operative endeavour by the proletariat, so Manuel is the nexus of the natural symbols in the novel: tree, earth and water. The 'magic wand' that he is believed to have brought back from Cuba, and that can discover streams and even hidden treasures (p. 129), is affiliated to the archetypal symbol of the tree. It has overtones of the staff of Aaron which miraculously sprouted, flowered and bore fruit, and which is associated with Christ, miraculous fruit of the Virgin's womb; it simultaneously recalls the tree of Jesse, which is an allied Messianic symbol. The magic tree or stick has phallic and creative reverberations, and may be linked with the idea of resurrection and with a forward movement in time. Yet paradoxically the tree suggests sacrifice, both through the cross of Christ, and through the passivity of its very wood, destined to be burnt by man.[24] And in *Masters of the Dew*, Manuel, the living tree, is the sacrificial victim through whom the fields of his native region will miraculously regain their green fertility.

The notion of sacrifice is an everyday one in Haiti, since animals – chickens, goats or bulls – are ritually killed in the voodoo ceremony so that their life and vigour may be transfused to the *loas*, replenishing their divine moral energy. Such sacrifices can, evidently, have specific immediate objects such as the expression of gratitude (as in the case of the cock offered to Legba on behalf of Manuel's parents), or the desire to influence or appease the gods (as in the case of the animals, half bribe, half propitiation, which the villagers offer in order to induce the *loas* to send rain). In the ceremony for Manuel's return, the phrase which Roumain uses to describe the sacrificed rooster, 'a burning bush' in which are concentrated 'all natural forces' (pp. 67–8), is in part an Old Testament echo curiously appropriate to the situation of Manuel, for it was from a burning bush that God spoke to Moses (a traditional prefiguration of Christ) telling him that he was destined to lead his people out of the hands of their oppressors and guide them into a land flowing with milk and honey.[25] And it is tempting to see this allusion as further evidence of the sustained identification of Manuel with Christ throughout the novel, culminating (in the view of many commentators) in the Messianic sacrifice of his death. This view is supported by Manuel's dying words, which echo his earlier Christ-like greeting to the hostile clan: 'I've come with peace and reconciliation' (p. 148). His final speech to his mother opposes the idea of animal sacrifice to human sacrifice:

> 'You've offered sacrifices to the *loas*, The blood of chickens and young goats you've offered to make the rain fall. That hasn't done any good – because what counts is the sacrifice of a man. The blood of a man. Go see Larivoire. Tell him the will of my blood that's been shed – reconciliation – reconciliation – so that life can start all over again, so that day can break on the dew'. (p. 158)

While the Christian reminiscences are inescapable here (the shedding of blood for peace, reconciliation and the resurrection of mankind),[26] it should also be observed that Manuel is no conscious imitator of Christ – his notion of the Christian heaven, expressed in heavily ironic terms on pp. 44–5, is of a racist's and colonialist's paradise – and that, unlike Christ, he does not voluntarily offer up his life for his fellow men. Indeed, what saves him from being a cardboard hero throughout the book is the engagingly modest and human nature of his emotions and ambitions. His first statement about the vanity of offering animals to the *loas*, in a conversation with Annaïse some time before the discovery of the spring, makes no mention whatsoever of the sacrifice of a man; he is simply attempting to combat the fatalism of the villagers by preaching a practical doctrine of individual effort. 'The blood of a rooster or a young goat can't make the seasons change . . . What counts, since you're asking me, is rebellion, and the knowledge that man is the baker of life' (pp. 87–8). He contrasts the active image of men as bakers with a passive image of the villagers as 'resigned dough', and the unromantic metaphor stresses his robust, down-to-earth common sense. He wants the peasants to stand on their own feet, and the village to recover the fruitfulness of his childhood memories; he does not see himself as some larger-than-life saviour, and is astonished and disconcerted when Laurélien calls him 'Chief' (p. 75). The simple, moving love story is firmly based in the human world of physical passion and tenderness. Manuel's personal dream is to live with Annaïse in a three-roomed hut on the edge of the woods, with a railing, two doors, and maybe a small porch. He will build the hut himself and paint it blue, because blue makes things look clean; he will make the furniture, and a shady arbour outside, and his grape vine will do well because he will fertilize it with coffee grounds. This is the fabric of everyday happiness, rooted in reality and not in the supra-human domain of heroic sacrifice. Manuel is not even killed for an abstract reason such as his political beliefs, or a supernatural one such as his infringement of the god Ogoun's warning; he is killed because Annaïse prefers him to Gervilen. His real sacrifice – and its true importance lies in the fact that it is an unprecedented one in the region – is that he renounces vengeance, and thus breaks the destructive chain of reprisal and counter-reprisal which has prevented the restoration of the *coumbite*. At the moment of his death, he acquires heroic stature by transcending his physical suffering and the anguish of his ruined hopes for a future life with Annaïse, in order to think only of the salvation of the village. The independent and dynamic spirit which he has shown throughout the narrative enables him to turn the negative, futile accident of his death into a positive and healing event. The moral energy which he displays recalls the symbolic function of the rooster sacrificed at the voodoo ceremony, 'one living entity' in which 'all natural forces' are concentrated (pp. 67–8). This aspect of the notion of sacrifice occurs in other contexts within the novel. We have seen that Manuel is identified with the sacrificial tree. His role as intermediary between the elements of earth and water is equally suggestive of a pre-Christian archetypal myth complex with which Roumain would have been familiar through his anthropological training, and which seems to have played an important part in his treatment of the theme of sacrifice. It is, above all, the physical fruitfulness arising out of Manuel's death which recalls the ancient vegetation cults of the Middle and Far East and of Central America, in which the fertility of the fields was ritually ensured by the annual slaying of a kingly or divine victim. Out of these ritual human offerings, the Christian concept of a redemptive sacrifice was itself to emerge.[27]

Water, frequently juxtaposed with blood in Roumain's narrative, has the dual connotations of the tree, associated with both life and death. Blood, water, sacrifice and fertility are symbolically fused in Manuel's thoughts when he is savagely beaten by the Cuban police and is sustained by a defiant endurance, the 'never-ending call of life' which is like a spring of blood deep within him and which consoles him with thoughts of the fruitfulness of revolutionary death: 'If you go down, you'll be seed for an unending harvest' (pp. 42–3). These associations may take on a negative value in the eyes of those bereaved by Manuel's death: his mother, who sobs 'Earth, Holy Earth, don't drink his blood!' (p. 156) – a phrase which reminds the reader of the sacrificed cock whose blood was dripped on the ground in a ritual libation – and Annaïse, who cries in protest, 'Can a man die like that . . . as fruit falls from a tree and rots?' (pp. 160–1). Manuel's own vision, however, is always a confident one: 'The fruit that rots in the ground nourishes a new life' (p. 42); 'What counts . . . is the blood of a man' (p. 158). From the time of his return to Haiti, he grasps the vital need for water, which he visualizes as a kind of life-blood, renewing the verdure of the burnt earth 'like a network of veins transporting life to the depths of the soil' (p. 53). When he learns about the vendetta, he perceives that the future irrigation canal would also create a moral transformation in the village: 'the water would bring them together again. Its cool breath would dispel the evil odour of spite and hatred . . . a brotherly community would be reborn' (p. 80). He sees it as a cleansing torrent which can wash away the memory of the past bloodshed (p. 124) and release the inhabitants from their stagnant bitterness. As bringer of the water, Manuel's function is thus reminiscent of that of the medieval Grail knights (themselves the literary heirs of the old vegetation gods) whose task was to heal the Waste Land of its mysterious malady, making its rivers flow once more and restoring the kingdom to its former green and fertile state.[28]

Imprisoned in their petty resentments, which have become almost as effective a drug as voodoo, providing a means of escape from physical problems and allowing the transference to a human target of their impotent anger against the elements (p. 131), the villagers are incapable of harnessing these elements and using them for man's benefit. Manuel alone approaches recalcitrant nature with both love and the determination to gain the upper hand, 'to overcome the earth's bad will every day, to bend the whims of the water to [his] needs' (p. 54). Water itself is as female and fertile as the earth: this double fecundity is suggested by the description of the spring at Mahotière (p. 143), which flows between the legs of the mountain in a cool ravine, its clear depths teeming with succulent crayfish. The theme of a sexual bond between the labourer and his land is reiterated through Manuel's belief that the capricious, feminine elements, recognizing a man's virile strength, will yield to him – 'Then the earth will call you, "Dear Master". The water will call you, "Dear Master" ' (p. 54). The idea of mastery over nature's great forces is poetically summed up by the title of the novel, in French *Gouverneurs de la rosée* (Governors of the Dew). For the Haitian reader, the title has a literal meaning as well as a symbolic one. In the Creole-speaking Haitian countryside, the peasant in charge of local irrigation (*arrosage* in standard French) is called the *gouvèné rouzé*.[29] It is typical of the novel's successful fusion of realism and symbolism that the title should be equally appropriate when read at either level, and that the four simple words should be rich with such diverse allusions. In choosing the old term 'governor', with its echoes of colonial rule, Roumain refers the reader obliquely to the political ideology underlying the book, and thus heralds Manuel's revolutionary dream of a black peasant uprising which would gain true independence for the Haitian proletariat. The metaphoric import of the title depends largely, however, on the use of the word 'dew', which evokes water in its most delicate and poetic form. The falling of dew has biblical associations of fruitfulness and divine blessing (as in Deuteronomy 33:13 and Haggai 1:10), so that control over the dew suggests a god-like authority over the forces of life and death. The dew that fell on Gideon's fleece (Judges 6:37–8) was taken in the Middle Ages to be a prefiguration of the Virgin's impregnation by the Holy Ghost, and thus became thematically linked with the Annunciation – the moment at which the Incarnation of Christ was believed to have taken place.[30] Hence dew is symbolically linked with virginity and the Saviour, and the triple association foreshadows that of Annaïse, Manuel and the spring in the ninth chapter of the novel. Dew is also linked with paradise, for it is present in Bienaimé's idyllic memories of the days of the *coumbite* (pp. 25, 102) as well as in his son's deathbed vision of an earthly Eden. On the human level, it forms a part of Annaïse's and Manuel's separate daydreams about the dawns they will share and the good life they will build together (pp. 116, 153).

Water in various manifestations is therefore simultaneously tied to the themes of sacrifice, healing, political power, and fertility. Human fertility in the novel parallels that of the land. The conception of Annaïse's child is carefully located at the site where Manuel has discovered water, and Roumain's choice of phrasing creates a bond between the man's sexual act and the water's fecundity: 'He had taken her by the spring where the sounds of the water had cut into her body like a fertile stream of life' (p. 160). This union has the quality of a ritual coupling, reflecting the ancient association of human fertility with that of the earth. The ritual element is enhanced by the fact that the attitude of the lovers' bodies duplicates the earlier gesture of symbolic union between Manuel, the earth and the water, when he finds the spring and lies down on the ground, embracing it with his whole body in ecstatic delight

(p. 109). It is further intensified by old Délira's posture as she begs the holy earth not to drink her wounded son's blood; when she falls to her knees, arms outspread, and kisses the earth in tears (p. 156), the text closely follows that of the earlier chapter where Manuel, lying down on the ground, kisses the earth with his lips and laughs. The gestures of both mother and son are natural ones in Haiti, where rapping ceremonially upon the earth, pouring libations upon it, kneeling and touching lips or forehead to it are acts of homage addressed not to the earth itself, but to the legendary cosmos beneath and within it where the gods, and the souls of the dead, reside.[31] But the allusion at these points in the novel is not specifically to voodoo ritual. Rather, the transition from laughter to tears, from Manuel's salute to the underground water – 'There she is! The good, sweet, flowing, singing, cooling, blessed life!' (p. 109) – to Délira's supplications on behalf of her son who is going off towards the grave and the dust (p. 157), creates the impression of two phases in an archetypal pre-ordained cycle of life, death and resurrection.

The final stage, that of resurrection, is heralded by a phrase which borrows the terminology of the Christian Gospels but transposes it to a secular plane. The peasants, burying Manuel, are described as 'carrying their brother off toward that earth that he loved so much and for which he had died' (p. 177). The secular nature of his resurrection is elaborated by Annaïse, who sees it as an eternal and sensual fusion with nature: 'It wasn't Manuel, that great, cold, stiff, lifeless body . . . The real Manuel was walking through the mountains and the woods in the sunlight. He was talking to Annaïse . . . taking her in his arms, enveloping her in his warmth. The real Manuel was making a canal so that the water might flow through the fields. He was walking in the harvests of the future, in the dew of early dawn' (pp. 162-3). The last scene of the novel shows us a double resurrection. The empty canal cut across the plain waits to be filled: the French text uses the word *saignée*, which means a small irrigation canal but derives from the common word for bleeding, and thus prolongs the figurative association of blood and water in Manuel's life, as well as the theme of sacrifice. As the water flows down into the plain, its surface sparkling in the sunlight,[32] it is accompanied by the new, triumphant *coumbite* with the drummer at its head. The ways of Guinea have been restored; the earthly paradise is to be recovered; the spirit of fraternity is now revived. The success of the *coumbite*, as Manuel foresaw, has resolved both the physical dilemma and the spiritual conflict within the village. Manuel lives on in the very presence of the water; but also in concrete, human form, through the child that Annaïse will bear him, and in whose blood the two hostile clans will be permanently reconciled. At the symbolic level, the birth of the child following on the death of its father prolongs the sense of a pre-ordained cycle, linking Manuel once more with the ancient vegetation gods who died and were mourned annually, only to be reborn with each fruitful spring. At the realistic level, the last words of the narrative stress the reassuring continuity of human life and effort: 'She took the old woman's hand and pressed it gently against her belly where the new life was stirring' (p. 188). The child will be born in a fertile garden. The barren earth and the untouched virgin have moved beyond the 'fallen', sterile present which set the tone of the novel's early chapters; the fruitfulness of both announces the redemption of the village and its access to the Promised Land.

Fall and Redemption

Notes

1 For the early history of Haiti, see Césaire, *Toussaint Louverture*; James, *The Black Jacobins*; James C. Leyburn, *The Haitian People*, with an introduction by Sidney W. Mintz (1941; rev. ed. New Haven and London: Yale University Press, 1966), and David Nicholls, *From Dessalines to Duvalier: Race, Colour and National Independence in Haiti* (Cambridge: Cambridge University Press, 1979). On the condition of the slaves before independence, see Gabriel Debien, *Les Esclaves aux Antilles françaises, XVIIe - XVIIIe siècles* (Basse-Terre: Société d'Histoire de la Guadeloupe; Fort-de-France: Société d'Histoire de la Martinique, 1974).

2 These Hymns are reproduced in Raphaël Berrou and Pradel Pompilus, *Histoire de la littérature haïtienne* (Port-au-Prince: Editions Caraïbes, 1975), I, 21-2, 26-9, 52-3.

3 Samuel Hazard, *Santo Domingo, Past and Present; with a Glance at Hayti* (New York: Harper & Brothers, 1873), p. 422.

4 See Naomi M. Garret, *The Renaissance of Haitian Poetry* (Paris: Présence Africaine, 1963), pp. 31, 36.

5 Bernard Diederich and Al Burt, *Papa Doc: Haiti and its Dictator* (1969; rpt. Harmondsworth: Penguin Books, 1972), pp. 38, 329.

6 Jacques Roumain, 'Propos sans suite', reprinted in *La Montagne ensorcelée* (1931; new ed. Paris: Les Editeurs Français Réunis, 1972), p. 72. All translations from this volume are my own.

7 'Préface à la vie d'un bureaucrate', in *La Montagne ensorcelée*, pp. 48-50.

8 See J. Michael Dash, introduction to *Masters of the Dew*, p. 7.

9 Eugénie Galpérina, 'Jacques Roumain, sa vie, son oeuvre', in Jacques Roumain, *Œuvres choisies*, ed. E. Galpérina (Moscow: Editions du Progrès, 1964), p. 261.

10 On Roumain and Haitian Communism, see Diederich and Burt, pp. 328-30.

11 'Bois d'ébène' (a poem of 1939), in *La Montagne ensorcelée*, pp. 233, 235.

12 *La Montagne ensorcelée*, p. 101.

13 Michel Serres, 'Christ noir', *Critique* 29 (1973), p. 18. On biblical symbolism in Roumain, see also Marie-Lise Gazarian-Gautier, 'Le Symbolisme religieux dans *Gouverneurs de la rosée* de Jacques Roumain', *Présence Francophone* 7 (1973), 19-23, and Léon-François Hoffmann, 'Complexité linguistique et rhétorique dans *Gouverneurs de la rosée* de Jacques Roumain', *Présence Africaine* 98 (1976), pp. 150-1.

14 On the importance of Guinea in voodoo belief, see Maya Deren, *The Voodoo Gods* (1953; new ed. St Albans: Paladin, 1975), pp. 42-3.

15 See Deren (pp. 117-20 for Agoué and pp. 141-2 for Loko), who cites earlier studies in comprehensive footnotes.

16 Roumain had, however, undertaken a detailed study of voodoo at the urging of the French anthropologist Alfred Métraux in the early 1940s, and published an account of the ritual associated with one of the voodoo drums, *Le Sacrifice du tambour Assotôr*, in 1943.

17 On Erzulie and Ogoun, see Deren, pp. 118-19. On Ogoun in general, see pp. 127-31; on Ogoun St Jacques, see also p. 77. On Aïda Ouédo, see pp. 114, 173, 175.

18 On the monomyth, see Joseph Campbell, *The Hero with a Thousand Faces* (1949; rpt. London: Abacus, 1975).

19 Galpérina, p. 265, and Garret, pp. 156-7.

20 See Leyburn, pp. 199-201.

21 On the archetypal symbolism of the tree, see Gilbert Durand, *Les Structures anthropologiques de l'imaginaire* (Paris: Bordas, 1969), pp. 391-9, and Campbell, p. 211.

22 See Deren, pp. 42-3, on the significance of trees in voodoo.

23 Georges Ngal, 'L'Image et l'enracinement chez Aimé Césaire', *Présence Francophone* 6 (1973), p. 5. The quotation from Césaire is on p. 7 (my translation).

24 See Hall, pp. 1, 169, and Durand, pp. 322, 398.

25 See Hall, pp. 213-14.

34

26 On the biblical symbolism of blood as the water of life, see Serres. pp. 20–1.

27 For a full discussion of vegetation myth elements in *Masters of the Dew*, see Beverley Ormerod, 'Myth, Rite and Symbol in *Gouverneurs de la rosée*', *L'Esprit Créateur* 17 (1977), 123–32.

28 On the relation between the Grail legends and vegetation myth, see Jessie L. Weston, *From Ritual to Romance* (Cambridge: Cambridge University Press, 1920).

29 See Hoffmann, p. 156.

30 See Hall, pp. 19, 138.

31 See Deren, p. 42.

32 See Dash, introduction to *Masters of the Dew*, p. 18, on the symbolism of light and darkness in the novel.

2

The Freeing of the Waters:
Edouard Glissant's *The Ripening*

'A river to protect me against
the corruptions of the dusk'
(*Cahier*, p. 37).

Edouard Glissant's most recent volume of poetry, *Boises*, is dedicated 'to every country which is diverted from its course and suffers the failing of its waters'.[1] The dedication, the book's sub-title (*Natural History of an Aridity*), and the concluding words of the final poem – 'So we must retrace the dried water-course and descend into many absences, to wind along to the place of our rebirth, black in the rock' – all refer us to the major themes of Glissant's work: the need to recapture, but also to transcend, a vanished, unrecorded history; and the struggle to preserve a sense of cultural identity in the face of metropolitan French policies that discourage and inhibit the onward flow of a specifically Caribbean tradition in Martinique and Guadeloupe.

The 'many absences' referred to in this poem are those of the slave ancestors: doubly absent, since the details of their lives, unlike those of their masters, were unchronicled in the past (the official registers dismissing them with the brutally terse formula: 'arrival, canefields, death'),[2] and since their memory is ignored, or even rejected, by their present-day descendants. At the heart of Glissant's writing there is the strong desire to restore and elucidate the vast areas of the Caribbean past which have been neglected by European historians or else recorded with an unjust bias. In the preface to his play *Monsieur Toussaint*, he says: 'For those who know, of their own history, only that obscure and diminished portion to which they have been relegated, the recovery of the near or distant past is an imperative necessity . . . A passionate determination to unveil the past which has been deformed or obliterated by others may sometimes give us a better sense of the meaning of the present.'[3] He sets out, therefore, to stimulate Caribbean memory and to force the reader to re-examine the past – not in a vain quest for dates or facts, but in an attempt to acquire a sense of the continuous flow of time which lies dormant in the Caribbean landscape: the sea with its memories of the middle passage, the canefields bearing perpetual witness to the experience of exploiter and exploited, and the mountain forests filled with the presence of the maroons, the runaway slaves. He visualizes the rocks of the countryside as holding within themselves secret caverns

. . . filled with lost corpses, phantom bodies
(Which, sown there in times long past, forgotten there, have infil-
trated the rock with their violent decay)
Bodies of those whom from the beginning we call our heroes, and
whom we truly praise,

Edouard Glissant's *The Ripening*

Those who do not blaze forth in the unique light of posterity's
verification
But keep watch in the deafness of this rock, waiting for our cry to call
them forth.[4]

This appreciation of the latent historical qualities of the landscape imparts a
bitter strength to his grief that areas once rural, and even the formerly
impenetrable forests which sheltered the maroons, are now falling before the
onslaughts of metropolitan development companies: 'right up on the very
heights with their tangled thickets, the landscape has been ravaged and wrung
dry'.[5]

Along with the image of the parched and devastated land, that of the dried
watercourse, with its suggestions of drought and sterility, has come to haunt
Glissant's latest works. Its meaning is twofold: as the river is a traditional
symbol of the passage of time, its ceasing to flow denotes the absence of a sense
of history and continuity in the French Caribbean islands today; and the failing
of the water also represents the inroads of modern industrialization, a destruction of the landscape that is itself symbolic, in the author's eyes, of the destruction wrought upon his race first by slavery and then by economic and cultural
imposition. Slavery, with its enforced separation from African roots, began a
long process of physical deprivation and emotional impoverishment. 'You
deport me to a new country (which is an island), you steal from my mind –
indeed, from the inmost depths of my being – the knowledge of my former
country, you further insist that the new country belongs only to you, and so I
must go down the ages, countryless' (*L'Intention poétique*, p. 196). This
historic loss of identity is paralleled by a divorce between man and the land
today which is, for Glissant, symptomatic of the state of alienation that charac-
terizes his country: the feeling of dispossession, the moral disarray.[6] The situation has been aggravated by the policy of assimilation to France which has
sundered, for French West Indians, the connection with a meaningful African
past and has disregarded the folk-ways of their slave ancestors. Glissant's
second novel, *Le Quatrième Siècle*, is an imaginative reconstruction of the
Caribbean past as it would have appeared to all those living through it, with
major emphasis upon the viewpoints of two interwoven families whose African
ancestors arrived on the same ship: one, Longoué, to escape immediately and
take refuge in the maroon forests; the other, Béluse, to accept his fate as a
plantation slave. Members of these families appear in his other novels: *La
Lézarde* (*The Ripening*), *Malemort* and *La Case du commandeur*. In the last
two, as in *Boises*, the maroon ancestor of *Le Quatrième Siècle*, who has refused
to accept the condition of slavery and thus represents an archetypal freedom, is
called *le Négateur* – the repudiator, the one who rejects. The path which he
traces back down from the mountain forest to rescue from plantation servitude
the woman he has chosen for himself assumes a symbolic importance in these
works: *perdre la trace*, to lose the track (or the trace), becomes synonymous
with the loss or rejection of ancestral memories. In *Malemort* (p. 219) Glissant
portrays his contemporaries as holding out their hands towards a treasure
which they can never grasp, following separate tracks which lead nowhere, for
the path taken by the primordial black ancestor has been forgotten: the
Négateur has 'withered away in people's minds and hearts. He [is] now no
more than a vague sense of pain'. Similarly, in *La Case du commandeur*
(p. 138), successive generations are portrayed as vainly 'seeking the way

through . . . seeking the track'. In a fusion of the images of the lost path and the vanished watercourse, Glissant writes of 'the track silted up not by fertile mud and red clay but by grey stony expanses destined for arcades or bungalows or helicopter pads. All of us asking: "But what should we do, then?" . . . soon to be lost in the yellow light of scattered earth where our yesterdays are buried but where tomorrow never dawns . . . The track lost found and lost once more' (*Malemort*, pp. 189–90).

An insistence upon the verbs *tarir* (to run dry, to cease to flow) and *dessécher* (to dry out, to wither, to parch) is counterpointed in Glissant's writing by references to the real river which flowed through the landscape of his childhood: the Lézarde, whose rivulets once filled the plain near Fort-de-France but have now all but disappeared in the name of industrial progress. The novel, first published in 1958, which bears the name of this river is dominated by the image of the vital, sparkling water linking the mountains, the repository of maroon memories, with the unfettered sea. The river then was characterized by vigour and energy: 'with the mud swirling up from its bed and the logs across it, it sang a chaotically savage song. [It] was calling out for life'.[7] Its impatient cascades and bright blue eddies, 'exultantly free', are compared to the exhilarating uprising of 'a people in revolt' (*The Ripening*, p. 31). These associations lend a grievous weight to the laconic note in the later novel *Malemort* (p. 190): '1960 The Lézarde dried up'. Glissant persistently forces the reader to confront the dismal spectacle of the plundered river; its rich broad stream, once teeming with insect and animal life, which was the focal point of his early, idyllic pleasures, has now dwindled to an insignificant trickle, 'a gutter . . . That childhood Lézarde no longer exists' (*L'Intention poétique*, p. 220). The mangroves of its former delta harbour no more crabs, the rivulets are 'betrayed by white rubble', 'bits of cardboard and chunks of debris lie on the skeleton of the Lézarde' (*Malemort*, p. 193). A system of cross-references exists between all of Glissant's novels, and enables him to underscore, in *Malemort* (p. 61), the fact that the river in *The Ripening* was already menaced, 'poisoned . . . soon to dry up in the derisory construction of what would later be called (a row of flimsy shops made of wood and corrugated iron, a de luxe slum for goods manufactured elsewhere and stored there) an industrial zone'.

Pain at the despoliation of the river is thus linked with other emotions: anger aroused by France's cosmetic attempts to provide the overseas Departments with a semblance of economic development; bitterness at the pitiable inadequacy of such gestures, which serve only to obliterate the natural relationship which should exist between man and the land. But Glissant acknowledges that this relationship, in any case, has never flourished in the West Indies, where those who worked on the land in past centuries had no hope of owning it and learnt to associate land ownership only with the negative 'pleasure of possessing and showing off . . . [of] spitting on one's fellow-men' (*Le Quatrième Siècle*, p. 168). So the freed slaves drifted to the fringes of the towns with their false promise of prosperity, and perpetuated the divorce between themselves and the tropical countryside, renouncing any attempt to become masters of their physical environment.[8] *The Ripening* records a moment in the history of Martinique when it seemed that the breach between the land and its inhabitants could be healed, that with the assumption of Departmental status the island could hope for real progress and fruitfulness; in the novel the river is depicted as curving around the town as if 'to enfold a portion of humanity, to reassure its people and help them' (p. 32). On the contrary, in *Malemort*, the

Edouard Glissant's *The Ripening*

title of which is a medieval word meaning cruel and tragic death, the predominant mood is a compound of grief, cynicism and disillusionment. The author sardonically exposes the contradiction between the lip service officially paid to the notion of fostering a sense of Caribbean cultural identity, and the true attitude of metropolitan France towards the islands: 'Of course there are problems here but a Frenchman's a Frenchman, whether he's a Breton, an Alsatian or a West Indian' (*Malemort*, p. 194). The crushing of independent private initiative and self-development is rendered in microcosm by the failure of a modest local attempt to create a commune which would have brought a few families back to the land. The area is requisitioned by a metropolitan company whose giant tractor charges noisily backward and forward, ripping the earth apart, fouling the freshwater pools and 'ravaging all this dream of land reform' (*Malemort*, p. 214). The tractor's blind attempt to uproot three tall ebony trees echoes an earlier moment in *Le Quatrième Siècle* (p. 169) when Saint-Yves Béluse (a descendant of the African who accepted slavery), desiring, like his former masters, to exploit the land, plans to uproot and sell the wood of three ebony trees, seeing only their commercial value and not the fact that they have looked down upon the lives of his ancestors and are a precious link with the past. Such indifference to the landscape is indifference to the meaning and importance of history. On the other hand, care for the land-scape and attachment to it are, for Glissant, essential means whereby a commu-nity cut off from its original roots and ties may slowly come to know its new country and take root in it, regaining through the landscape a lost sense of historical continuity and of nationhood, '*suffering* the land and becoming worthy of it' (*L'Intention poétique*, p. 196).

The Ripening is the story of an initiation into the meaning of a landscape. It is set in Martinique at the time of the 1945 elections, which paved the way for the island's assumption of Departmental status; but this is not established until late in the narrative, when the novel specifically invites interpretation as a political allegory. At the outset it is the poetic and mythical qualities of the narrative which are most in evidence, and its primary impact is that of a fabulous adventure. The fiction is built upon traditional, archetypal motifs: the departure from a known region into the unknown; the encounter with an alluring woman; the questing journey through a mysterious forest; the descent, in darkness, to a magic spring; the tests of skill and endurance; the killing which frees imprisoned waters and lifts a curse from a community; the final, difficult return of the hero enriched and matured by his initiatory experiences. When the work is reconsidered with hindsight, however, in the light of its precise setting in time and place, the reader becomes aware of multiple parallels between the mythical situation of the protagonist and the awakening consciousness – the 'ripening' – of his country. This deft intertwining of poetic fiction and political thesis is in keeping with Glissant's conviction that the function of his art is not merely to reflect the Caribbean environment, but to support and illuminate the stages of its growth, to testify to the slow forma-tion of a nation whose existence is not yet recognized even by its own nationals, and still less by those who contest its right to independence.[9]

Although written in conventional novel form, *The Ripening* is for the most part as bare of everyday domestic detail as a classical French tragedy. Few concrete events are described: the author's main concern is the intellectual and emotional development of his characters, and the growth of their sense of commitment to the land. The tone of the book is abstract, and much of it takes

The Freeing of the Waters

the form of conversation and debate. In addition, Glissant persistently reverts to evocations of the river and the countryside, elements which are closely connected with the symbology of his fiction. The events of the story unfold through a series of journeys, each of which represents a progressive stage in self-knowledge and in the exploration of various dimensions of human experience. The opening pages stress the themes of genesis, change and exploration. The main protagonist, Thaël, sets out from his mountain home in the early morning. Place and time are those to which the novel will return at its end. The landscape is idyllic: the paradisaic motifs of dawn and mankind's birth are suggested by the sunlight playing on the dew, the magnificent poinciana tree which dominates the space above, and the 'primeval heat of earth's first day' into which the hero steps. But the sun leads Thaël forward and downward along a muddy track towards a second tree, the plum-tree ('tree of misfortunes', p. 70) which 'marks the boundary between the known and the unknown'; as Thaël stops beneath it he is conscious of standing on the very brink of a venture whose 'blood and sweat' are still to come. The sense of being guided and instructed by the elements of nature around him – the trees, the sunlight and shadows, the river, the sea – is one that will accompany Thaël throughout his journeying. Already, as he descends into the lowlands, he is aware of inner change, of a transition from a private world of mystery and isolation into a public world of factual analysis and enumeration. He has crossed a decisive threshold into a sphere of rebirth.

This initial journey brings Thaël to the town of Lambrianne, to meet and become involved with a group of young people, led by Mathieu, who entrust him with a mission which they themselves cannot safely undertake. The group, which has been campaigning on behalf of a new political party representing the interests of the countryside and the agricultural workers, is threatened by the arrival of Garin, a former local man and hired killer turned government official, who has been sent to stamp out political dissent in the area. They ask Thaël to arrange the apparently accidental death of this man. Through Mathieu's group, Thaël is introduced to aspects of the landscape which were unfamiliar to him, and which, like the river, assume a symbolic importance in the narrative: the flatlands planted in sugar-cane, and the sea beyond. His next journey takes him upriver to Garin's house in the hills, the House of the Spring, which is built right over the source of the Lézarde. The situation of the house, which confers on its owner the power to withhold from others the flow of the river, symbolically indicates Garin's role as the representative of a menacing, exploitative authority and as an archetypal figure of evil. Thaël's return downriver with Garin ends in the drowning of the latter when Thaël overturns their boat upon the treacherous sand bar in the bay. Finally, acquitted of responsibility for Garin's death, he travels back up to his home, taking with him Valérie, the girl he has met in the canefields of the plain. But on their arrival she is attacked and fatally mauled by Thaël's dogs, and the novel ends not upon a peaceful return, but on the prospect of a further journey back to the House of the Spring, where Thaël intends to starve his dogs to death in expiation of their crime.

The French title of *The Ripening, La Lézarde*, relates both to the plot and to the theme of the birth of political awareness, since Thaël's journey upriver is synonymous with his acceptance of political responsibility, and the river's downward flow 'toward evening and the dark sea, thereby perfecting its knowledge and accomplishing its death' (p. 32), mirrors his growing insights and foreshadows the death of his adversary in the bay at the mouth of the

Edouard Glissant's *The Ripening*

Lézarde. The course of the river, rising in the northern highlands and cascading downwards with the 'swift rapids of its youth' (p. 31), slowing to encompass the town and to learn 'the grey realities of the plain' (p. 33), running past 'the sinister fields of sugar-cane' (p. 31) to end in the mud-streaked delta, parallels the path of discovery which Thaël follows. Its 'irreversible flow' takes it from its source amidst 'the legends of the mountains' – a lofty place of origin which suggests a symbolic superiority over the fallen flatlands of cane – down to its meeting with the sea, which is 'the dawn of true and painful knowledge' (p. 33). In the same way, Thaël springs from the mountains, with their historic maroon associations: 'he knows the old legends, he cares for the mysteries' (p. 23); but he has come down to seek 'order and clarity' (p. 21), and ultimately, to seek self-knowledge. When Mathieu says that Thaël is there in order 'to join the murmurous past to the bitter present' (p. 80), he underlines both Thaël's closeness of spirit to the ways of his ancestors, and his ignorance of the misery that still prevails in the flatlands. Thaël's early remoteness from the life of the plain echoes that of the ancestral *Négateur*: 'in this country, where the mountains are everywhere subject to the temptation of the sea, to be a man of the mountains presupposes a supreme vocation for refusal. [The mountains are] a last refuge of solitude, untouched by the abrupt light and dark of passion' (p. 12). This spiritual affinity with the past, however, carries with it the danger of too great a detachment from one's fellow men. Mathieu is drawn to Thaël by his own fascination with history and yearning for contact with his lost ancestors; yet he is also 'a rebel against the stultifying influence of the past' (p. 25), and his role is to force Thaël into contact with the present. It is he who opens Thaël's eyes to the cruel contrast between the splendour of the tropical landscape and the deep-rooted poverty of the peasants who work the land, a poverty summed up for Mathieu by a sight which continues to haunt him: the spectacle of a 4-year-old child gravely guiding his father's emaciated oxen across a sterile field, while just beyond the river swirls and sings its joyous song. It is through Mathieu and his friends that Thaël comes to see Garin as a corrupt and self-seeking traitor to his race and class, who has murdered in the past and is now 'preparing for a career of exploitation' (p. 203). Thaël's fear that Garin's actions will intensify the people's suffering is the decisive factor which persuades him to bring about the latter's death; and this decision transforms him 'from a man of the mountains into a man of the countryside' (p. 55). When he travels beyond the town into the canefields that surround the sugar factory, he is conscious of having 'left the realm of myth and entered the wasteland of everyday living . . . the stifling confinement of commonplace misery' (p. 70). It is a transition which Glissant considers essential; he continually stresses the twin imperatives of recovering a lost history and simultaneously 'living in and bearing witness to the present, along with all those who are living through it' (*L'Intention poétique*, p. 38).

Thaël's encounter with the canefields is a striking example of the power that landscape has, in Glissant's hands, to evoke the forgotten past. In *Le Quatrième Siècle* (pp. 46–7) old Papa Longoué, the last descendant of the original *Négateur*, looks down towards the plain and sees, in his mind's eye, its successive transformations throughout the centuries: the virgin bush meeting the sweeping descent of the hillside acacias, and then being progressively thinned out in order to accommodate the rigid manmade squares of the canefields; and he reflects that all of Caribbean history is illuminated by the land before him and its changing appearances down the ages. The same idea is present in *Malemort* (p. 61) where the woodland once traversed by the *Négateur* is 'at first intact original then cleared burnt over then filled with cane rotting under water then dried out choked with sand metalled over, a recorder of time finally struck down beneath its own branches'.

The mountains are one repository of the epic past; the sea is another, which brought to the New World, 'nailed to the tall ships, a people whose flesh was sold, hired out, bartered', and which bore the Haitian liberator Toussaint back in the opposite direction, to die in the 'white sea of the Jura'.[10] And, as in Césaire's *Cahier*, the canefields hold the ancestral memory of captivity and suffering. When the young Mathieu Béluse comes to Papa Longoué to hear him recount the past, the old man tells him to open his eyes to 'the things of the past which are planted in the ground to speak to you . . . Take a single cane plant, watch it grow in the earth till its arrow rears up against the sky, follow its path to the Central Factory and see how it turns into molasses and syrup, sugar or rum . . . then you understand what pain is, and hear beneath the official records the true voice of the past which for so long has remained unchanged' (*Le Quatrième Siècle*, p. 220). Thus when Thaël approaches Lambrianne for the first time, it is appropriate that the road into the town should be bordered on either side by canefields; his passage along it symbolizes his initiation into the realities of toil and affliction that characterize the plain. Later, more fully aware of his own ignorance, he visits the distillery 'like a tourist', consciously 'acquainting himself with the penetrating odour of death', and runs down an alley between two fields of densely growing cane 'in order to know at first hand this prison, to feel, between its whistling walls, the full weight of its tyranny' (p. 70).[11] The same claustrophobic effect is reproduced in *Le Quatrième Siècle* (p. 223) where the canecutter's physical and mental horizons are bounded by the 3-metre height of the cane above his head and the line, just above ground level, along which the stalks must be cut. Yet *The Ripening* suggests that those who work in the canefields, as they live through the accursed and never-ending cycle of planting and harvesting, are slowly, like Thaël, moving towards full awareness, are maturing with the maturing cane and coming 'to find in this place, this time, a taste for life and liberty' (p. 51). The members of Mathieu's group, with all the idealism and enthusiasm of youth, respond to this new mood in the country, seeing their island still as a captive feudal society but also as 'a newly ripening fruit, slowly opening . . . and offering up its riches to those who seek, to those who suffer' (pp. 32–3).

The canefields form a major leitmotif throughout *The Ripening*, and their tragic function in the history of Caribbean slavery is kept before the reader by repeated references to the 'death-dealing stalks' which tear at the lips of the starving children who suck them (p. 51), the 'devouring cane' (p. 132) and the 'factory of death' in its midst (p. 69), the 'sinister fields' (p. 31) with their 'odour of sweat and death' (p. 119), the rum and sugar which hold the population in their grip like a pair of torturing pincers (p. 237). Even in the town it is impossible to escape the omnipresent cane, which is transported on a railway line running appropriately by the cemetery and the slaughterhouse, and crossing the central square of Lambrianne. The strident passage of a freight-car, a 'hideous yet everyday vehicle', is a brutal interruption to the town's holiday festivities, an 'assault of naked reality' reminding the inhabitants of the industry that dominates their lives (p. 173). In the third part of the novel, where political statement is more overt, cane is explicitly associated with past slavery and present economic exploitation. The spirit of social protest which impels

Mathieu and his companions is shown to be founded on an indignant perception of the majority of their compatriots as 'a nation of canefield beasts, victims of scorn and exile' (p. 178). In the mood of euphoria after the election victory of the reformist party, the peasant Lomé, who exemplifies the dawn of political consciousness among the poor, turns his back upon the cultivation of cane and joins with the student Pablo and the policeman Tigamba to plant vegetables and bananas and keep livestock. It is a measure of the gap of disillusionment between the era of *The Ripening* and that of *Malemort* that in the later novel, Tigamba is no longer working alongside Lomé but is a corrupt police brigadier casually shooting down street protesters and lending his support to the representatives of an oppressive regime. Lomé, however, is now 'solidly planted in the earth', having achieved that desirable sense of harmony with his physical environment which is beyond the reach of the alienated cane workers; and he is one of the few who 'has not lost the track which leads from the mountains down to the sandy shore' (*Malemort*, p. 204).

The contrast between the northern mountains and the southern canefields is sharply delineated in *The Ripening* as Thaël, the mountain-dweller, takes the road out of town that leads to the sugar factory. It runs in the opposite direction to the road that had led him to Lambrianne, the winding mountain road with its atmosphere of leisure, beauty, shade and silence, and its ancestral association with freedom. On the contrary, the flat, dusty southern road, unrelieved by verges, hedges or human habitation, runs 'straight as fatality' across the plain to the factory, its 'inflexible tarred surface seeming to salute the workyard of death' (p. 69). The low, monotonous scene with its ugly buildings and skeletal iron bridge is totally foreign to Thaël's experience, and is as oppressive as the cloying, fruity smell of the cane, the suffocating fumes of the boiling syrup, and the dense rows of plants rustling and crackling in the breeze. It is in this alien, menacing setting that he first encounters Valérie and, hemmed in on all sides by the walls of cane, is inexorably driven towards her as she stands 'like a flash of light in a long, narrow prison cell' (p. 76). An underlying motif of the novel is the danger of Valérie's beauty, which first distracts Mathieu from his political purpose and his true love of Mycéa, and then threatens to beguile Thaël into forgetting his new commitment to the cause of the suffering poor. She seems, to Thaël, to represent 'a synthesis of the conflicting forces' within him (p. 183) – his urge towards the plain, and his desire to retreat to the fastness of his home. He is convinced of her instinctive goodness, and believes that she alone can save him from his feelings of helplessness and confusion; but he also detects in her a certain disdain for the peasantry, a lack of understanding of their 'innate, smiling grandeur'. It is significant that her beauty is associated with the canefields from the moment when Thaël first sees her, laughing and confident, amid the ripe arrows of cane. When he takes the road through the canefields for the second time, he thinks of her as 'the true daughter of the lands' around him. The association is an ominous one, for in Glissant's work it is 'the plain . . . set in mud, [which] cries to us of death'.[12] Arguing bitterly with Mathieu about his right to involve Thaël in his political cause, she stands silhouetted against the plain and her face 'melts into its green depths. Mathieu looks into the distance, but it is Valérie that he sees before him. The horizon is empty' (pp. 105–6). This fusion of Valérie with the southern landscape is consolidated by Mycéa's ironic description of her as 'a flower amid the flowers and coolness of the valley . . . standing out above all others, like an arrow of sugar cane in a field of vegetables . . .

making cakes and jams and doing a little needlework – that's real life – while all around there is ruination' (p. 205).

Valérie's spiritual isolation in her 'dream land, a place of peace where everything can be forgotten, where there is no motion or drama or sorrow', parallels Thaël's initial remoteness from the life of the flatlands and absence of commitment to any cause.

It is on his second journey towards the factory, 'amid the smell of burnt sugar', that he realizes for the first time that he will not be able to return to his insulated way of life in the mountains, that he has already unconsciously committed himself to 'the paths of his countrymen's toil and endeavour' (p. 183). Yet, under the influence of his love for Valérie, he does attempt such a return. Climbing away from the town with her, he interrupts her domestic chatter in an effort to explain to her the importance of the canefields in his new apprehension of reality: 'When I first came down here . . . I didn't see the distillery. It was there, all the time, but I didn't see it. All along the way there were fields of sugar-cane, but I didn't see them or know what they meant' (p. 238). His encounter with Garin and assumption of responsibility for the latter's death are the factors which have heightened his awareness, so that when he once more treads the path across the canefields he sees them as 'a prison of sugar-sweat, of meager salaries and fat dividends, of ignominy and exploitation built upon a verdant base' (p. 184). But Valérie, in whom familiarity has bred indifference to the fields' 'permanent message of sweat and hunger' (p. 72), turns him gently away from such talk. Thus the loss of Valérie, unexpected and unlikely as it first appears, assumes an implacable logic when viewed as a final initiatory rite which forces Thaël into full maturity and makes it impossible for him to resume his secluded hillside existence. Her death reveals to him the naivety of his assumption that a single political act, the killing of Garin, could solve all problems and eradicate all suffering: 'How false it is to believe that our task is done. We have only just begun it' (p. 252).

Like Manuel in Roumain's *Masters of the Dew*, Thaël has many of the traditional attributes of a saviour. He is a humble mountain shepherd, lacking the experience and sophistication of Mathieu's group, yet he has come from afar to help them: his 'is the wisdom and the power of decision' (p. 80). He 'speaks like a prophet' (p. 23), and his real name, Raphaël, recalls the biblical function of his namesake (whose name means 'God heals') as guardian angel and protector of the young and of all pilgrims and travellers.[13] His message is that of Glissant himself: 'We must reconquer the land . . . A man must take root before he can set out' (p. 63). His gravity and reserve are such that it is easy to overlook the fact that he is only 18 years old, three years younger than Mathieu, and that he is unsure of his own motive for leaving his home, 'drawn towards the town by some force that spurred him on' (*Le Quatrième Siècle*, p. 285). Mathieu suggests at the outset that he may have come to Lambrianne in order to find himself (p. 22); and involvement with Mathieu is, indeed, the catalyst that transforms Thaël's vision of himself and of his role in the world. The relationship between the two is translated in terms of an interplay of light and dark, of contact with the past and lucidity in the present. Mathieu sees Thaël as his 'nocturnal and essential counterpart: a Mathieu of the deep night' (p. 116). Darkness and mystery are associated with the past, both with the lost motherland of Africa and with the fugitive, unrecorded history of the early slaves and maroons in the West Indies. In *Le Quatrième Siècle* Mathieu is portrayed as an adolescent eager to penetrate the mystery that surrounds his Béluse ancestors and their traditional enemies, the descendants of the

Négateur, whose sole survivor, Papa Longoué, is Mathieu's only link with the past. Thaël, whose maternal ancestor arrived in the same slave-ship as the *Négateur* and the first Béluse (*Le Quatrième Siècle*, p. 166), and who himself lives in the mountains, exercises the same fascination over the older Mathieu and shares the same legendary prestige as Papa Longoué. As Thaël is identified with the mountains, so Mathieu identifies himself with the town, as if 'his name summed up all the reality which blossomed on its red rooftops' (p. 14). Like the plain with its 'heavy, dazzling light' and its blazing, blinding sun, Mathieu is a 'torrid zone', 'a cascade of light, a luminous body, set apart by the sun' (pp. 24-5). Here, as in Glissant's long essay *Soleil de la conscience*, the sun is symbolic of knowledge, self-awareness, lucidity, a sense of order, a revolutionary consciousness.[14] It is for Mathieu's cerebral, didactic qualities and his long acquaintance with the poverty-stricken plain that Thaël is drawn to him; he counters Mathieu's 'I want to know and teach' with his own desire 'to live and learn this misery, to endure and combat it' (p. 29). Thaël is a foil for all Mathieu's group, 'clear-thinking, methodical men [who] seek after legend', while Thaël seeks 'order and clarity' (p. 21).

Yet Mathieu is not simply a cool scholar interested in history. He and Thaël are 'assailed by the same passion' (p. 30), 'moved by some force beyond [their] understanding' (p. 22). And Mathieu himself is intensely ambivalent about his love of the past: justifying his work as an archivist by his belief that self-knowledge, for his fellow Martinicans, lies in knowledge of their lost history (p. 79), but also half resentful of the hold that Papa Longoué has on his imagination, fearful that he will be tempted to linger too long, his will numbed, in the realm of shadows and mystery which the old man inhabits: 'I'm tired of your shadows! People are dying of hunger and they can't eat shadows . . . A man must fight!' (p. 139). Through Mathieu's inner conflict, Glissant explores a problem to which he repeatedly returns in his later writing: that of the weight which West Indians should give to their history. Forgetfulness of Africa, the 'infinite country' of which Papa Longoué can grant Mathieu only tantalizing glimpses, and forgetfulness of the middle passage that brought the slaves to the Caribbean, must result in a sterile, doomed endeavour to fill the vacuum thus created with the ways of an alien culture, 'hands daily stretched out towards the manners of another whose voice and gesture can never quite be captured' (*Le Quatrième Siècle*, p. 31). This denial of the *Négateur*'s path may lead a whole nation to 'disappear, run dry, with no true descendants, no future fertility' (*Le Quatrième Siècle*, p. 264). To shoulder the weight of the past, however, is a difficult and at times a self-defeating enterprise. Médellus, the visionary and failed commune leader of *Malemort*, rediscovers but cannot support the *Négateur*'s track, which 'opens up in him ravines of shade in which he founders'; his moods oscillate between sudden inexplicable outbursts of violence and 'a gentle, contented laissez-faire attitude' (*Malemort*, p. 213). The same fatalistic passivity is present in the young Mathieu who is drawn into Papa Longoué's world of shadow and suffering as he had once fallen, a terrified and unresisting child, into the blue depths of the sea, that other witness to a forgotten history (*Le Quatrième Siècle*, p. 257). It is an attitude against which the author warns: 'The fervent rediscovery of ourselves should not lead to a sterile and exclusive preoccupation with the past' (*L'Intention poétique*, p. 142).

Papa Longoué ultimately represents a retrograde force. As a *quimboiseur*, he keeps alive the African tradition of healing and prophecy handed down to him by his maroon forebears. But by this very fidelity to the spirit of the

Négateur, he also prolongs the maroons' old, vain hope of a return to Africa, which, as long as it survives, prevents full acceptance of and commitment to the new country.[15] A balance must therefore be struck between past and present.

At the beginning of *The Ripening*, Mathieu's inability to reconcile the two is remarked by Thaël: 'he goes from the poinciana tree to the distillery and from the distillery back to the tree, and he still hasn't found what he's after' (p. 80). The distillery, symbol of present-day economic exploitation and injustice, of the fate of an abased people, is opposed to the poinciana tree or *flamboyant* whose brilliant red blossoms make it a 'tree of splendour' (p. 219), a 'symbol of glory' (p. 70). In the novel the poinciana which guards the path to Thaël's house in the mountains is associated with 'night' (p. 77) and specifically with 'the splendour of memory' (p. 70); it is 'the hearth where the life of the hills burns brightly' (p. 250). Through these associations, it represents the past, like the hieratic silk-cotton tree (legendary haunt of ghosts) further down the road.[16] But at the same time it represents the future goal towards which Mathieu equally strives: 'to free the country from the poverty and shame and above all the pettiness which had for so long been imposed upon it . . . to reach the poinciana and the terrifying silk-cotton tree, to go beyond the dazzling sand bar' (p. 219). Like Thaël, Mathieu undergoes an initiation; but in his case it is twofold. As the adolescent of *Le Quatrième Siècle*, listening to Papa Longoué, he has sought to remount the river of time. Now his work for the electoral campaign leads him to cross another river 'which separates one shore of life from another' and which will enable him 'to arrive at true knowledge of the land, to taste its full savour' (p. 115). The end of this initiatory process is the election victory through which his group 'attains the tree of splendour and the magnificent, boundless sea' (p. 219); and it is significant that this coincides with the death of Papa Longoué, which 'means farewell to old Africa' for Mathieu (p. 223). In their discussion of the old man's death, the members of the group try to define his place in their endeavour and to arrive at a solution to the problem of history. Mathieu feels that Papa Longoué's error was to cling exclusively to the memory of Africa, disregarding the existence of other things. These unspecified 'other things', which in fact, paradoxically, 'include Papa Longoué . . . which stem from Papa Longoué' (p. 223), imply both recognition of the African past and fidelity to the Caribbean present. If the claims of the latter are ignored, there can be no end to rootlessness and alienation, no dynamic impulse towards a fruitful and healing cultural synthesis. And the path to such a synthesis lies in the landscape itself, which holds the key to past, present and future; within which Thaël sees his people 'reaching out, through so many mirages, to the expression of their own essential qualities' (p. 183).

As Mathieu reveals the realities of the plain to Thaël, so Garin draws him back to the mountains, up to the source of the Lézarde, and then down again to the moment of crisis upon the sand bar beyond its mouth. Thaël's journey upriver through the shadows and splendours of the forest, his senses heightened by hunger, takes on the nature of a ritual quest for a legendary enemy. As he follows the hidden paths, the silvery snakeskin shed on the ground before him prefigures his encounter with Garin, the antagonist 'more dangerous than a snake that has just sloughed its skin' (p. 87), whose fate has crossed his own. The landscape itself seems to direct his will and communicate its strength to him. The river imposes upon him the task of locating its source – 'that gentle gushing forth which will soon flow strongly and bring fecundity' (p. 87) – as a prerequisite for the accomplishing of his mission. The forest is alive around him in a 'fusion of rising sap, darkness and flashes of light' which gives him the exalted sensation of being 'a branch of the universal tree' (p. 88); here, as in *L'Intention poétique* (p. 48), the tropical tree represents 'a vigorous surge, a seething density'. The same 'sombre exaltation' (p. 90) holds him as he enters the upper level of Garin's house, makes his perilous way around the unrailed inner balcony and follows the dark ramp down towards the sound and coolness of the concealed spring: 'the imprisoned source of the Lézarde, guarded by thick walls, surrounded by marble flagging, like an idol weighed down with finery'. 'Everything begins here', thinks Thaël; and the walled spring within the cavernous house, bathed in a 'fabulous cool' (p. 96), recalls the archetypal well, the ancient mirror of the self which, when contemplated, brings self-knowledge and knowledge of the world without.[17] The vocabulary of this passage stresses the sacred and arcane nature of Thaël's experience. The moment when he discovers the spring is one of 'religious expectation before an altar streaming with water' (p. 91). He spends the night which follows in a state of vigil, 'like the neophyte of some secret cult' (p. 94), and is conscious of having fulfilled an initiatory requirement: 'It is true that I have found both the source of the river and the man to be killed. Here, in this proud darkness, the river is born and he has his dwelling' (p. 91). Thus the slaying of Garin becomes synonymous with the freeing of captive waters, another archetypal motif which confers upon the conflict between the two men the dimensions of cosmic myth. Garin, 'planted in the spring', is like 'a tree attempting to usurp the fertility of the Lézarde . . . to sully the river and its surrounding fields and men' (p. 94). Thaël, the defender of the river, becomes the age-old hero of quest-romance, moving from the pastoral safety of his innocent youth, through a period of searching, into a death-struggle against a monstrous foe whose defeat will restore life-giving waters to a fallen and sterile land.[18]

The winding path which Garin and Thaël follow along the Lézarde's downward course is linked, in *Malemort* (p. 49), with the twisting track which the *Négateur* took down to the plain to rescue his future wife from the yoke of slavery. The identification of these two 'sinuous destinies' underlines the significance of Thaël's mission: it, too, is an act of liberation, undertaken to free the community from the corruption which Garin represents. Garin's definition of freedom is based entirely upon self-interest. Born into poverty, he has risen in life on the principle that money, whatever its source, is the only key to success and superiority. Like the European plantation owners before him, he now seeks to exercise power through the acquisition of private property, and at the expense of others; he has bought the House of the Spring 'in order to be quite free: to command the whole river' (p. 93). His complicity in the schemes of his former employer, a local white planter who attempts to persuade him to use his political contacts in order to appropriate the lands bordering the river, highlights a moral issue which Glissant debates elsewhere: the opposition between the interests of the individual and those of the community. Glissant sees this issue in terms of a discord between two systems of thought which have both influenced the Caribbean. On the one hand, the African ideal of collective participation sets a supreme value on sharing, on social and cultural co-operation, and thus prizes the community above the individual. On the other hand, the European cult of personality and free will fosters the pursuit of private goals and jealously defends the individual's right to personal possessions; it thus militates against the concepts of generosity and universal participation.[19] In the context of these notions, Garin's enjoyment of his 'power to release one piece of land and requisition another' (p. 93) takes on the aspect of a betrayal of ancestral values, an adherence to an alien model of personal ambition, domination and exploitation. His attitude to the land, which he himself has never worked, is one of calculation and of obscure resentment: 'with an assurance born of hate he put his finger on the most fertile areas, those with a future in store' (p. 97). He observes, but has no sympathy with, its appeal to the sensibilities of others; he simply deplores its lack of mineral wealth. In him, the sense of divorce between man and his environment is carried to an extreme. The idea that there is a 'true greatness in living with the land, patiently, and conquering it like a beloved woman' (p. 103) is remote from his considerations, as is Thaël's belief that the soil should belong to those who till it. He detests the town because it 'is a continuation of the land' (p. 125); and while Thaël feels that the town-dwellers are ennobled by their inner awareness of the countryside around them, he despises them as simpletons, incapable of revolt against the system which he himself has successfully turned to his account. His ruthless code of each man for himself promises disaster for a region which has already had its full share of suffering. His vision of society is presented as warped and tainted. Like Thaël and Mathieu, he is 'not merely a man but an instrument of his country's fate, an exemplary destiny' (p. 104); and Thaël's conviction that he should die stems from the fact that the example he sets is impure and morally unacceptable.

Yet in the course of their journey downriver a state of truce arises between the two men, and an unexpected bond is forged. The river appears to transform them both: Garin is clad in a new dignity, as if 'his past crimes, his betrayals, his ignorance are all cleansed, effaced, obliterated by the descending water' (p. 109); while Thaël is spiritually carried away by the flow of the Lézarde, which seems to penetrate him, as it does the land, like a symbol of 'hope and restitution' (p. 118). Despite the irreconcilability of their moral stances, they are united in their response to the call of the sea, which represents for both an open horizon, a dynamic future. Yet, paradoxically, the sea is 'the negation of all human purpose' (p. 147); the transition from riverside to seashore is felt as a transition from flux and mutability to a timeless immobility, an infinite spaciousness, and induces in both men a sense of surrender to the inevitable. An inner compulsion leads them 'heavily forward, in a straight line, twin embodiments of fatality' (p. 145), like the river which goes unresistingly towards its death in the sea – the sea, 'pitiless and eternal' (p. 101), which holds the memory of ancestral deaths during the middle passage, 'the smell of seaweed, of hot wood, of bitter blood' (p. 147): and Thaël's attack on Garin in the boat echoes, perhaps, that of the *Négateur* in *Le Quatrième Siècle*, who threw himself, as the slave-ship rode at anchor, against the first Béluse, who had betrayed him into captivity. But, again like the *Négateur*, Thaël does not actually kill his opponent, except in so far as he is responsible for the overturning of their boat. Garin drowns in the raging surf at the sand bar beyond which he had wanted to pass, 'to laugh in the sunlight on the other side, in defiance of Thaël and of the sea'. Glissant later suggests, in fact, that Garin goes to his death consenting, 'like an overseer secretly weary of towing the sugar factory along, resolved to elude life and to sail beneath the foam of the open sea', who has 'chosen the foaming sand bar as the table for his last repast' (*Malemort*, pp. 49, 59). Thaël does not even know, until he reaches the shore, that Garin is dead. The importance of the episode lies primarily not in the removal of Garin (who accurately predicts, as he disappears, that there will always be other Garins), but in the crystallization of Thaël's political commitment, the attainment of a definitive stage in his initiation. The crossing of the sand bar is established early in the novel as a ritual test of masculine strength, a feat of endurance which, like the splendid upward thrust of the poinciana tree, symbolizes the aspirations of Mathieu's group. When they teach Thaël, the mountain boy, to swim, each of them is 'a link in the chain that soon [will] bind him to the sea'; and the sea itself, the 'force that holds him captive', is the pre-ordained site of an essential rite of passage, having reserved for Thaël 'a place obscurely preappointed for his use since the beginning' (p. 45). His triumph over the sand bar is the final step in the ritual process which began at the House of the Spring; as he kneels, afterwards, upon the beach, trying to gather the threads of his experience together and make sense of it, he 'understands that he has entered into life' (p. 154). The symbolic and mythical qualities of the incident are underscored by the fact that for the first time in history, the waves cease to rage over the sand bar, as if the sea is placated and satisfied by the death of Garin.[20] Lomé, the spiritual heir of the Longoués, whose profile so astonishingly reproduces that of the *Négateur* (*Le Quatrième Siècle*, p. 274), confirms Thaël's accession, through his struggle with Garin, to the adult world: 'You are entering life, you have the necessary knowledge. Your work is just beginning' (p. 169).

Although the third part of the novel is more directly orientated towards political events than the first part, which deals with Thaël's descent to the plain, or the second, which relates his encounter with Garin, it is nonetheless linked by theme and metaphor to the motifs of emergence from shadowed isolation, of initiation and of spiritual renewal which dominate Thaël's adventure. Election day, the first Sunday of September 1945, is the moment when the people see at last an end to the 'long years of shadow and denial' and hope for an 'intoxicating affirmation of their birth'; on the outcome of the voting depends 'the drying up of the night, the long-awaited dawn' (p. 191). The vote in favour of Departmental status, so much criticized in later years by advocates of full independence for the islands, seemed at the time to offer an immense step forward from the colonial conditions of the pre-war period. The years of World War II had themselves been an era of intense hardship and indignity for the French Caribbean territories. Their suffering was entirely caused by their French affiliations: France, occupied by the Nazis, was enemy territory for the Allies, who regarded Martinique and Guadeloupe in the same hostile light and set up blockades which prevented the importation of essentials such as food and drugs. The island colonies, run as a virtual sugar monoculture, were incapable of supplying the population's needs. At the same time, thousands of French sailors, unable to get back to occupied France, were billeted in the islands, thus exacerbating the problem of supplies and, by displays of prejudice, creating grave racial animosities. In all his novels Glissant touches upon the privations of this period: the endless queues for a tiny amount of salt or cassava; the nightmare world of the hospital, lacking all but the most primitive of remedies; the racism of Pétain's sailors and their thefts of crops from small farmers' plots; and along with the physical starvation, the sense of isolation and emptiness, of imprisonment by the closed, sterile, uncrossable sea.[21] Thus the war nurtured in the inhabitants of the islands a sense of the desirability of a new social order and a wish to assert their own right to political and personal dignity. In *The Ripening* (p. 17), the mood of the immediate post-war period is suggested by images of a winged metamorphosis: the casting off of old forms, the unleashing of dreams; emergence into dazzling sunlight and unbridled upward flight.

At the end of the war, the belief was strong that once the islands had become full-fledged Departments of France, they would enjoy those metropolitan privileges which were absent under the colonial regime. Césaire has called this the period of the myth of social justice and equality, the myth of the miraculous benefits that full French citizenship would confer.[22] In fact, the centralization resulting from the conferment of Departmental status meant the loss of what measure of regional administrative autonomy previously existed. At the same time, the extensive powers of the new Prefect (a metropolitan political appointment) were not, and still are not, seen to differ greatly from those of the previous colonial governors. While family allowances and other government subsidies ensure a minimum standard of living which the majority of voters today are reluctant to set at risk by pressing for separation from France, in the years since 1946 there have been persistent manifestations of disenchantment with the Departmental relationship. The recurrent riots, in protest against unemployment, inadequate wages or working conditions, which have been brutally put down by the police; the strikes and civilian demonstrations crushed through the intervention of metropolitan security forces, are viewed by Glissant as a kind of continuation of the movement of revolt against slavery inaugurated by the first maroons. In *Malemort*, he dramatizes this ongoing struggle through the evocation of an unbroken series of figures of protest. From 1788 (date of the arrival of the *Négateur* in Martinique) to 1974, the year of the novel's completion, they rise up in rebellion against their exploiters, are cut down by the authorities, but rise again in resurrected form, as the chain of courage and defiance is prolonged down the years, 'unfurling time like a cane leaf down its stalk with at every node the portrait of those who have fallen, their strength, their hidden name which will be our mark in time' (*Malemort*, p. 129).

The Ripening – already, in 1958, a historical novel – looks back with implicit sadness to the hopeful illusions of 1945, when it seemed that a nation had 'fought its way out of the labyrinth' (p. 229), had conquered its forlorn obscurity, just as Lomé's post-election song symbolically puts the dusk to flight. The innocent euphoria and the false sense of security that this moment encouraged are summed up in the person of Thaël. His trial at an end, his mission accomplished, his girl in his arms, he is one with the rejoicing crowd in the streets on election night, celebrating a 'total liberation' (p. 218). The Lézarde, rising in spate and flooding the plain, seems to echo the forward surge of the people and underwrite his and their achievement. During his adventure Thaël has been increasingly likened to his countrymen, 'newly awakened to their own identity' (p. 18). His striving towards spiritual maturity and political accomplishment has been inspired by their own: 'in his soul their common effort was slowly taking shape and coming to life . . . The birth pangs of his people were now agonizingly implanted in his spirit . . . each one of them incarnating a portion of the common treasure' (p. 183). Like the members of Mathieu's group with their excited talk of a future Caribbean federation and their immediate plans for rural reform, Thaël regards the election mandate as the start of real power for the people of the island: 'After this election, there won't be a governor from outside any more. They'll have to remove him' (p. 197). His naive faith is untouched by Mathieu – the novel's symbol of clearsightedness, and the only pessimistic presence on election day – who already has a foreboding that the people's elected representatives will have no genuine control over future events; that, governor or no governor, the reality of life will be unchanged. Not until the final pages of the novel is Thaël shocked by Valérie's death into a reconsideration of that reality; and this ultimate lucidity is the true end of the process of initiation which he had wrongly believed to be completed with his defeat of Garin.

An underlying theme of the novel, connected with the motifs of journeying and initiation, is the theme of suffering, through which the individual may arrive at a state of illumination and a spiritual dawn. Apart from Garin, all the main characters, whose youth is constantly emphasized, are engaged in a voyage of discovery and a time of testing: Thaël and Mathieu are not alone in undergoing rites of passage. All are 'apprentices' following secret paths which 'must one day cut across the main road and melt into the great flow' (p. 133). Mycéa, retreating from Mathieu's hurtful emotional defection, walks all night through terrifying shadows, 'ascending a nave of mysteries towards the altar of morning' (p. 57), to be found at dawn by Lomé, whose kindliness, abject poverty and inexplicable everyday joy reveal to her the humble, sane way of life that lies behind a misleading legend. Valérie, drawn yet repelled by the unknown mountains from which Thaël comes, climbs fearfully at twilight up the steep, dark track to Papa Longoué's hut to ask for his enigmatic knowledge of the future. Tigamba and Margarita follow in the footsteps of others, attempting to come to terms with unrequited love and conflicting loyalties. The paths they take are those of questing adolescence, 'fragile . . . invisible roads, which a man leaves behind when he attains the true age of reason, when he shares the fruit of his land and takes the measure of the universe around him' (p. 104). These roads, which join the past to the future, are compared to the path which joins the river to the sea, and the comparison reminds the reader that the Lézarde, throughout the novel, is a natural correlative of man, from the moment of its carefree birth, through its impetuous downward course and its slower, contemplative flow past the grievous actuality of town and plain, until it reaches that state of complete knowledge which is symbolized by its death and fusion with the dark sea. Its muddy delta represents the painful imperfections of existing conditions, which Mathieu works to eliminate, looking forward to a day when the Lézarde will arrive crystal clear at the sea 'like a confident nation coming to its meeting with other nations' (p. 81). Thus a metaphorical crossroads links three forms of achievement: the river's attainment of a 'true and painful wisdom' (p. 33); the individual's survival of an initiatory ordeal; and the country's accession, after the centuries of suffering, to a state of dignity and maturity. Thaël is aware, even after his gruelling conflict with Garin, that the daily misery which he observes on the plain is something which his own flesh has never endured; as Valérie, too, has never fully known 'the dark dregs of life' (p. 183). The horror of her violent death is the price he must pay for definitive wisdom. When, keeping vigil by her body, he renounces his rosy vision of the future, and realizes the contradiction between the metropolitan view of his land as 'a not very serious paradise' (p. 16) and the evidence of destitution, disease and madness around him, his rejection of the comfortable lies in the patriotic song he had learnt at school signifies his decisive step from the realm of childhood into the rigorous climate of adult experience.

The agents of Thaël's final anguish are his own dogs, creatures with 'legendary names' who represent the essence, the 'passion' (p. 12), of the mountains – and here the word 'passion' keeps its ancient connotation of suffering, because of the maroons' long struggle to survive in the hilltop woods which were so poignant a reminder of the 'famished yet magnificent forest' (p. 189) of their distant, lost homeland. From the beginning the dogs are associated with shadows: both with the literal shade of the poinciana tree which is their habitual place of rest, and with the figurative shadows of history, the world of night and memory which the poinciana represents and of which Papa Longoué is the heir and interpreter. Their waiting presence at the end of the novel underlines the significance, in the novel's moral scheme, of Thaël's return home. At the outset he had gone forward, in the 'first heat of the first day', to meet the challenge of an unfamiliar setting and an unknown venture; to learn the bitter truths of life on the plain. The final section opens upon his departure from the plain in the 'last light of the day' and his retreat into a world of 'calm shadows' (p. 237). At the end of his passage through the initiatory process, instead of moving onwards, he has chosen to withdraw into the apparent safety of the past. In thus seeking reintegration with the world of the past, he repeats the error of Papa Longoué, an old man who has preferred to 'live in the shadows' (p. 139) all his life, 'walking day and night in the paths of memory' (p. 189), advocating a spiritual return to the ancestral forest, but making no attempt to reconcile this past world with the concrete needs of the present. The fact that Papa Longoué discerns in Valérie, too, a yearning after the past ('for she had the forest in her heart', p. 190), is a warning of her future end. Like Papa Longoué, wedded too exclusively to history, and like Garin, who attempts to perpetuate an old, unjust pattern of exploitation, Valérie is fated to disappear: '[she] too will have been only a shadow' (p. 252). From the time when Thaël tracks Garin up to the House of the Spring, the thought of Valérie is associated in his mind with the mood of that dark quest, 'the smell of blood', 'the odour of sacrifice' (p. 88); and as the memory of Valérie presides over the killing of Garin, so, for the reader of Glissant's novels, the memory of Papa Longoué's wife Edmée (a blood relative of Thaël's) presides over the death of Valérie. For Edmée, too, is rolled helpless down a hillside slope, caught up by hurricane winds, her limbs torn apart by the rocks as she falls; 'having gone up the mountain and been sent back lifeless, like a ball, by the descending gale' (*Le Quatrième Siècle*, p. 230).

The instrumentality of the dogs in Valérie's death is a frightening reminder of a half-forgotten era of terror and vulnerability. They are represented in the novel as monstrous forms, and epitomized by the hallucinatory animal that Papa Longoué sends as a warning to Thaël and Garin, bounding 'with immense, silent leaps' through the darkness like 'a fragment of the night itself fated to return mysteriously over and over until it finally faded away, leaving only fear and trembling as the traces of its passage' (p. 122). The dog is universally regarded in ancient mythologies as a magic animal with power over life and death, and is often credited with contradictory qualities: guardian and protector, it is also a scavenger and devourer.[23] Thaël's attitude towards his animals, one of simultaneous esteem and repulsion, reflects an archetypal unease. In addition, in the Caribbean context the dog has had more specific associations with dread, violence and mutilation, having been traditionally used by plantation owners to track down runaway slaves. Glissant attributes to the dogs of the past the same greed for plunder and profit that inspired their masters, men and animals having come alike from Europe to take possession of a land not their own (*L'Intention poétique*, p. 7). The baying of hounds and

Edouard Glissant's *The Ripening*

mastiffs, in *Le Quatrième Siècle*, pursues the first fugitive Longoué as he reaches the safety of the densely wooded hills; their menacing cry is repeated when the *Négateur* is again evoked in *Malemort* and *Boises*. Failure to escape the dogs meant, for the slave, not simply return to the plantation, but an exemplary punishment, ranging from the lopping of a limb to the blowing apart of a body by gunpowder. The nightmare of the maroon chase – the distant howling of the massive beasts, their nearer panting, their savage display of strength: and the gasping, frantic effort of the hunted human animal to elude their seemingly inexorable advance – is re-created at the end of *The Ripening* when Valérie, already panic-stricken by the sombre and unfamiliar mountain scene, seeks vainly to escape the attacking dogs which mercilessly harry her back down the dark slope. Their triumph over her pathetic attempt to flee is symbolic of the power to cripple and destroy which is still held, in parts of the Caribbean, by those persons, public or private, who have inherited the authority of a vanished plantocracy. In *Malemort* (p. 45) the police dogs hunting down the fugitive Beautemps are the logical descendants of the giant mastiffs which pursued the maroons, and their function is identified, here as in *Boises* (p. 39), with that of the gendarmes themselves and of the metropolitan security corps, the later agents of repression. In animal or human form, the armed forces of tyranny accompany their symbolic opposite, the defiant maroon, down the Caribbean ages. Thaël's discovery that 'the land still harbours secret corners where two dogs are able to kill . . . where despair and solitude are installed' is the conclusive factor which obliges him to leave his home once more, 'to begin again: the quest, the choice, the house to be built, the life to be put in order' (*Le Quatrième Siècle*, p. 284).

Thus Thaël's animals, like the white Great House of Garin's former employer, represent the anachronistic lingering on of an oppressive era which must finally be laid to rest if there is to be any dynamic forward thrust in the country. The source of the Lézarde is an image not only of the past, but of the starting-point of the future, and the preservation of its free, unsullied flow is the purpose towards which the narrative action tends. Thaël's decision to take his dogs there is in keeping with his early intuition (p. 98) that the House of the Spring is like his own home, and stresses the link that these mountain sites retain with the past. His plan for the dogs' expiatory death may be seen as a vengeance exacted not only for Valérie, but on behalf of all the unknown dead of maroon history. The Lézarde, by keeping the starving dogs from swift extinction, demands their suffering as retribution for historic wrongs: it is, in a sense, a closing of accounts. Thaël's intention to await their death and remove their rotting carcasses before they can pollute the river is a pendant to his earlier mission to dislodge Garin, the 'traitor [and] dog' (p. 47), from his sinister ascendancy over the river's source, which he threatened to befoul. This final act of cleansing is in accordance with the functions of salvation and purification that are attached to Thaël's role in the novel. It also reunites his path with that of Mathieu, whose stated goals are to clear the delta of mud and to free his countrymen from all that hinders their emergence into the 'kingdom without frontiers' (p. 61) which the sea perpetually promises. Throughout the story, the ideals of Thaël and of Mathieu are presented as complementary, not as alternatives. Thaël perceives his country's needs as 'the heritage of the past [and] the free use of the land'; Mathieu defines them as 'knowledge and self-expression' p. 140). The two young men are 'different, and at the same time similar. Like night and day' (p. 199), and both are equally necessary to the novelist's vision of future reform.

The threat of defilement to the Lézarde, against which, at different levels of the narrative, both Thaël and Mathieu are seen to strive, is comparable to the obstruction and defacement of the *Négateur*'s track, which has led to the sorry spectacle of a race deprived of integrity and become indifferent to its own alienation: 'the placid banality of a tragic situation which is no longer even perceived' (*Malemort*, p. 193). The ancestral track itself is envisaged by Glissant as a second river. Both the *Négateur* and the Lézarde once descended from the mountains 'so as to know the land', but the contours they followed are today unrecognizably altered, the vegetation ravaged; ironically, even the canefields, the most sombre link with the past, are now 'dried up' (*Malemort*, p. 137). And as the Lézarde's course has been corrupted by industrialization and reduced to a futile dribble, so the *Négateur*'s path has silted up and become 'two thin trickles of water choked with mud and refuse' (*Malemort*, p. 189), with a corresponding failure of man's natural bond with the earth he treads and with his primordial roots. The message of Glissant's later work is that the waters freed by Thaël, once symbolic of hope and future fruition, are now again imprisoned. 'Malemort', in *Boises*, becomes the very name of the island, no paradise but a land of death, its former rivers fading and sinking through the rubble and the sterile sand.

Notes

1 Edouard Glissant, *Boises* (Angers and Paris: Editions Acoma, 1979), p. 9. The *boise* was a form of shackle used on slaves. All translations from Glissant's work are my own, except those from *La Lézarde* (Paris: Editions du Seuil, 1958), which are taken, with some emendations, from Frances Frenaye's translation, *The Ripening*.
2 Edouard Glissant, *Le Quatrième Siècle* (Paris: Editions du Seuil, 1964), p. 219.
3 Edouard Glissant, *Monsieur Toussaint* (Paris: Editions du Seuil, 1961), pp. 7–8. For further comments on Glissant's view of history, see Jean Corzani, 'La Négritude aux Antilles françaises', in *Négritude africaine, négritude caraïbe*, ed. Jeanne-Lydie Goré (Paris: Editions de la Francité, 1973), pp. 126–7; Vere W. Knight, 'Edouard Glissant: The Novel as History Rewritten', *Black Images* 3, 1 (1974), 64–79; and Beverley Ormerod, 'Beyond *Négritude*: Some Aspects of the Work of Edouard Glissant', *Contemporary Literature* 15 (1974), 360–9.
4 Edouard Glissant, *L'Intention poétique* (Paris: Editions du Seuil, 1969), p. 39.
5 Edouard Glissant, *Malemort* (Paris: Editions du Seuil, 1975), p. 200.
6 See Edouard Glissant, 'Action culturelle et pratique politique: propositions de base', *Acoma* 4–5 (1973), 16–20. The search for a lost past and the sense of rootlessness in contemporary Martinique are the central themes of Glissant's latest novel, *La Case du commandeur* (Paris: Editions du Seuil, 1981).
7 *The Ripening*, p. 27. In this translation the river's name is rendered as the Lizard, but the meaning of *une lézarde* is a crack or fissure.
8 On the alienation of the Martinican from his physical environment, see the opening paragraphs of the essay 'Poétique et inconscient' in Glissant's *Le Discours antillais* (Paris: Editions du Seuil, 1981), pp. 276–8.
9 See *L'Intention poétique*, pp. 185–6. The difficulty, in Martinique, of attaining a sense of nationhood and of Caribbean identity is a major theme of Glissant's *Le Discours antillais*.
10 Edouard Glissant, *Les Indes* (1955), reprinted in *Poèmes* (Paris: Editions du Seuil, 1965), pp. 143, 88.
11 See the discussion of this episode in F.I. Case, 'The Novels of Edouard Glissant', *Black Images* 2, 3/4 (1973), p. 8.
12 Edouard Glissant, *Le Sel noir* (Paris: Editions du Seuil, 1960), p. 19.
13 See Hall, p. 260.

14 Edouard Glissant, *Soleil de la conscience* (Paris: Editions du Seuil, 1956).

15 For a discussion of Glissant's views on the negative function of the *quimboiseur*, see Bernadette Cailler, *Proposition poétique: une lecture de l'œuvre d'Aimé Césaire* (Sherbrooke: Naaman, 1976), pp. 22–3.

16 'The silk-cotton tree which at midnight escapes from all vegetation and enters the circle of the ancestral powers' (*L'Intention poétique*, p. 48).

17 See Durand, p. 237.

18 See Northrop Frye, *Anatomy of Criticism* (1957; rpt. Princeton: Princeton University Press, 1971), pp. 186–206, on the archetypal patterns of romance.

19 See, in particular, *L'Intention poétique*, pp. 40–2. For further discussion of these concepts, see Ormerod, 'Beyond *Négritude*', pp. 362–3, and Bernadette Cailler, 'Un itinéraire poétique: Edouard Glissant et l'anti-*Anabase*', *Présence Francophone* 19 (1979), pp. 110–11.

20 For another interpretation of Garin's death, see Knight (p. 74), who takes the sea at the sand bar as symbolizing a step into the politics of the future – a step which is impossible for Garin, the agent of reactionary political forces.

21 See *Le Quatrième Siècle*, pp. 256, 260–1, 266, and *Malemort*, p. 22. For a further account of the situation of wartime Martinique, see Frantz Fanon, *Toward the African Revolution* (*Pour la Révolution africaine*), trans. Haakon Chevalier (Harmondsworth: Penguin Books, 1970), pp. 32–4.

22 See Aimé Césaire, 'La Martinique telle qu'elle est', *French Review* 53 (1979), p. 187. For a full discussion of the issue of Martinique's political status, see Richard D.E. Burton, *Assimilation or Independence? Prospects for Martinique* (Montreal: Centre for Developing-Area Studies, 1978).

23 See Beryl Rowland, *Animals with Human Faces: A Guide to Animal Symbolism* (London: George Allen & Unwin, 1974), pp. 58–66, and Durand, pp. 92, 428.

3

The Plantation as Hell: The Novels of Joseph Zobel and Michèle Lacrosil

'Where is the healer to suck . . . the poison at the root of the open wound?'
(*Cahier*, p. 82).

'Every rich black is a mulatto; every poor mulatto is a black.'[1] This nineteenth-century Haitian aphorism, still current today, is based upon two implicit assumptions: that social class is determined by race (although wealth may serve to redeem lowly origins), and that the black man is normally to be ranked below the mulatto. Although Haitian society, after independence in 1804, differed in composition from that of the other islands (a mulatto élite having largely taken over the role of the departed white plantocracy), the social principles inherent in the aphorism were generally accepted throughout the Caribbean in the colonial period, for in every island the interplay of race and rank was dependent upon the hierarchies of plantation life. And those hierarchies, in turn, were created and upheld by a dominant fair-skinned minority who accorded to the black slave the status of a chattel or an animal.[2] In every island, the presence of the auction-block symbolized this prevailing attitude. 'For centuries,' says Césaire in his *Cahier*, 'this country repeated that we are brute beasts; that the human heart-beat stops at the gates of the black world; that we are walking manure hideously proffering the promise of tender cane and silky cotton, and they branded us with red-hot irons and we slept in our shit and we were sold in public squares and a yard of English cloth and salted Irish meat were cheaper than us' (p. 67). Once purchased, a slave belonged body and soul to his master, who was legally permitted to inflict upon him savage punishments; who, despite the provisions of the *Code noir*, might (and in many recorded cases, did) torture and kill him with impunity; but against whom his own evidence was inadmissible in a court of law.[3] To strike any member of his master's family was punishable by death; to attempt to escape was punishable by mutilation. His living conditions were in accordance with his inferior status, and were reflected by a high mortality rate. Malnourished and poorly housed, overworked and mistreated, slaves brought from Africa were particularly vulnerable to disease and epidemics: in the eighteenth century the French planters in the West Indies expected to lose 50 per cent of their African-born slaves within eight years of their acquisition.[4] Racial inequality lay at the very heart of the plantation system, for the view of the typical planter was that 'the black man, left to himself, will never and can never be anything other than a brutish creature given up to purely animal instincts'.[5]

'Brutish' and 'animal': the words occur over and over again in relation to the black slave, in the surviving letters of the white estate owners, managers and overseers of past centuries. This historical perception of the black man as a dehumanized object was a function of his employment as an expendable canefield beast. In consequence, the modern Caribbean writer tends to portray canefield work as an ongoing agent of degradation which continues to deprive the labourer of human attributes. In the twentieth-century plantation communities depicted by Joseph Zobel and Michèle Lacrosil, black estate workers still stand at the base of the social pyramid as did the faceless, anonymous mass of their slave ancestors. The overseers in Zobel's autobiographical novel, *Black Shack Alley*, distinguish their workers, registered under their first names only, by epithets denoting their physical – animal – peculiarities: thus Maximilien-dog-teeth is opposed to Maximilien-big-calves. When they come in from the fields on Saturday afternoons to collect their wages, the labourers do not emerge as individuals, but as an 'earth-stained bunch', a 'pack of foul-smelling, dung-coloured beings'.[6] Among them, the narrator's grandmother, a canefield weeder, with her battered rainsoaked hat looking like a cap of manure, and her cracked, muddy, swollen hands and feet – their nails 'thicker, harder and more shapeless than the hooves of God knows what animal that had galloped on rocks, in scrap iron, in a dung heap' (p. 181) – is stripped of her identity as 'the best and most beautiful of grandmothers' and becomes 'a frightful sight, who did not in any way resemble a *maman*, an old woman, a black woman, nor even a human being' (p. 51). The same loss of personal identity is implied by Michèle Lacrosil when, in *Tomorrow Jab-Herma*, she portrays the crop-time workers as a team of mechanical scarecrows:

> Canecutters in shorts and hessian shirts were bending down. Coarse straw hats hid their heads; arms and legs were wrapped in rags; neither their faces nor their hands could be seen, only tattered bundles which stooped, cut, rose up, lopped off the tops of the stalks, with two machete strokes removed the leaves, stalks on the right, leaves on the left; moved forward and began again the traditional gestures, about the only lesson dating from slave times, the same gestures repeated for three centuries.[7]

The passage is very reminiscent in tone and content of a celebrated paragraph in which the seventeenth-century French moralist La Bruyère, with a humanitarian vision unusual in that era of aristocratic urban literature, offers us a glimpse of the peasants in the fields of rural France:

> One sees certain wild animals, male and female, scattered over the country, black, livid, and burned by the sun, who are chained, as it were, to the land they are always digging and turning over with an unquenchable stubbornness; they have a sort of articulate voice, and when they stand up, they exhibit human features: they are men. At night they retire to their burrows, where they live on black bread, water and roots; they spare other men the trouble of sowing, tilling the ground, and reaping for their sustenance, and, therefore, deserve not to be in want of that bread they sow themselves.[8]

Their situation puts into a new perspective that of the African slaves who were their contemporaries, reminding us that Europe, too, was then the scene of grave social injustices, and giving us some insight into the mental conditioning which enabled the colonial plantocracy to regard with such callousness the plight of the enslaved. There is, however, an important difference: the European peasantry was not condemned by the mere fact of race, as were the slaves in the Caribbean, to a permanent state of dispossession and dehumanization.

The Plantation as Hell

The plantation novels of Zobel and Lacrosil are both dominated by the social and racial stratification established in the era of slavery. Characters of every class and skin shade still retain ancestral memories of the estate hierarchy with its privileges and its disparities, and their behaviour is very largely determined by traditional responses. In order for us to understand much that is taken for granted by these authors rather than explicitly stated, we need to bear constantly in mind the fact that the plantations of the past were complex, self-contained organizations, in which social attitudes were not always contingent upon race alone. The documents which survive from former times are not only the correspondence of planters and their employees, but also accounts and inventories, bills of sale and records of the progress of work and distribution of tasks. From these various pieces of paper a composite picture can be built up which indicates that for both white and black members of an estate community, factors such as the nature of a person's employment or his country of origin would modify the role played by colour in the assignment of social status. The written evidence is, of course, the work of whites alone, but the behaviour of slaves, on which so much of their masters' daily life depended, is constantly mentioned. A young Frenchman, for example, taken on as an apprentice refiner on a Haitian sugar estate in the late eighteenth century, writes to his mother complaining that the black laundresses reflect their master's contempt for his white overseers by ruining the latter's linen. A traveller to Martinique in the same period reports that black Creole slaves (that is, those born in the West Indies) scorn those born in Africa, regarding them as 'human machines'.[9] Other considerations such as economic standing, degree of authority over others, mode of housing and nourishment, freedom of choice of sexual partner, might also come into play in the assessment of rank. Some plantation occupations were common to members of both races: white artisans such as carpenters and smiths might work alongside equally skilled slaves, distinguished from them only by their legal freedom and the payment of a very small wage.[10] But while mulatto and black tradesmen formed an élite group among the slaves, white tradesmen were near the bottom of the white social order.

Thus persons of the same race might, on the estates, be distinguished from each other by a number of social nuances. Almost everything comes back in the end, however, to that obsessive preoccupation with skin colour which, along with extremes of poverty and wealth, was to be the poisonous legacy of the plantation system to the Caribbean. Sexual behaviour, for instance, can seldom have been free of racial undercurrents. A mulatto mistress was a status symbol for white males, more difficult to acquire and more highly prized than a black mistress. Marriage was a different matter. White tradesmen were occasionally known to contract marriages with coloured women, but a formal union of this sort was almost unthinkable for a planter, manager or overseer, who would thereby bring about his own sure social ruin. For a black female slave, the state of concubine and the conception of a child by a white man were almost the only hope of better living conditions and social mobility for her descendants. But she had probably less freedom of choice in such matters than anyone else on the estates, since slavery deprived her of the right to dictate the sexual uses of her own body; she was required to fulfil the role of a breeding machine for future labour, and was widely regarded as fair game for any male in a position of authority over her, from the white sailors on board the slave-ships to the white plantation staff and those slaves who enjoyed a privileged status.[11]

The Novels of Joseph Zobel and Michèle Lacrosil

On all West Indian plantations, whether of cane, coffee, indigo, cotton, tobacco or cocoa, the hierarchy of white and black personnel was headed by the resident planter or, in the case of absentee owners, by a manager (called a *gérant* or *géreur* in the French islands). If the owner lived in Europe, he would have his appointed agent in the island: the attorney, or *procureur*, usually a businessman or another planter, who was paid by a commission on the plantation's income and might also hold a contract to furnish slaves, food, wood and other supplies. The attorney did not, however, normally reside on the estate, and visited it only from time to time; in such cases, therefore, it was the manager who was the effective head, and held power over the slaves' daily lives: who, in the owner's absence, was the real master of the plantation. His responsibility to the owner was to make the greatest profit possible; his private goal, to make money for himself. The means to both these ends was to exact as much work as he could from the slaves at his disposal. But a resident owner or his manager generally played an administrative role and seldom supervised slaves directly, leaving this to one or more of the overseers (*économes*). The multiple duties of overseers included book-keeping and secretarial work, the superintendence of the sugar-mills or the coffee-mills, the inspection of work in the fields, and, during crop-time, when the sugar factory worked twenty-four hours a day, the direction of both day and night shifts in the preparation of sugar, molasses and rum. Under the overseers were the drivers or *commandeurs*, who, up to the end of the seventeenth century in the French islands, were usually drawn from the ranks of white indentured workers, and only later from among the slaves themselves. In addition, many plantations employed white tradesmen – a head boilerman (*maître-sucrier*), a distiller, carpenters and coopers, millwrights, smiths and ploughmen – until, by the middle of the eighteenth century, the era of greatest prosperity, most had acquired or trained slaves able to take over these skilled positions. Although the overseers, hard pressed, ill paid and treated as social inferiors by the planters and managers, felt themselves to be on the lowest rung of the white ladder, the tradesmen ranked below them, as did white domestic servants.

The social distinctions and variations of privilege among the white plantation staff set a pattern of dominance and subjection that was to be echoed in the ranks of the slaves. The relationship between manager and overseer, in particular, was often one of dissatisfaction on the manager's part and envious resentment on that of the overseer. The manager resided in the Great House itself (*la grand'case*) or in a house of his own, upwind of the factory boilers and the slave quarters; accompanied by his family if he was married, but often living with a mulatto 'housekeeper', an arrangement which could lead to trouble among the slaves if she sought and received special favours for her own friends and relatives. The overseers sometimes ate with the owner or manager, but were expected to sit at the far end of the table, to volunteer no conversation of their own, and to leave when the dessert was served. Their living quarters were sparsely furnished and their small salaries allowed of no luxuries. Unlike the manager, they did not have the diversion of frequent journeys to town, and sought entertainment through casual liaisons with slaves. As the supply of would-be overseers was always greater than the demand for their services, they might be dismissed on the slightest pretext; but two out of three left voluntarily because of illness, a sense of isolation, or plain dislike of the job or of the manager. This frequent turnover had an adverse effect on the slaves, since new overseers always tended to overwork the field gangs so as to impress the manager with their productivity. The latter, however, was just as likely to be critical of the overseers' excessive zeal as of any negligence on their part in handling the slaves. In theory the owner or manager had to preside over the meting out of severe punishment, but the definition of severity was fluid: it was legal in the eighteenth century for an overseer in the French islands to give a slave up to fifty lashes, and a blind eye was usually turned to the drivers' use of the whip. Below managerial level the white staff had no common interest save their need to maintain control over the slaves. Like the overseers, the white artisans felt no sense of personal commitment to the plantation, and had no source of recreation except slave women; their wages were very low and they, too, were forever moving on elsewhere. The white drivers of the seventeenth and early eighteenth century were more privileged than the tradesmen, since they ate from the master's table and were empowered to give orders to all the servants, whether white or black. But as they cost more to keep than slaves, caused complaint by their sexual relationships with women in the field gangs, and often exceeded their authority by punishing field workers with extreme harshness, they were phased out in favour of black drivers, who inherited many of their privileges and thus came to head the hierarchy of slaves.

This black hierarchy was not so much created by the slaves as determined for them by the varying degrees of physical comfort or hardship, and moral authority or abasement, decreed for them by their white masters, according to the amount of favour which they enjoyed in the latter's eyes. This favour depended upon their usefulness to the plantation, their obedience, industry and loyalty, and to some extent upon their colour: mulatto slaves were seldom branded and were more likely to be given employment as domestic servants or apprentice tradesmen than to be relegated to the field gangs. Most authorities, on the evidence of planters, managers, and white visitors to the colonies (the slaves themselves having had no opportunity to record their own opinions), assert that the position of house slave (*esclave de case*) was regarded by the blacks as more desirable than that of field slave (*esclave de jardin*, also called *esclave de l'atelier, de terre, de houe, de place* and *de bêche*), although it has been contended that the field slave preferred the independence of his lot, despite the backbreaking toil it involved, to a domestic role which kept him constantly at the mercy of a master's or mistress's personal caprice.[12] Certainly, apart from the drivers themselves, who were granted special privileges designed to reinforce their command over the other slaves, those who worked on the land were worse off than house slaves, and for domestics to be sent back to the fields was considered to be a punishment and a disgrace. House slaves were better fed (being entitled to their masters' leftovers), better clothed, better housed, and often better treated than field labourers, since they came directly under the owner's or manager's orders and were thus removed from the despotic rule of the drivers. The slaves of the *grand'case* were intensely involved in the life of their masters, and appear to have been often devoted to them; few were runaways (*marrons*), unless they were demoted to the gangs. They internalized many of their masters' attitudes to work and to colour, darker-skinned domestic slaves commonly deferring to lighter-skinned ones, and all of them regarding physical labour on the land, even the cultivation of a personal allotment, as beneath their dignity. Field slaves, on the other hand, lived in the *cases-nègres* in spartan conditions, and their protein-deficient diet was largely composed of the roots and vegetables that they had to grow in their spare time, a small quantity of salt fish or beef being supplied by their owner. Inability to adapt to this unfamiliar diet, lacking in the game meat which they had enjoyed in Africa, was a frequent cause of illness and even of death among new arrivals. Their working hours were long, starting towards 5 a.m. when they were awoken by the driver and their presence checked by an overseer's roll-call. Within half an hour they were at work, unless they were allowed to eat breakfast first; in some cases they took this meal with them to the fields. At eleven or at midday there was an hour's break, which they sometimes spent cultivating their own plots, though more often at rest. They generally worked until sunset, and it was already dark by the time they returned to their huts. At crop-time, when the canes had to be crushed and the juice processed as soon as possible after harvesting, they were frequently required to work a further four-hour shift in the sugar-mill and the factory, though they were rewarded for this by extra food and rations of rum; because of the inadequacy of their normal provisions, there was no lack of volunteers for these wearisome and hazardous additional tasks. Unless they were prevented from work by torrential rain, their life was a ceaseless routine of hoeing and holing, weeding, cutting, gathering and transporting the cane which was itself the principal reason for their existence as slaves.

The advantages of being a driver were both physical and psychological. The authority of drivers was challenged by no other slaves except the head boilermen, who, in their key position in charge of sugar-making, knew themselves to be equally essential to the successful functioning of the estates. Their prestige was upheld by overseers, who supported them in public and reprimanded them only in private so as not to undermine their influence over the field gangs. Armed with a whip or a stick (the *coco macaque*), each driver was responsible for the overall discipline of his gang, composed of about thirty slaves; and while the overseer dictated the gang's workload, it was the driver who deployed individuals within the group to particular tasks according to his estimate of their strength, a function which allowed him to display both favouritism and vindictiveness. In theory he did not have the right to seduce the women of other slaves, but in practice he used his rank to take his pleasures where he wished: one head driver on a Haitian estate is recorded as having fathered over sixty children. A driver's responsibilities included knowing personally how to perform the various jobs he supervised, and advising the owner or manager on the choice of new slaves. His living quarters were better furnished than those of the other slaves, and he was better dressed and fed; moreover, since he was fully occupied supervising the field gang, other slaves were detailed by the overseer to cultivate his provision ground for him. When he reached the age of around sixty, if he had given satisfaction throughout his career, he was rewarded with a plum job such as gate watchman, given permission to travel outside the estate boundaries, and sometimes freed outright.

The slave trades – those of boilermen and distillers, masons, sawyers, carpenters and coopers, millwrights and wheelwrights, blacksmiths and cart-drivers – were often reserved for men of mixed blood, a fact which reflects the pervasive influence of colour prejudice on the plantations, and the advantages for a slave of being born a mulatto. Tradesmen, like house slaves, escaped the oppressive, monotonous labour and menial status of the field gangs, and enjoyed a better diet. But occupational mobility was very restricted on a plantation, as there were comparatively few jobs for apprentice artisans or domestics; the majority of slaves were destined to the canefields. Women slaves, in any case, were not apprenticed to trades, and their only hope of avoiding field work was to be taken on among the limited number of domestics, or in the hospital. They were therefore numerous in the gangs and were generally forced to work even in the last stages of their pregnancies. This, and the fact that they were frequently obliged to take their very young children to the fields and keep them there all day in the sun, contributed to the high mortality rate among infants. By all accounts no other slave envied the lot of the field gangs. Père Labat, writing in the first half of the eighteenth century, notes that tradesmen such as coopers 'pride themselves on not being among the ranks of those who work on the land, and on having other Negroes beneath them', and elsewhere remarks that 'the child of a driver or an artisan will not want to marry the child of a field worker'.[13] After slavery was abolished, it was this type of work which was most shunned by the freed slaves, so that the estates were obliged to import thousands of indentured workers (between 1852 and 1885, 70,500 East Indians, 15,000 Africans and over 1,000 Chinese were brought to Martinique and Guadeloupe); and in all the islands the unskilled black labourer retained the low status which had been attributed to the *nègre de jardin*. Even today in the Caribbean, agricultural work is unpopular because it is widely regarded as degrading; more than any other occupation, it still holds the stigma of slavery.

Up to the very eve of emancipation, slavery remained a dehumanizing experience on the estates. The Haitian slaves had freed themselves at the start of the nineteenth century, but although slavery was briefly outlawed in the French islands soon after the Revolution, it was swiftly re-established; it was not until the middle of the nineteenth century that it was finally abolished, and meanwhile slave-owners went on abusing their power. In Guadeloupe alone, between 1841 and 1842, eight masters were accused of excessive cruelty, outright torture, or the actual murder of a number of slaves. The majority of them were acquitted or escaped with a fine. A French abolitionist wrote in 1845 of the planters' ineradicable conviction of their racial superiority, and of their continued practice of locking up their blacks after work, as they locked up their animals, for in their minds there was a 'perfect assimilation of the slave to the beast of burden'.[14] Even when slaves were not ill-treated, their private lives were dictated by their masters' wishes, and the majority of them were either forbidden to marry (since a married slave could not be sold without his wife and young children) or else allowed to marry only a slave on the same plantation, often in an unwitnessed ceremony which could later be declared null if it suited the planter's interests. The emancipation of slaves in the British West Indies, which took place in 1833, had some beneficial repercussions on the conditions of slavery in the French colonies. The slave trade there had been stopped in 1831, and over the next ten years other edicts forbade the mutilation and branding of slaves and reduced the legally permitted number of lashes. An official attempt was also made to introduce elementary schooling for slave children from the age of 4, but this met with an outcry from the plantocracy, and in practice it was free coloured children who benefited from the new schools in the towns; the majority of slave children were kept at work on the estates until abolition came to the French islands in 1848.

The racial prejudice inherent in the master–slave relationship also militated for more than a century against freed slaves. The *Code noir* of 1685, while it fined white men for having illegitimate children by slaves, permitted marriage between a master and his slave mistress: such a marriage freed the wife, and automatically freed and legitimized her children. Furthermore, freedmen were granted the same rights as persons born free. However, by the early eighteenth century the French monarchy was officially discouraging mixed marriages, and by the middle of that century no coloured person could hold public office in the French islands. They were also excluded from other occupations: for example, in 1765 an edict was published in Martinique forbidding notaries and attorneys to employ coloured clerks, since such duties could be entrusted only 'to persons whose probity is recognized, a condition which cannot presumably be met in the case of a birth as base as that of a mulatto'.[15] The growth and ambition of the free coloured population so alarmed the white colonists (already in a state of permanent apprehension over the superior numbers of blacks) that a host of legal restrictions were imposed upon persons of mixed race limiting their freedom of movement, prohibiting their presence in theatres and inns frequented by whites, and even prescribing the mode of dress they should adopt. A royal decree of May 1771 stipulated that they were to be kept in a 'state of humiliation'.[16] Racial discrimination was thus perpetuated and encouraged by public statutes aimed at defusing the potential strength of the free coloureds, for the prosperity and peace of mind of the planters depended not only upon the docility of their slaves but on the acceptance by freedmen of a permanently inferior status. Only in 1833 were civil and political rights granted to the free coloureds. Themselves the objects of racial scorn, the free coloureds were often as prejudiced as the whites against the black slaves at the base of the social structure. The slaves were known to respond by regarding them as hybrids without a country.[17] Most mulattos passionately desired to dissociate themselves from the black part of their ancestry and be identified only with the white part, and the women among them commonly preferred to be a white man's mistress than to marry another mulatto.[18] The notion of the advantages of a light skin, inherent in the ranking system of plantation life, was thus ineradicably implanted in Caribbean social structure. Many free mulattos are recorded as having been cruel to their own slaves; and in their internalizing of the racial values of the white plantocracy, they were said to be as contemptuous as the latter of white men who threw away their social status by marrying mulatto women. Alienation, a poor self-image in relation to whites and a disdainful attitude to darker skin shades were thus common features of the free coloured caste, who even away from the estates adhered to the hierarchical notions prevailing there.

The end of slavery did not mean the end of a paternalistic and authoritarian attitude on the part of the master class to those who continued as paid labourers on the estates. Even when plantations were taken over from individual planters by large companies, the relationship between employers and employees remained a far more personal one than that occurring in other fields of work, and in the case of estates staying in the control of a planter family, the social gulf between the planter and his labourers was a logical consequence of their relative status in the past. Those blacks who went in for small farming on their own were still dependent on the plantations for seasonal work to help them make ends meet, and often relied on them, in addition, to buy their cane and other produce. Rather than a self-sufficient peasantry, emancipation created large numbers of under-employed agricultural workers whose unstable social patterns, endemic poverty, low educational level, fragile conjugal relationships and fatalistic approach to life may be seen as the distressing heritage of the field slave's powerless and abject condition. Where men of mixed race assumed positions as manager or overseer (a development which began in the nineteenth century), they adopted the attitudes of the old white staff towards the casual labourers in the fields. Until recent times, positions of control in the cane monoculture were the guarantee of political and economic power in the Caribbean; and the scarcity of work and low wage structure of the sugar industry meant that the majority of black employees had no share in the profits and were systematically denied the chance of social advancement.[19] Status, therefore, continued to be identified, for all practical purposes, with an individual's place in the colour spectrum; wealth and privilege continued to be associated with lightness of skin. In mid-twentieth-century Martinique, plantation and factory ownership and top management were still in the hands of local whites (known as *békés*), while in Guadeloupe most of the sugar industry was controlled by metropolitan companies who generally sent out managers from France.[20]

Zobel's *Black Shack Alley* is centred on an estate village in Martinique between the two world wars, while Lacrosil's *Tomorrow Jab-Herma* concerns events on a Guadeloupe *habitation* (the French colonial term for a plantation) in 1952. Both novelists employ the traditional device of the newcomer who takes the reader with him as he penetrates and explores the physical and emotional responses of a closed universe. In Zobel's novel it is the black child José, born on the estate but too young at first to understand the frustration of the labourers and the quality of their despair, whose eyes are gradually opened to the interaction of colour and class, first in rural Martinique and later in the Route Didier of the capital. This street with its rich *béké* villas and appendage of domestics' shacks mimics the contrast of the master's *grand'case* and the slaves' *cases-nègres* on the plantations, as the Rue Cases-Nègres itself, where José first lives – the 'street of Negro huts' which gives the novel its French title – reminds the reader, by its very name, of the inequalities and injustices of slavery. In Lacrosil's *Tomorrow Jab-Herma* it is the *métropolitain* Philippe Bonnier, engineer and heir to a French sugar company that has bought the plantation of Pâline from its local owner, who arrives in Guadeloupe to inspect Pâline and be confronted for the first time with the nuances of a colonial society in decay. Through his encounters with Constant Sougès, the white planter who resents his intrusion; with Cragget, the mulatto labourer for whose neuroses he is the catalyst; with Pilou, the mulatto secretary who desires him because he is white; and with Jab-Herma, the black chauffeur and witch-doctor who waits in the wings to manoeuvre him, Philippe is transformed from an apparently diffident young man into an autocrat who consciously sets out to supplant and destroy Sougès, the anachronistic survivor of the old Creole plantocracy.

The child narrator of Zobel's *Black Shack Alley* is largely unaware, during his first seven years, of the subtle class and colour distinctions which are the heritage of plantation society. The divisions within José's own community are simpler, though no less rigidly hierarchical. On the one hand, there is the small and uniform group of black estate workers among whom he lives with his grandmother, M'man Tine, the canefield weeder. On the other hand, there are a few remote figures of authority whose power, in the child's eyes, derives principally from their adult status and their occupation on the estate. Their race is irrelevant to him; it is only in passing that he mentions that the overseer is a mulatto, and the care which he and his fellow urchins exercise in avoiding this man's attention during their forages into the canefields is due above all to their fear of parental punishment if they get into any trouble. In José's mind the distance between the management and the labourers is to be measured

The Novels of Joseph Zobel and Michèle Lacrosil

principally by the visible evidence of their dwelling-places: the latter live in some three dozen ramshackle wooden huts perched on a hillside above the canefields; higher up the hill is the overseer's house; and at the very top stands the manager's larger house, tile-roofed and majestic, presiding over the *casesnègres* and the great expanse of cane beyond them.

Those of the children who are too young to work in the *petites bandes*, the youthful weeding gangs, have little contact with the realities of estate labour until the day when, as a consequence of their setting fire to one of the worker's gardens, the overseer decrees that they may no longer remain at play in Black Shack Alley while their parents are away, and must accompany them to the fields. Before this point in José's childhood, his life is one of endless excitement and adventure, shadowed only by adult retribution for his more destructive exploits. His contact with the natural environment is direct and exhilarating. The plantation is an infinite source of delight, with its wealth of fruit-trees to be raided for guavas, plums or mangoes, its river in which to catch crayfish, its ox-drawn carts on which to hitch illicit rides, its pleasurably sinister tunnels of tree-ferns to be explored, and its fallow fields offering the chance of forgotten bits of cane, half shrivelled but still juicy enough to be enjoyable. The children have no sense of their own poverty and privation; in the absence of the adults, they are 'free, responsible only for [them] selves, and masters of Shack Alley' (p. 38). José's narrative is punctuated by a recurring sense of intoxicating independence as M'man Tine and the others go off to work: 'Not an adult left in Shack Alley! . . . We were alone and the world was ours' (p. 12).

Zobel portrays this childish universe as one of mingled innocence and cruelty, harshness and generosity. The children rejoice in uprooting plants, raiding birds' nests, stoning cows, mutilating dragonflies and nailing lizards to fences. Forever forgetful of the likelihood of punishment, they throw pebbles into barrels of drinking water and ransack their parents' empty huts for hidden tins of sugar. Forever hungry, they willingly share with their playmates their meagre lunches of cassava flour and codfish, or breadfruit and pig snout. Lords of creation during the day, they are constantly and mercilessly beaten in the evening for their misdeeds, and their twilight apprehension is underscored by the vulnerability of the animal world around them: the mules returning from the fields, brutally whipped by their swearing drivers; the moths darting into the flame of the lamps only 'to tumble backwards on the table, dead or singed beyond ever flying again' (p. 9). The weary, short-tempered adults re-entering Black Shack Alley seem to José 'like ghosts coming out of the darkness for some unknown gruesome ritual' (p. 21), and the weapons of corporal punishment – switches, broomsticks, pieces of rope – are, for the children, the inescapable instruments of that ritual. Yet the adults are not resented by them; on the contrary, they are admired; their incompletely perceived emotions and actions are endlessly intriguing, and to the young onlookers their Saturday night dances are an irresistible carnival of food and alcohol, insistent drumbeats and wild, passionate dancing. They are envied, too, as the masters of their own fates, inhabiting a mysterious sphere which is the antithesis of powerless childhood: 'where one procured one's own food, where one was not beaten . . . where one did not fall as one walked nor as one ran, where one did not shed tears' (p. 27).

There are, however, intimations of unease in José's small world. The 5-year-old child at the beginning of the narrative is baffled and saddened by his grandmother's bitter ramblings about the past – 'those things I didn't fully understand, but which I felt so cruelly' (p. 25). As the translator of *Black Shack Alley* has pointed out, the author avoids the artificiality of having a young boy comment on the state of his society by placing such remarks in the mouths of other characters.[21] Thus it is M'man Tine who, in one angry monologue, provides the reader with an encapsulated account of the typical black female labourer's destiny. Left defenceless by her mother's death, she is placed by her uncle in the children's weeding gang, while he takes possession of the plots of land which her grandfather had given to her mother. The passing reference to the fact that this grandfather was an old *béké* indicates to the West Indian reader that he must have had his daughter by a slave woman or black domestic servant on his property. M'man Tine herself, as an adolescent, suffers the fate which so often befell the field-gang women when she is raped by the headman (still called the *commandeur*, the old term for the driver), who, 'seeing how I was built, held, rolled me over on the ground and drove a child into my belly' (p. 24). Refusing to let her own daughter go the same way, she finds her a job as a domestic servant, but the girl is made pregnant by a coachman who then disappears, and she leaves the grandchild, José, with M'man Tine and goes off to find work in the city. M'man Tine, continuing to work as a weeder, is impelled by her passionate determination to save the boy from plantation labour, to break the chain which binds successive generations to the canefields, for 'how will it all end if the blasted fathers place their sons . . . in the same misfortune?' (p. 45). Along with José, she represents the disadvantaged condition of the rural poor, and together they form a standard West Indian matriarchal household.[22]

This stereotyped case history, rather clumsily inserted into the narrative flow, is socially informative, but mechanical; it is the small descriptive touches within the fiction – the grandmother's perennial grumbling about working in 'the white people's cane'; the strange, intimate smell of sweat, 'the smell of plantation workers', which attracts the children to the forbidden territory of the adults' small, dark bedrooms during the working day; the frenzied hips, glassy eyes and fixed smiles as the Saturday night dancers give themselves up to the drug of the drumbeat – that convey the sense of oppression, the endless, unrewarding, unrewarded physical exertion, the absence of creature comforts, and the feeling of being at the mercy of forces beyond one's control which characterize the cane workers' lives. And it is through M'man Tine's unremitting fatigue, her effort to prepare José's evening meal when she returns from the fields in the evening, her intense, silent pleasure in her nightly pipe of coarse tobacco, her unpredictable swings from brutal chastisement to a rough, despairing tenderness, that the child comes to apprehend, dimly at first and then with increasing clarity, the nature of her work and its constant ravages upon her body and emotions. Later, when he goes with her into the canefields, he is struck by the solitude and silence in which she toils and the painful difficulty she has in loosening the weeds from the hard ground; his own childish playfulness is reduced to muteness and immobility. José's gradual realization of what estate labour means is similar to that of an earlier Zobel hero (in the novel *Diab'-là*, written in 1942) who, as a child, is puzzled by the sullen depression of the adult labourers in his district, and only later, when he joins their ranks, comes to see the *békés'* canefields as robbing a black man of dignity and joy.[23]

In the absence of a father, José attaches himself to one of the canecutters of

Black Shack Alley, 'the oldest, most wretched and most abandoned on the entire plantation' (p. 29), who becomes his mentor. Through conversations with Médouze, José hears of the slave past, the capture of Médouze's African father, and the existence of a remote paradise, the ancestral Guinea, where misery, weariness and hunger do not exist; which is contrasted with the hell of the Caribbean canefields. Médouze, one of the author's adult mouthpieces, represents the disenchantment of all those who once believed that the abolition of slavery would mean the end of servitude. From his father he has learnt that emancipation changed little for the freed slaves: 'I remained like all the blacks in this damned country: the *békés* kept the land, all the land in the country, and we continued working for them. The law forbade them from whipping us, but did not force them to pay us our due . . . We remained under the *béké*, attached to his land. And he remained our master' (p. 33).

Too proud in his old age to leave his strenuous job and join the disrespectful young ragamuffins of the *petites bandes*, Médouze is found one night dead among the canes. His death, and his symbolic importance as Christ-like victim of the canefields, have been foreshadowed on all the Sunday afternoons when José has come upon the old man asleep on his bed, which is a bare plank propped up at one end on a stone. Lying in the shadows, his bearded body dressed only in a loin-cloth, rigid and elongated on the narrow plank, Médouze already has the posture of a corpse and the familiar attitude of the crucified Christ. The unspoken comparison is later made explicit by the author when José goes into a church with his grandmother and sees a statue of Jesus on the Cross. Unacquainted with the Crucifixion story, he senses the tragedy latent in the strange figure (so incomprehensibly that of a white man) and relates it to the only domain of suffering and martyrdom that he knows: the world of blacks and of animals. The Christ figure reminds him of the lizards that he and his friends transfix to fences, and at the same time of Médouze, lying emaciated on his hard plank in his tattered loin-cloth (p. 50). The dead Médouze, carried back from the fields by the other labourers ('It's the canes that killed him'), takes on the dehumanized aspect of his slave forebears, becoming 'a thing black, long, bony and half-dressed in rags'; stretched out for the last time upon his too-narrow plank, his rust-coloured teeth showing in a stiff, fixed smile, he is once more compared to an animal, the dead rat that a country child might find in the middle of a road (pp. 56–7). The wake for Médouze marks the transition from José's earliest years to the start of his schooldays; and the memory of the old man's lonely death returns to haunt him later as he witnesses his grandmother undergoing the same 'showers, storms, sunstrokes . . . weeds, cane stalks, cane leaves' which struck down Médouze (p. 77) and fears that she, too, is 'dying a slow death in those fields of sugar cane' (p. 122).

José's entry into primary school in the nearby village of Petit-Bourg alters his view of race and class, which was formerly based on the simple black/white dichotomy that Médouze had taught him and that he could relate to his own limited experience of life. School is a kind of mirror which shows him a number of racial types playing a variety of roles, and he himself is one of them, acquiring for the first time a sense of his social identity. Studies of children's racial attitudes in recent years indicate that in many cultures the pre-school child, from about the age of 3, is already aware of ethnic differences, and that between 6 and 8 years of age, 'concepts and feelings about race frequently include adult distinctions of status, ability, character, occupations, and economic circumstances'.[24] José is 7 when he goes to school, and in a community already hyper-sensitive to colour and class it is not surprising that he should be portrayed as constantly alert to differences of skin complexion, hair texture and parental status among his small companions. But his thumb-nail sketches of his friends are also a didactic authorial device which apprises the reader of the divisions within Martinican society, divisions which are always related back to colour, and in most cases to the ranking order of the plantation. Thus José's friend Vireil, who has a tanned complexion and long, soft black hair, and is one of the few pupils to wear shoes to school, turns out to be the son of an estate manager. As if repeating the pattern of casual and exploitative sex indulged in by the *géreurs* of the past, Vireil ends up making a country girl pregnant, and then disappears from the novel. Another friend, Raphael, is of a lighter colour than José, with smooth black hair. Both boys wear shabby clothes and go shoeless, but José, the cane-weeder's grandchild, is regarded with suspicion and disapproval by Raphael's grandmother, who does not work on the land but sells cakes in the village.

The most detailed portrait is that of Jojo, brown-faced, stiff-haired, well-dressed and forever unhappy. Jojo is the son of a mulatto foreman at the sugar factory, who has all the attributes of wealth: a fine house with many shuttered windows, full of new furniture; a car, and a wife who does not work. But although Jojo lives with them, he is not the son of Mme Roc, and the role of unwanted, alien outcast to which she consigns him is symbolic of an entire society's tendency to reject all those of dark skin and lowly origins. Before becoming head foreman at the factory, Jojo's father had been a plantation manager, and 'as nothing was easier for the managers and overseers than to do what they wanted at the whim of their desires, tastes and appetites', he had had a child by one of the estate weeders, 'a young, plump, beautiful octoroon with an amber-coloured complexion' (p. 88). Because of her beauty he had made her his mistress and acknowledged the child. Zobel is careful to underline both society's view of her situation – that she was lucky to be chosen as the mistress of a mulatto and a foreman (an attitude dating from the era of slavery, when such a situation offered an escape from field drudgery) – and the reality of her position, which is the unequal and precarious one of a maid sleeping with her master. This pleasant but uncertain period of Jojo's life comes to an end when his father marries a woman of his own social class. He keeps Jojo with him, while the beautiful Gracieuse remains alone in a one-room dwelling and, through the spite of Roc's new wife, is gradually cut off from the company of her son. Mme Roc's descriptions of Gracieuse as 'a true black woman from the plantation', a 'dirty, vulgar black girl' (p. 89), reinforce the atmosphere of class and colour prejudice in which Jojo grows up, and his sad confidences reveal to José a state of affairs the latter had only half grasped when M'man Tine used to ramble on in denunciation of mulattos (the overseer at Black Shack Alley was one) as being 'always quick to flatter the *békés* and betray the blacks' (p. 45). Jojo's mother eventually leaves the village to live with a small farmer in another district, and the boy remains at the mercy of his stepmother and her black maid, the object of their perpetual contempt and physical abuse.

Unsupported by his father, who believes Mme Roc's spiteful tales against him and is constantly punishing him, and victimized by his uncle, the school principal, Jojo can only take refuge in dreams of a time when his father and stepmother will be dead, and he himself will have attained a position which, in his childish mind, is the epitome of adult power: that of foreman at the sugar factory. But finally he runs away to join his mother, and decisively abandons the middle-class world his father and uncle inhabit. The plantation symbolism latent in his life story is fully brought out when his flight is compared to that of a runaway slave, who, out of sheer despair, has taken to the bush to seek freedom (p. 115). The school buzzes with the old term for fugitive slaves – '*Georges Roc a marronné!*' – and the event haunts José's imagination as Médouze's death had done. Some years later, when José is a high school student in Fort-de-France, Jojo turns up once more, working as a gardener and houseboy in Route Didier, the suburb of the rich *békés*. José, at first shaken by his former friend's enormous drop in status, eventually reflects that Jojo, having renounced his mulatto father to follow in his dark-skinned mother's footsteps, has 'taken the road fatal to all the little boys whose parents work in the canes' (p. 165). Jojo's career is thus emblematic of the black man's struggle to break away from the state of deprivation and humiliation which was his lot in slave times. His brief encounter with plantation work, when he attempts to rouse the other labourers to protest against the illegal reduction of their wages, and spends six months in prison for assaulting a manager, confirms his symbolic importance in the novel's moral scheme. This act of defiance represents both a social and a racial revolt. Jojo now identifies with his mother's race and with his black co-workers on the plantation. The mulatto manager whom he attacks belongs to the world of his father and uncle, which he has rejected for its prejudice and cruelty: 'A mulatto (and I have a bit of the blood in me, alas!) is always ready to shout "dirty nigger" and to threaten to kick' (p. 165). His audacity and his powers of endurance make him, in José's eyes, a hero beside whom the narrator's life is 'insignificant' (p. 166).

During the formative years he spends in primary school, José's perspective on the social world is attained not only through observation of his fellow students, but through the pressures which society begins to exert on him, and the image of himself which is reflected back by other people. He meets with race and class discrimination in his relationships with the lighter-skinned Raphael and Jojo, not from the boys but from their guardians: Raphael's grandmother looks askance at him when he plays outside her house, and Jojo is not allowed to play with him at all, and can do so only clandestinely. Jojo's stepmother's maid, herself black, epitomizes both the sense of innate superiority which historically separated the house slave from the field slave, and the alienation of those who internalized their masters' racial values. When she calls José 'this little black boy' there is no sense of a shared racial identity; a monolingual Creole speaker herself, she scorns José for speaking Creole; in her opinion, his place is 'to remain in [his] mother's shack instead of coming here to teach other people's children vices' (p. 102). Thus José learns to be cautious and mistrustful in his dealings with the adult world, for 'people [are] so suspicious of black children!' (p. 114). And at the same time, he learns that the very word 'black' is associated with a negative emotional climate and a hostile stereotype.

The old plantation hierarchies operate against him also in his daily contact with the hypocritical Mme Léonce, in whose house his grandmother had arranged that he should eat his packed lunch. Mme Léonce is of the same complexion as M'man Tine, but considers herself socially superior to the estate weeder, for she is the wife of a foreman at the sugar factory, and once employed José's mother Délia as a servant. She puts José to eat in a corridor and tells him to fetch his water from the standpipe by the road. When he has finished eating, he is to wait in front of the house until school reopens. He is hurt and mortified by her treatment of him, which he cannot really understand, and which contrasts so sharply with her kind promise to his grandmother that she would welcome him each midday: 'I felt like a little dog in front of her' (p. 66).

Things seem about to improve when she offers to provide his meals herself and lets him eat in her kitchen, but this turns out to be a pretext for using him during his entire lunch hour as an unpaid servant to wash dishes, clean shoes, run errands and sweep the yard. Afraid to tell his grandmother, since her attitude to Mme Léonce is one of humble gratitude, José suffers in silence. The social humiliations and emotional anguish of the underprivileged black child, propelled by an anxious, well-meaning mother into an alien milieu where he can no longer turn to her for support, form a particularly poignant motif in Zobel's work. There are unforgettable vignettes in his *Laghia de la mort* of two estate children for whom, like José, early schooldays bring a bitter realization of poverty and inferior social status. One child, in a passion of grief and anger, is dragged away by his gentle, intimidated mother from a condescending shop assistant who has refused to give her a reduction of price on the schoolbook which the child desperately desires, which the teacher chides him for not possessing, and which his mother simply cannot afford. The other, shamed by the taunts of his better-dressed schoolmates, fixes two dirty bandages over nonexistent sores on his legs, in a confused, pathetic attempt to compensate for his lack of shoes.[25] As for José, he continues to be patronized and exploited by Mme Léonce until he finally rebels and runs away from her. He is then reduced to raiding fruit-trees for his lunch during the remainder of the term, afraid of his grandmother's anger if he tells her that he no longer eats at Mme Léonce's.

From this time on, the presence of acute hunger is an accepted, though intermittent, fact of José's existence: when his grandmother is away in hospital; when, at high school in Fort-de-France on a quarter scholarship, he has no money to buy food from the caretaker's stall during recess; when his mother goes to live in at her employer's house and leaves him alone in an urban slum to survive on a haphazard and unhealthy diet. Before his famished eyes, the pretty, light-skinned primary school mistress at Petit-Bourg dips her elegant spoon into a bowl of fragrant chocolate; later, the affluent, fair-complexioned high school boys around him stuff themselves with cake and gingerbread. Food, like so much else in his life, becomes an attribute of colour and class. Lack of good clothes is another factor which excludes him from many festivities and ceremonies destined for children; lack of any shoes at all delays his First Communion by a year and gives him the painful impression of being left behind by his village classmates. Yet he is destined to overtake and outstrip them; he alone moves on from the village school to the *lycée* in the capital.

His relationship with M'man Tine is of central importance to this achievement. Her tenacious ambition to keep him out of the *petites bandes* fuels his own desire to escape the plantation, and her proud satisfaction at his every scholastic success inspires him with the wish to retain her respect and admiration.[26] She instils in him the notion that education is the only way out of the canefields, and it is through this that he alone, of all the children and adolescents portrayed in the novel, avoids 'follow[ing] in its natural stages the destiny of one born in Black Shack Alley' (p. 149). In the final section, when he is attending high school in Fort-de-France, his circumstances are favourably contrasted with those of his two friends and contemporaries, Jojo the gardener, and Carmen the chauffeur. All were born on plantations, and Carmen, like José, grew up in an estate worker's wooden shack. But his parents had no ambitions for him; at the age of 7 he was leading ox-carts along the plantation roads, and from there progressed to being himself a mule driver. The accident of national service brought him from the plantation to the city, where he stayed on, cheerful and illiterate, as car driver to a *béké*. José, who makes no close friends among the high school boys – the social distance is too great for him to bridge: no one else there has parents who wield a spade or a cutlass – depends upon these two boys for comradeship and emotional support. Like his own mother, they are menials on Route Didier; and only with them does he feel at ease.

The social structure of Route Didier dominates the last part of the novel, and represents a transposition of plantation hierarchies to an urban setting. It is there that one finds 'the richest white people and the best black servants' (p. 126). The Route de Didier is a real road whose name is synonymous with an elegant suburb above Fort-de-France largely inhabited by wealthy *békés*, descendants of the white plantation-owning Creoles, a few of whom still dominate the economic life of the island.[27] José is delighted with its bright, smart villas and large, luxuriant gardens; it is as foreign to him as his first experience of the primary school in Petit-Bourg, and he explores it with caution on his visits to his mother in the servants' quarters of her master's residence. Later he and his mother move to a rented room in an agglomeration of shacks clinging to the hillside below Route Didier, all occupied by chauffeurs and maids who work for the *békés* above – as the occupants of Black Shack Alley had worked for the manager and overseer whose houses loomed over their huts. José then comes to see these servants as spiritual descendants of the house slaves of the past: submissive, obsequious and self-effacing, convinced of the superior power and virtue of the whites, prostrated before their masters in a way he had never observed even among the down-trodden estate labourers of Black Shack Alley and Petit-Bourg. Even his friend Carmen takes it for granted that his *béké* employer's black mistress is lucky to be able to 'lighten the race' with her two mulatto children; and Carmen himself, when he begins learning to read and write, forsakes the black maids with whom he formerly slept, to become the lover of a mulatto woman whose husband owns a café in town. José gradually perceives the street as a microcosm of Martinican society, in which a tiny group of local whites, however ignorant or uncouth they may be as individuals, constitute a 'rare, precious species', presiding over the inferior 'grafted species' of the mulattos and the much more numerous and less valuable blacks, 'the cheap, common lot' (p. 152). Later still, in a state of dawning sociopolitical awareness, he regards it as a privileged enclave unfairly built upon the sweat and suffering of labourers like his own grandmother, whose blemished hands bear mute witness to 'the fierce cuts inflicted by the cane leaves to create Route Didier' (p. 181). As a child on the plantation, he had given little thought to its remote, invisible *béké* owner. Only in the city is he personally confronted with the wealth, power and arrogance which characterize those at the top of the hierarchy. In the sequel to *Black Shack Alley*, José, now a student in Paris, is still preoccupied with the tripartite nature of Martinican society, dominated by the sugar aristocracy of the Route Didier. When a friend and compatriot of his is about to return to Martinique to take up a post at the *lycée* in Fort-de-France, José bitterly predicts that he will soon turn his back on those of his class and colour: 'Although you're as black as the ace of spades . . . you will become, so to speak, a mulatto, because of your job. Whether you wish it or not. Your chief feature in your own eyes, and those of others, will be your superiority to the black who slaves away in the *béké*'s canefields – and who can't even speak French.'[28]

At the middle-class *lycée*, where the other pupils' parents are doctors, schoolteachers, cabinet-makers, office workers, tailors, seamstresses and pharmacists, José is conscious of shame when required to give the profession of his next of kin. He does not even know whether the name of M'man Tine's humble job exists in French; he knows it only in Creole, and finally glosses it over by declaring that she is a farmer. But he never loses his sense of loyalty to her. She, much more than Délia, is his real mother, and his earliest, most unrealistic ambition, to own a large fruit and vegetable property and employ many well-dressed, well-housed workers, was built about the presence of M'man Tine: freed from the plantation, she would be there taking care of his hens and gathering their eggs. This dream was punctured by Jojo, who pointed out first of all that only a *béké* could own all that, and secondly that if workers were so well treated, 'niggers' would no longer exist – a state of affairs which is clearly impossible. José's early fantasy fades, but his desire to take M'man Tine away from her life of unremitting toil is intensified as he sees her declining in health and energy with every passing year. His letters to her from Fort-de-France attempt, in a youthful way, to reassure her that a better life is ahead: 'Soon I'd be big, I'd be successful in my examinations and she'd not have to work in the sugar cane fields, or anywhere else' (p. 134). But on his summer visits he is grieved and ashamed to observe once more her abject poverty, the smelly, grimy shack where she has to live, her constant exposure to rainstorms which send her home shivering with fever. Life becomes a race for José to finish his schooling before it is too late to rescue her from servitude; back in Fort-de-France, he is impelled by 'dreams of becoming a man, so that M'man Tine wouldn't have to work any more on the sugar cane plantations' (p. 137). When he passes the first part of his *baccalauréat*, his success is not meaningful until he can give the news to his grandmother in person and remind her that she has 'only one more year to wait before being delivered from the cane fields' (p. 170). In the novel's pathetic conclusion, she dies during that year, with José far away in Fort-de-France, unable to offer her even the comfort of his presence. With her passing, the story ends. Her life has had two functions: one, to ensure José's safe removal from the destitution which she herself never escapes; and the other, to open his eyes for ever to the injustice of a social system which continues to condone the existence of inequalities almost as intolerable as those of slavery itself.

Through the central figure of M'man Tine, Zobel rejects the European myth of the plantation as a natural paradise of sunlight and sensual abandon, where vigorous labourers and their exotic girls move through the canefields to the rhythmic beat of charming traditional work songs. In *Black Shack Alley* the plantation of the 1920s is an image of hell:

> a damnable place where executioners, whom you couldn't even see, condemned black people from as young as eight years old, to weed, to dig, in storms that caused them to shrivel up and in the broiling sun that devoured them like mad dogs – blacks in rags, stink with sweat and dung, fed on one handful of cassava flour and two cents' worth of molasses rum, who became pitiful monsters with glassy eyes, with feet made heavy by elephantiasis, destined to collapse one night in a furrow

The Novels of Joseph Zobel and Michèle Lacrosil

and to breathe their last breath on a dingy plank on the ground of an empty, grimy hut. (p. 122)

Against the flat and occasionally stilted tone which prevails in much of the novel, such passages stand out by their anger and distress, reminding the reader that the author's chosen point of view is above all that of the black field worker who, for centuries, was the lowest creature on the sugar estates, and the one most consistently denied the opportunity of speaking out against his own dispossessed condition. Thus Zobel seeks to redress a historic wrong and, like Césaire (*Cahier*, p. 50), to be 'the mouth of misfortunes which have no mouth'.

The presentation of plantation society in Michèle Lacrosil's *Tomorrow Jab-Herma* differs from that of *Black Shack Alley* in that the black field labourer remains in the background, and is viewed, with one exception, through the eyes of characters who stand above and apart from him: Philippe Bonnier, the visiting French engineer; Constant Sougès, the white West Indian whose family owned Pâline for centuries, and who has been retained as assistant manager of the estate by the French firm to whom it now belongs; Jab-Herma, Sougès' black chauffeur, whose reputation as sorcerer and healer gives him a prestige in the estate village as great as that of Sougès himself. The exception is Eric Cragget, himself a labourer, but one whose mulatto blood and middle-class childhood cause him to detest and despise his black fellow-workers. Although the narrative standpoint is ostensibly a multiple one – for the novel attempts to portray a variety of racial and social types embracing the entire spectrum of plantation life – most of the characters surface only fleetingly and superficially: it is Bonnier, Sougès and Cragget who dominate the scene. The novel shifts continually and rapidly between the unexpressed thoughts of these three, and the thinker's identity often remains unstated, obliging the reader to deduce it from the emotional content of the particular stream of consciousness being recorded; the cumulative effect of such passages is to build up a complete moral portrait of each of the men. Curiously, Jab-Herma himself, upon whom the story opens and closes, remains an opaque and somewhat two-dimensional character, although he gives the novel its title and is presented as a figure of great symbolic importance to the evolution of the plantation.

Two separate dramas unfold simultaneously within the brief space of days that the events occupy, and Philippe Bonnier, the newcomer and outsider, is at the centre of both. His relationship with Constant Sougès, the local white (the Martinican term *béké* is little used in Guadeloupe, and Lacrosil refers to Sougès as a Creole), is a dramatization of the struggle for power between French capitalist interests and the Guadeloupean planter class, which was to end with the takeover of most of the island's agricultural land by metropolitan companies.[29] Set in 1952, the novel shows us a plantocracy in decline: poverty has forced Sougès to sell out to Philippe's uncle Arbrissel, the distant, invisible managing director whose company controls half of the world's sugar market from its Paris headquarters. Arbrissel has sent out a manager, Georges Robérieu, whose policy has been a tactful one of allowing Sougès to remain in charge of the work force and thus retain an illusion of power which is essential to his pride. Robérieu discovers Philippe's relationship to Arbrissel, but Sougès, who is unaware of it for most of the novel, treats Philippe with the patronizing arrogance of an aristocratic eighteenth-century planter dealing

73

with one of his white employees. Robérieu uneasily foresees the inevitable clash between them as a 'conflict of authority between the representative of the central power, and the Creole who wants to be master on an estate he has sold' (p. 67).

Constant Sougès has the instincts of a feudal lord: not only the habit of mastery, but also an automatic concern for the survival and well-being of those whose ancestors were the slaves of the Sougès family in past centuries. It is a paternalism which takes for granted the abject poverty of the labourers' shacks, but which provides food and shelter for the pregnant adolescent thrown out by her family, or the ignorant sharecropper who has lost his cane crop by failing to protect it against borers, and who would have had his lease revoked by a more impersonal landlord. The labourers, too, take for granted Sougès' ancestral rights and duties, his power to protect and to punish: as far as they are concerned, 'Mr Constant' is still the real boss of Pâline. The patterns of obedience, respect, resignation, and abdication of personal responsibility which were laid down in slave times are unchallenged by the majority of those who live in the estate village. There is an intimate interdependence between the workers' shacks and Sougès' house; the domestic servants he could not afford to employ are unpaid volunteers from the ranks of the village adolescents, and the food on his table is a gift from the labourers' provision grounds. These time-honoured practices serve to conceal the reality of his financial destitution, and in the faded splendour of his residence nightly dinner parties are held for the white staff with all the style of the traditional Great House gatherings. Family jewels, handpainted Sèvres porcelain, chandeliers, wall hangings, priceless antique furniture and carpets create an illusion of colonial luxury which has no basis in economic reality. The final eviction of Sougès from Pâline merely confirms a downfall which had been delayed by Robérieu's kindness, but which was none the less unavoidable from the moment when financial control of Pâline was transferred to Paris.

For Sougès, Pâline is 'a separate world' (p. 33), a self-enclosed entity resistant to time and change. Although he is only 27, he is as conservative as a much older man, and hates any alteration in his environment, even the minor one of his wife dyeing her hair without consulting him. This apparently insignificant incident is in reality symptomatic, to him, of the unwelcome innovations that the Paris head office, represented by Philippe, is threatening to force upon him; and his growing exasperation at Philippe (which is somewhat reminiscent of the angry suspicion in which the nineteenth-century plantocracy held metropolitan abolitionists) is complicated by sexual jealousy over the interest his wife, Joëlle, has shown in the visitor. Her new blonde hair is meant to outrival Philippe's. Sougès is affronted by 'this wish to wear another's colour'; but his reaction goes still deeper: his 'universe is disrupted', the world about him is 'stirring' (p. 105). Philippe is shaking up the formerly static way of life in what was once Souges' exclusive domain, and the latter's need to dominate, to have everyone within his reach dependent upon him, becomes progressively more difficult to satisfy. As psychological insecurity overtakes him, he also sees his financial recovery growing more unlikely. He had hoped to restore his fortunes by increasing the number of his sharecroppers, whom he regards in much the same way as his forebears had regarded their slaves: 'A sharecropper, once he's settled in, means peaceful, reliable labour; you rent them a tiny plot of land, they do all your field work, there's no chance of a strike, and you have no cash problems, thanks to the estate shop' (p. 33). This shop, from which the workers buy everything on credit against their wages – which they therefore seldom see in cash – is a traditional plantation monopoly. Sougès views the 'good old system' of barter, the exchange of piece-work for goods from the shop, as 'relieving the men of money worries' (p. 112), not as preventing them from being in charge of their own finances, nor as depriving them of the desire to make provision for the future. He is satisfied that none of his workers will ever die of starvation while he is alive, and that the young ones have their guitars, their cockfights, the moonlight and the old folk-tales to keep them quiet.

Sougès' deepest conscious feelings are for the land he possesses, his private 'Eden' (p. 98). When, at the end, he knows that he is to be evicted, his bitterness is directed against the Parisian intruder who, without roots in Guadeloupe, will never become attached to the country. He is convinced that no one on the plantation cares for it as much as he does (the sharecroppers 'could not love as he did a land which they did not own'). But his real grief is at the loss of power:

> He was fond of the slaves on the property . . . He couldn't imagine living without them, without their courage and their resignation. He needed to have someone at hand who would raise towards him a face hollowed by hunger and anxiety, begging him: 'Please, Mr Constant?' Someone on whose shoulder he, Sougès, would place his hand, to improve some wretch's lot by the mere pressure of that hand, and to feel himself a god. (p. 241)

In his own house he keeps his young wife under his thumb, believing that 'to display authority in the home [is] an essential requirement for gaining people's respect outside it' (p. 149). He patronizes the seedy French book-keeper, tolerating him at dinner every evening because he is part of Pâline, but never permitting him to address Joëlle by her first name. He is gracious to the Robérieus until they come into conflict with him over his treatment of Philippe; then Cécile Robérieu berates him as 'the slave of a furious appetite for domination, of a violent legacy of abominable, indecent despotism' (p. 167). It is Sougès' despotic nature and function that the novelist emphasizes: descendant of plantocrats and slave-owners, governed by the conviction of his hereditary rights, he is presented as the epitome of arrogance and selfishness. Through him, the author passes judgement on the white Creole landowning class, which promised its slaves liberation but gave them no material compensation for their past sufferings, merely turning them into landless labourers, 'domesticated, humiliated, consenting' (p. 241), slaves still in all but name. Philippe, whose early reservations about Sougès are swept away by his admiration for the other man's artistry as a pianist, is none the less alienated by his autocratic conduct and ends by resolving to destroy 'the past, the time of the Creoles' (p. 208). In his own mind Sougès, the king about to be deposed, compares Philippe (p. 222) to Saint-Just, the young eighteenth-century revolutionary who was intransigent in his call for the execution of the French monarch.

Alongside the conflict between Sougès and Philippe, a relationship arises between Philippe and Eric Cragget which dramatizes another aspect of Caribbean life: the mulatto's historic obsession with whiteness. Cragget is the male counterpart of the coloured heroines of Michèle Lacrosil's two previous novels.[30] Like them, he sees himself as the prisoner of his skin and the pre-ordained victim of those fairer than himself. Socially and emotionally insecure, he incarnates the alienated West Indians of Césaire's *Cahier* (p. 86) who 'never get over being made in the likeness of the devil and not in the likeness of God'. He corresponds to a fictional stereotype of the mulatto that is perhaps more frequently encountered in West Indian writing in English, and that is characterized by certain predictable traits: a yearning desire to be white, a wish for sexual union with a light-skinned partner, an attitude of submissiveness and admiration (sometimes coupled with latent or repressed hostility) towards white people, and a concomitant attitude of superiority and scorn towards blacks.[31] Such features may, in fact, be present in any fictional character of mixed race, and not merely in the mulatto, who is strictly speaking half white and half black; Lacrosil's first heroine, for example, is a *câpresse*, the daughter of a mulatto woman and a black man. They are also often accompanied by psychological instability and social maladjustment. This literary stereotype of the coloured person has its roots in the plantation system, wherein mulatto slaves were often favoured over blacks and deferred to by them; wherein liaisons with white persons might be, for the slave, a means towards better living conditions and even towards freedom; wherein a pattern of social and racial stratification, imposed by the white plantocracy, was accepted by those slaves who internalized the values and prejudices of their masters. The prejudice against agricultural work, perceived as degrading and fit only for the blackest of slaves, is of particular importance in Cragget's case since he is himself obliged to work as a field labourer, a situation which he loathes.

Cragget is an atypical version of the literary stereotype in that he spent his childhood not in colonial society, but in France. For this reason, his white ideal is not the Creole, Sougès, but the metropolitan, Philippe. Although his personality so closely conforms to that of the nineteenth-century free coloureds manoeuvring for social mobility and full civil rights in the Caribbean context, Lacrosil attributes his behaviour to an individual experience of injustice at the hands of one particular person. In realistic terms, the story of his life is implausible, but it must be seen as a carefully contrived narrative designed to meet the requirements of social allegory. Born to working-class poverty – his West Indian mother is the domestic servant of a wealthy Frenchwoman, his English father is a criminal in jail – Cragget is romantically projected into the life of a 'young prince' when his mother falls fatally ill. Her capricious employer informally adopts him and he enters a world of private governesses, music and horse-riding lessons, and, later, the classrooms of a top French *lycée*. Over-indulged in everything, including his tendency to petty theft, and led to expect a higher education and a successful career, he is shattered when his guardian dies and leaves her money not to him, but to charities concerned with juvenile delinquency. Her will provides only for him to become a labourer on a farm in Normandy. Unable to stand the racial and social hostility of the other farm workers, who dub him the Black Aristocrat, he hitchhikes back to Paris and struggles for existence in a series of unskilled jobs, unable to get enough time or money to complete his education. One day, sweeping a street outside the Arbrissel company's head office, he glimpses the young Philippe going in for an interview with his uncle. His imagination is caught by this fleeting image of the perfect Other: 'the straight nose, the pure mouth, like the models offered in drawing lessons or the pictures in catechism manuals during his childhood and adolescence; he wanted to be a true replica of that heavenly gaze, that innocent face . . . The engineer was an ideal . . . like a dream that one is glad to have had' (pp. 84–5). On impulse, Cragget signs on with the company and finds himself 'repatriated' as a canecutter to an island which is utterly foreign to him. Philippe's arrival at Pâline three years later is an unbearable reminder of his own failed ambitions. Philippe represents everything that Cragget would like to be: a white man, a university graduate, a professional, an independent being. The close proximity of this unattainable type of perfection exacerbates Cragget's frustrations and finally drives him over the edge into suicidal despair. His final words, shouted to the distant Philippe over the noise of the floodwaters in which he is about to drown himself, seem to acknowledge the extent to which he is a case history of alienation: 'I am not a person, I am a situation . . . I am an intolerable situation, from which I must escape at any price' (p. 247).

The figure of Cragget is of central importance to the narrative, both as an image of Caribbean racial tensions and also as the author's chief mouthpiece for protest at the conditions of the cane workers' lives. These conditions are initially presented through the eyes of Philippe, the newcomer who is appalled by the contrast between Sougès' colonial mansion and the ramshackle wooden huts perched on stones above the open gutters of the estate village. When the engineer first walks through the village, his shocked gaze makes the labourers momentarily aware of their own destitution; but they, like him, soon relapse into the indifference, the 'age-old blindness' (p. 47), which is the only way to tolerate the intolerable. Cragget, on the other hand, never ceases to resent his wretchedly inadequate shack, unpainted, with no bathroom or electricity; and his indignation is fuelled by the fact that for half the year a row of comfortable bungalows lies empty, reserved for twenty Dutch technicians who live at Pâline only during the season. He longs for red meat, in place of the labourers' monotonous diet of cassava, salt cod and dumplings; as his sense of grievance grows, he is depicted knocking over his bowl in a fit of rage and trampling on 'this slave food designed to weigh down body and mind, and force slaves into resignation', indignant that Philippe is doubtless 'dining on lobster, steak or chicken' (p. 198). He is the only one of the labourers capable of analysing his economic situation and perceiving the ways in which the organization of the plantation perpetuates the psychological and financial evils of the slave system: the workers forced to accept a minimal wage, resigned to being forever in debt to the estate shop, and dependent on the goodwill of the management for permission to grow a few subsistence crops on small pieces of estate land.

However, it is evident that Cragget's anger is purely on his own account; he feels nothing but contempt for his black fellow workers, who serve only to remind him of his failure to be white. They, on their side, resent his educated speech and cannot comprehend his objections to the management's paternalistic stance. In the forced intimacy of the shop, over the midday meal, this mutual animosity is never far from the surface. Accused by his chief antagonist, Clovis Parche, the workers' union representative, of trying to ape their masters ('Talking like white people isn't going to make you white'), Cragget is provoked into a passionate diatribe against both white oppression and black apathy:

'I live in their world! I work my guts out for their factory. I have to talk like them so that they can understand me, don't I? . . . Do you think I can create a world of my own, Clovis? With values that are *ours*, coloured people's values? What are you all doing, if not submitting to their laws and whims, the working hours they force on us, the ways of thinking that they impose? . . . You think you're free? You bloody idiot.' (p. 61)

He has no ambition to strive for the improvement of the cane workers' lot; what he wants is to occupy a position of privilege in white society.

Cragget is clearly the character that the author finds most interesting. He is seen as a victim of racial prejudice, rather than as a subscriber to it; as a doomed individual, not as a warped one. It is he who is portrayed with the greatest degree of sympathy and poetic insight, as he moves from unhappy isolation into increasing mental disturbance:

> The Other is at home anywhere; Cragget is an outsider everywhere. The leaves around him are strange: prickly, hostile! They are a barrier, he can't get through them. Where can he find in this country, whose lands were distributed to the Others two or three centuries ago, a little plot, a shelter, and a mental attitude which would allow him to pull himself together, to be himself? His only refuge is in fantasy, and he knows that is close to madness . . . since he must destroy himself, or dream himself another person, in order to try and exist. (p. 197)

His obsession with Philippe, the ideal Other, has been seen as an existentialist theme, in accordance with Sartre's concept of human relations as a battleground where the individual and the Other struggle for psychological supremacy.[32] Philippe's view of Cragget as a man vanquished by white society ('We control the world he lives in and the image he has of himself. He judges himself according to criteria imposed by us, he desires to be what he is not', p. 159), and Cragget's constant preoccupation with the notion of the Other (it is the only term by which he designates Philippe in his thoughts), would seem to bear out the hypothesis of an existentialist element in the novel. However, fascination with the white Other is also, of course, a key element in the Césairean definition of alienation; and in Frantz Fanon's *Black Skin, White Masks* it is argued that to apply Sartre's theory of the Other to a black consciousness is fallacious, because to the black, the white man 'is not only the Other but also the master, whether real or imaginary'.[33] Cragget never questions Philippe's superiority; he regards him with an envious yet tender admiration that is very close to love. He spies on the Frenchman compulsively, contrives encounters with him, but is tongue-tied when given a chance to speak to him. Philippe takes as his mistress a mulatto girl who is a secretary at the factory; Cragget aspires to be this girl's lover also, not for love of her, but because Philippe has embraced her. Taking the Frenchman's place in her bed, he will be able to imagine that he has *become* the Other: ' "Close your eyes, imagine that it's Him, don't cry out, don't be afraid, tell me how he kisses." No lover could wish for more complete self-negation' (p. 141). But the girl Pilou, herself an example of the mulatto literary stereotype who takes pleasure in being subservient to a European lover, angrily rejects Cragget, an act which he correctly interprets as a rejection of his colour. In rage and humiliation, he must leave her room with nothing 'to nourish his dream'.

Tomorrow Jab-Herma is not only a portrait of plantation life; it is also a detective novel, and here again, Cragget is at the centre of the plot. Philippe has been sent out from Paris not only to assess the estate's viability, but also to investigate a series of mysterious thefts of barrels of rum. Shortly after his arrival, his young maid Clarine is murdered, and then his mistress Pilou. Cragget is the author of all these crimes, but his guilt is not revealed until the final section of the novel. Meanwhile, Philippe is the principal suspect, and the consequent suspense provides much of the book's dramatic interest. Sougès, who not only sees Philippe as a threat to his authority over Pâline, but also mistakenly believes that Joëlle is about to run off with him, is quick to accuse the engineer of the murders. He uses all the habitual imperiousness of the upper-class Creole in attempting to persuade the black police superintendent of Philippe's guilt, and, when Pâline is cut off from town by floodwaters, threatens to lock Philippe up in a cellar and have a confession beaten out of him by four of his men. The superintendent puts the Frenchman under police protection, fearing for his safety as much from an attack by Sougès (whom he describes as 'a mongoose . . . a bloodthirsty creature. A wild animal [that] can't be tamed in this part of the world', p. 175), as from one by Cragget, whom he suspects but against whom there is insufficient evidence for an arrest. Philippe, who is not told the reasons for his police guard, misinterprets it as a sign that the superintendent will co-operate with Sougès in torturing him till he admits to the murders. He sees the two men as compatriots, and therefore mutually supportive: this misapprehension is an aspect of one of the novel's minor themes, the inability of the white foreigner to grasp the delicate shades of feeling which spring up within West Indian society as a result of the interaction of race and class. In consequence, Philippe suffers agonies of fear and anticipated humiliation; and when he is vindicated, he takes his revenge by forcing Sougès to choose between the closure of the sugar factory, or the destruction of his ancestral home and his own departure from Pâline. Ingrained pride, and his traditional acceptance of responsibility for the workers' welfare, both compel Sougès to choose his own ruin rather than theirs.

Thus Cragget's crimes are the indirect cause of the palace revolution which ends the long reign of the Creole plantocracy at Pâline. Although Cragget's motives were entirely personal and selfish, his own justification of his actions – 'stealing, a form of protest; killing, a cry of revolt' (p. 244) – is ironically ratified by their social consequences: Sougès, the novel's symbol of past oppression, meets his downfall, and 'something irreversible' is started, 'a change, perhaps a disturbing one, another era' (p. 253). Lacrosil does not go so far as to predict that this new era will improve the workers' situation. Indeed, although the novel is set in 1952, it was published in 1967, by which time the decline of the sugar industry and the increasing dependence of the population on social security were already apparent. However, Philippe's awareness that the Paris shareholders' profits from the estate are acquired at the cost of the labourers' wretched living conditions (p. 48), and his replacement of Sougès by Jab-Herma as the liaison officer between the village and the French management, convey the author's apparent hope that there will be some future effort by the metropolitan company to remedy the evils of the old plantation system. The greatest remaining stumbling-block, perhaps, to social progress will be the villagers' long habit of dependence upon white authority. This is suggested, though never explicitly stated, by their readiness at the end to accord Philippe the same submissive admiration and affection which they have always granted to their Sougès masters. It is Sougès, manoeuvring in a desperate attempt to reinstate himself with the Frenchman, who ensures that the workers take 'Mr *Philippe*' to their hearts as the hero who has saved them from the floodwaters; but their immediate willingness to set Philippe alongside 'Mr Constant', their conviction that he will protect their future interests because he is 'much too handsome to be wicked' (p. 249), the languishing, 'consenting' glances which the village girls now begin to cast at him, all hint at the difficulty of eradicating the ancient patterns of white domination and black subservience. These plantation patterns which Lacrosil highlights may be seen as the root cause of the situation today in which the majority of French West Indians are content to leave all social, economic and cultural initiative to the metropolis.[34]

In contrast with the labourers' habitual passivity is the restless dissatisfaction of Cragget, the throbbing sense of injury which spurs him on to crime. Like everyone on the estate, he believes in the legendary treasure which is said to lie buried on Tirêha, the forbidden island across the river from Pâline. The origin of the gold is bound up with folk memories of a West Indian hero, and with the world of magic and the supernatural. When, in 1802, Napoleon decided to re-establish slavery, which had been abolished in 1794 as a consequence of the French Revolution, Louis Delgrès, a Martinican mulatto and an officer in the French republican army, who was in command of the region of Basse-Terre in Guadeloupe, led a revolt of black soldiers and peasants against the French regiments which had arrived to impose Napoleon's decree.[35] After a fierce resistance, Delgrès was finally surrounded at Fort Matouba by a force of several thousand French soldiers. He waited until they made the assault and then blew up the powder magazine, killing not only himself, his Guadeloupean junior officer and three hundred of his men who had insisted on dying with him, but also the two columns in the vanguard of the besieging troops. The rest of Delgrès' army was destroyed: a thousand executed, two thousand imprisoned or deported. But Delgrès, by his heroic suicide, became a symbol of glorious self-sacrifice and dynamic black leadership, 'the hope and the model' (p. 17) for future generations of slaves and their descendants. In *Tomorrow Jab-Herma*, Delgrès' last retreat to Matouba, and his careful planning of the final, deadly explosion, make up a tale which the Pâline workers never tire of retelling as they sit in their open doorways on dark evenings, 'fleeing from themselves through this story of a flight' (p. 24). For Cragget, however, Delgrès' story is much more than an escape from reality: it is a parallel with his own life and a source of inspiration. Delgrès, a mulatto like himself, was first granted entry to the free, white world, and then denied it. Crying out against injustice, rousing up the countryside, commandeering the estates on his path, fighting with his back to the wall, refusing to surrender in the face of hopeless odds, he violently repulsed all attempts to enslave him. Cragget is able to identify with him in a way which is impossible as regards the ideal Other, who is white. More importantly still, the ghost of Delgrès seems to beckon him towards the hidden treasure which will restore his fortunes.

According to local legend, Delgrès had stolen Guadeloupe's gold reserves in an attempt to prevent payment of the French soldiers and thus bring about their disaffection. The Pâline villagers believe that during the retreat to Matouba, his wounds obliged him to stop and rest on the island of Tirêha, where he had two of his soldiers secretly bury the gold, and then killed them and buried them beside it. A century and a half of assiduous searching has failed to reveal the site of the treasure, which is now said to be guarded by the ghosts of Delgrès' soldiers. It is supposed that the bridge to the island is haunted also, and cannot be crossed save by someone armed with a fetish, a magic object, that has been brought from across the seas. Even such a person cannot recover the gold unless he sacrifices a male child and pours a libation of

The Novels of Joseph Zobel and Michèle Lacrosil

302 litres of rum in order to appease Delgrès and his dead. Some years before, there was a plan afoot to sacrifice a child on Tirêha, and Jab-Herma prevented it by placing a ban on all visits to the island. The villagers' imagination still dwells on the paradise, the future Golden Age, which the treasure could open up to them; but their ambitions to paint their huts or build bigger ones, to install electricity, to send their eldest sons to high school in town, are not proof against Jab-Herma's prohibition. Tirêha becomes the symbolic antithesis to their destitution, 'the fertile island that none dares touch' (p. 24).

Cragget, who scoffs at their superstitious fears, conceives his own plan for finding the gold. By devious means, he acquires a fetish from Africa; but his imperfect knowledge of the legend leads him to plan the kidnapping of a female child, the small daughter of Philippe's maid Clarine. To bargain for her daughter's life, Clarine steals the box containing the fetish, and is killed by Cragget. Later, he accidentally drops in Pilou's room the key of the unused vault where he has stored the stolen rum, and then kills her, also, when she frustrates his attempt to regain it. These murders are partly motivated by his racial obsessions: in strangling Clarine, he is punishing his own black mother for bringing him into the world; in strangling Pilou, he is killing himself, the mulatto who yearns to attain union with the Other. At another narrative level, both women are simply obstacles in the path to Delgrès' treasure. For Cragget, as for the other villagers, the legendary gold represents a 'way to live out his fantasies, his only possible strategy' (p. 198) in the battle against white domination. But his ambitions, unlike theirs, are abstract and unattainable, the product of a disordered mind: to 'become another person', to 'seize hold . . . of an ideal state of innocence', to find and punish the one responsible for 'the curse' pronounced on him and his race (pp. 244–5). In the last section of the book, a childhood memory surfaces which is offered as the origin of his alienation, the moment he has never been able to transcend. At school in France, he was once wrongly accused of breaking a window and expelled from the company of his white classmates. The adult Cragget, 'chasing after lost innocence', forever 'reaching outside himself', is still the 7-year-old outcast humiliated by the white schoolmaster who sharply reminds him of his racial difference, the 'angel thunderously forbidding him paradise' (p. 246). The biblical analogy is intentional: Cragget sees innocence as an attribute of whiteness, sin and ugliness as attributes of darkness, according to the images of his Christian childhood. In his mind, innocence and happiness are reserved for the white race, while the 'black pariah' (p. 197) is debarred from all forms of paradise. It is in these last hours of his life that he feels for the first time a sense of affinity with the other labourers, and regrets having shunned them. They, like him, are the victims of an ancient curse. In recalling the fall from grace of Noah's son Cham (p. 246), Cragget evokes the long centuries when European prejudice against the Negro expressed itself in the popular belief that his blackness was a divine punishment.[36] Thus the author subsumes the particular difficulties of the mulatto in the larger issue of the black condition, and the problems of both are finally related to the evils of the plantation system: 'the factory and the society created by it' (p. 247), which have corrupted Sougès, perverted Cragget, and made slaves of almost everyone at Pâline.

Even more than *Black Shack Alley*, *Tomorrow Jab-Herma* dwells upon the complexities of skin shade and social class in the Caribbean. But the theme of social change, towards which all the narrative tends, is associated above all with the two figures at opposite ends of the racial spectrum: the white metropolitan, Philippe, and the black medicine-man, Jab-Herma. Of all the characters in the novel, they are the least implicated in the plantation system: Philippe because he comes from France, Jab-Herma because he has used an African heritage of witchcraft and healing to acquire prestige, inspire fear, and command the respect of both the blacks and the white Creoles. Both are ultimately symbols of independence and power. It is Philippe who initiates change at Pâline, who is the catalyst for Cragget's obsessions, who weakens Sougès' influence over his wife, spoils his friendship with the Robérieus, and finally puts a stop to his control over Pâline. It is Philippe, too, who elevates Jab-Herma to an official position of power for all in the estate village. However, this merely consecrates an already existing authority: Jab-Herma has always acted as intermediary between Sougès and the workers, and has always been consulted and obeyed by the latter in both moral and practical matters. With Sougès he enjoys a special relationship. His mother was Sougès' nurse; the two boys, inseparable friends, once made a blood pact of eternal loyalty which neither has forgotten. Constant Sougès has confidence in Jab-Herma's 'absolute power' (p. 133) and relies on him for advice and support. Jab-Herma is known within and outside the plantation as 'the liegeman and all-powerful twin of lord Sougès' (p. 173). In fact, he carefully balances his personal commitment to Sougès against the advantages which Philippe's take-over would bring to the blacks at Pâline. Cool and reserved with Philippe, he does what he can to mitigate the Frenchman's antagonism to Sougès; but his main concern is for the workers of Pâline, and so Philippe's advent must be welcomed. The metropolitan, like the Creole, is a 'stage in a necessary evolution' beyond which lies 'freedom, ardently desired and not yet within reach' (p. 237). The notions of change and evolution are thus, in the case of Jab-Herma, directly connected with the idea of black liberation.

In the opening paragraphs of the novel, Jab-Herma appears as an ambiguous figure: a uniformed chauffeur dreaming in his car as he waits for the arrival of Philippe's boat; a man of mysterious and menacing arrogance, whom the customs officers are anxious to conciliate. His sleeping vision is of a town set ablaze, an army of dead, an unquiet ghost; of gold and blood and a ditch. This dream of Delgrès is a recurring one with him; but whereas Cragget sees Delgrès as a mulatto defying the white world, and Sougès identifies with him as a West Indian leader destroyed by a French intruder, for Jab-Herma Delgrès represents the thousands of blacks who rose up against the re-establishment of slavery, and whose revolt was bloodily suppressed – whose suffering still 'echoes like a cry' (p. 236) within the souls of those who now live in the region where they died. Jab-Herma's visions of the past are linked with a coherent view of the history and the modern predicament of the black West Indian. The physical horrors of the past, when Guadeloupe was 'the country of choice for cruelty and despair' (p. 236), are long since past, but he knows that the psychological wounds inflicted then continue to damage the slaves' descendants. Cut off from their African history and cultural traditions, Caribbean blacks have in desperation accepted white values, white ethics, white standards of beauty, despite the fact that all of these hold them up to ridicule. This is because they have never been free agents: 'The trouble is that we are plunged into the world of the whites and have no place in which to be ourselves. For three and a half centuries, they have been making us see things through their eyes' (p. 40). Most important of all is the economic deprivation which was set in motion by the circumstances of abolition: the ex-slaves were launched into 'a closed economic system' (p. 133), in which all the good land was already in the hands of the white population; starting from a penniless position, the blacks found it virtually impossible to acquire land of their own. Jab-Herma's sharp awareness of the urgency of social reforms authenticates his role as protector of the village interests, and explains his emblematic presence in the novel's title. There is a moral contrast between his path of action and that of Cragget. Cragget's pursuit of the white world is both unviable and self-destructive; he 'has never had a future' (p. 243). Jab-Herma, on the other hand, seeks to establish the black man's right to dignity and equality of opportunity; he 'is the future' (p. 237).

Although Jab-Herma's character is lightly sketched in the novel, Lacrosil is at pains to stress his ambition, his pride, his calculating intelligence, his intimidating height and strength, and the distance at which he holds others. His chauffeur's livery and menial job are a useful cover. They cause outsiders like Philippe to overlook or underestimate him, and protect the reality of his power, which is based upon his ancient, secret vocation: the practice of magic. The craft of the African witch-doctor, sorcerer or medicine-man, whose European names give only a debased idea of his importance to the physical, social and moral life of the tribe, lives on in some form in every Caribbean island. The Haitian voodoo priest, the Jamaican obeah-man, the *quimboiseur* of the French Antilles, are all heirs, to a greater or lesser extent, of the witch-doctor with his arcane knowledge of the properties of plants, his alarming faculties of healing and harming, his terrifying ability to communicate with the distant and the dead. Jab-Herma's gift of prescience, the reputed potency of his charms against accident and misfortune, his impassive, uncommunicative manner, and the awe-inspiring atmosphere of ritual which prevails at his consultations, all secure him an immense prestige. He uses this in a planned way to manipulate his environment; his choice of *métier* was deliberate, for he is convinced that 'every Negro needs a strategy in order to survive among the whites' (p. 146). No local person views his magic in this detached light: 'all, including Constant Sougès, believe in [him] or fear [him]' (p. 69); but Philippe, revising his initial impression of the chauffeur, comes to see him as 'a leader for whom the occult [is] a strategy, nothing like the traditional witch-doctor' (p. 253). Although he himself is only half convinced of his own supernatural powers, he is sure of his dominion over other men. Alone among all the characters, he has no moments of emotional weakness; even when he is secretly appalled by the poverty of his clients, he still takes their money, 'so as to be feared' (p. 96). Detached and invulnerable, he is the first to divine the identity of the murderer, but he plays no part in the pursuit of Cragget. His function is to 'wait, with unfailing certainty, for the right moment to intervene' (p. 254), the moment when destiny will have removed his obligation to Sougès, and his own sovereignty will be recognized by the metropolitan management. The novel ends with Philippe's order to Sougès: 'Ask Jab-Herma to come in.' The future which he represents is about to begin.

Whether a man of Jab-Herma's calling can ever, in the long run, be an influence for good in Caribbean society is a debatable point. By encouraging popular beliefs that human life is controlled by dangerous, unseen powers, he contributes in his own way to the prolongation of a moral climate in which the adult abdicates responsibility for his own actions. If sickness, failure at studies, loss of employment, disappointment in love, the miscarriage of hopes and

The Plantation as Hell

projects, in fact all forms of breakdown and decline are habitually blamed on supernatural forces, against which the individual cannot prevail without magic help, then – as is the case with Roumain's Haitian peasants – entire communities will remain handicapped by fear, lack of self-esteem and a fatalistic resignation. It is not possible for the twentieth-century West Indian to return to an African tribal existence, in which illness and misfortune are perceived as a result of intangible malice, and diagnosed and treated in accordance with magical procedures that derive from hallowed tradition – that are not concerned with European concepts of evolution and progress. He now lives in a world where success springs from the individual's moral energy, and man's capacity for achievement is fuelled by the implicit conviction of his own free will. Jab-Herma's vocation as witch-doctor ties him, in theory, to a stultifying past (although it should be noted that the author does not use him to embody a back-to-Africa message, as a writer of the *Négritude* movement might have done). Because he is an unorthodox and self-questioning witch-doctor, it is possible for him simultaneously to be regarded as a social revolutionary. But it is perhaps by personal example, rather than benevolent dictatorship, that Jab-Herma is intended to heal the open wounds of plantation society. Described in the novel as 'a symbol and a guide' (p. 176), he is offered by Lacrosil as a model of the new, ideal breed of West Indian, independent of white authority, confident of his own gifts, and able to transcend the brutalities, the shames and the deviations of Caribbean history.

Notes

1 'Nèg riche cé mulat', mulat' pauv' cé nèg'. According to Michel Leiris, in *Contacts de civilisations en Martinique et en Guadeloupe* (Paris: Unesco, 1955), p. 31, this now proverbial saying was first uttered in 1843 by Jean-Jacques Acaau, leader of a peasant revolt in the south of Haiti.
2 An eighteenth-century court order in Haiti (then Saint-Domingue) requires the sale of 'Negroes, pigs and other objects' belonging to an estate. It is cited in Antoine Gisler, *L'Esclavage aux Antilles françaises, XVIIe-XIXe siècle* (Fribourg: Editions Universitaires, 1965), p. 100.
3 See Gisler, pp. 44–5, 48–51, and E.V. Goveia, *The West Indian slave laws of the eighteenth century* (Kingston: Caribbean Universities Press, 1970), pp. 31, 41, 45, on legal cases and regulations concerning slaves and their owners. The slave laws were not identical in the various Caribbean colonies, but in practice slave conditions were relatively uniform.
4 Debien, p. 345.
5 Statement of an eighteenth-century French colonist, cited in Gisler, p. 38. All translations from Gisler and Debien are my own.
6 Zobel, *Black Shack Alley*, pp. 34, 154.
7 Lacrosil, *Demain Jab-Herma*, p. 72.
8 La Bruyère, *Characters*, trans. Henri van Laun (London: Oxford University Press, 1963), p. 206.
9 Both cases are cited in Debien, pp. 91, 301.
10 See Michael Craton and James Walvin, *A Jamaican Plantation: The History of Worthy Park 1670–1970* (London: W.H. Allen, 1970), p. 145. Information on the structure of plantation society in the following paragraphs has been drawn from the works of Debien, Gisler, Goveia, Leiris, and Craton and Walvin already cited, and also from K.O. Laurence, *Immigration into the West Indies in the 19th century* (St Lawrence, Barbados: Caribbean Universities Press, 1971); Orlando Patterson, *The Sociology of Slavery* (London: MacGibbon & Kee, 1967), and Richard Sheridan, *The*

The Novels of Joseph Zobel and Michèle Lacrosil

Development of the Plantations to 1750 (Kingston: Caribbean Universities Press, 1970).

11 Edouard Glissant, in *Le Discours antillais* (pp. 293–302), sees contemporary patterns of sexual behaviour in Martinique as the consequence of a type of sexual alienation imposed by slavery.

12 See Patterson, pp. 57–8.

13 Cited in Debien, pp. 98, 126.

14 Cited in Gisler, p. 69.

15 Gisler, p. 93.

16 Gisler, p. 97.

17 See Patterson, p. 64.

18 For an account of the social attitudes concerning mulattos, see Leiris, p. 23, and Mavis Christine Campbell, *The Dynamics of Change in a Slave Society: A Sociopolitical History of the Free Coloreds of Jamaica, 1800–1865* (New Jersey and London: Associated University Presses, 1976), especially pp. 39–70.

19 On plantation social structure after emancipation, see Elena Padilla, 'Les Types sociaux de la campagne antillaise', pp. 31–6, and Vera Rubin, 'Les Problèmes de la recherche anthropologique dans la Caraïbe', pp. 103–9, both in Jean Benoist (ed.), *Les Sociétés antillaises: études anthropologiques* (Montreal: Département d'anthropologie de l'Université de Montréal, 1966).

20 Leiris, p. 27.

21 See Warner, introduction to *Black Shack Alley*, p. v.

22 Edith Clarke analyses West Indian matriarchal households headed by a grandmother in *My Mother who fathered me*, 2nd ed. (London: George Allen & Unwin, 1966), pp. 133–9, 178–81.

23 Joseph Zobel, *Diab'là* (Paris: Nouvelles Editions Latines, 1946), pp. 33, 123, 169–70.

24 See David Milner, *Children and Race* (Harmondsworth: Penguin Books, 1975), pp. 61–100. The passage cited (from p. 84) represents the findings of an American study by H.G. Trager and M. Radke-Yarrow. Compare the study by Errol L. Miller, 'Body Image, Physical Beauty and Colour among Jamaican Adolescents', *Social and Economic Studies* 18, 1 (1969), pp. 72–89.

25 'Le syllabaire' and 'Mapiam', in Joseph Zobel, *Laghia de la mort* (1946; rev. ed. Paris: Présence Africaine, 1978).

26 See Randolph Hezekiah, 'Joseph Zobel: the Mechanics of Liberation', *Black Images* 4, 3/4 (1975), p. 49, on the importance of M'man Tine as a mother figure and a 'symbol of the Black Martinican essence'.

27 See Leiris, pp. 39–40, on the 'Blancs de la route de Didier'.

28 Joseph Zobel, *La Fête à Paris* (Paris: La Table Ronde, 1953), pp. 235–6 (my translation).

29 By 1973, only 14.35 per cent of Guadeloupean agricultural land remained in local hands, as opposed to 88.87 per cent in Martinique (Burton, p. 13).

30 Michèle Lacrosil, *Sapotille et le serin d'argile* (Paris: Gallimard, 1960) and *Cajou* (Paris: Gallimard, 1961).

31 On the fictional image of the mulatto in Caribbean writing in English, see Kenneth Ramchand, *The West Indian Novel and its Background* (London: Faber, 1970), pp. 39–50. For a sociologist's account of the 'white bias' in a mid-twentieth-century mixed-race Caribbean community, see Fernando Henriques, *Family and Colour in Jamaica* (London: Eyre & Spottiswoode, 1953), pp. 42–63.

32 See Jack Corzani, *La Littérature des Antilles-Guyane Françaises* (Fort-de-France: Désormeaux, 1978, 6 vols), vol. 5, pp. 256–7.

33 Fanon, p. 138. Although Lacrosil places at the start of the novel epigraphs from Sartre and Simone de Beauvoir, both of these quotations relate to the book's portrayal of social evils.

34 On the problems of cultural and economic dependence in the French Caribbean, see Glissant, *Le Discours antillais*, in particular pp. 166–84, 458–61.

35 For a historical account of Delgrès' revolt, see Oruna Lara, *La Guadeloupe dans l'histoire* (1921; new ed. Paris: L'Harmattan, 1979), pp. 131–56.

36 The story of Cham (or Ham), which occurs in Genesis 9:20–7, was adduced in past centuries by Europeans as an explanation of the Negro's colour. In punishment for Cham's disrespect to his father Noah, his own son Canaan was condemned to be 'a servant of servants unto his brethren'. The original Vulgate text used the word *servus*, which means a slave. Early Christian commentators saw Noah's nakedness as a prefiguration of Christ's nakedness upon the Cross, and Cham's mockery of Noah was therefore interpreted as the act of an unbeliever. The name Cham was taken to mean 'hot', and so in patristic writings Cham was stated to be the father of the African race. See, for example, *Patrologia Latina* (ed. Migne) 41, pp. 477–8 (St Augustine); 83, p. 236 (St Isidore): 111, p. 34 (Raban Maur). These various patristic traditions led to the apocryphal belief that God had cursed the black race, which was popularly associated with paganism and slavery.

4

Paradise Redefined: The Marxist Vision of Alexis' *Comrade General Sun*

'Golden with a sun no prism has sampled, a fraternal earth where all is free'
(*Cahier*, p. 50).

Were it not for the manner of his death, Jacques Stéphen Alexis might be remembered today primarily for his compelling depiction of life in the slums of Port-au-Prince. A passionate champion of the Haitian masses, he himself was born into the small black middle class which, until the Duvalier era, knew only an intermittent political power and coexisted uneasily with the economically dominant mulatto élite. His paternal grandmother was said to descend from Dessalines, the black general who led the final phase of the revolt against the French and proclaimed the independence of Haiti in 1804 at the northern town of Gonaïves, which was to be Alexis' own birthplace in 1922. His father Stéphen, a diplomat and writer, was the Haitian ambassador to Brussels and later to London, and was once rather unkindly described by a friend of his son, the poet René Depestre, as being 'too much the black academician, the Third World gentleman, Sir Stephen'.[1] But Stéphen Alexis' fiction, despite its conservative flavour and old-fashioned tone, reveals a genuine preoccupation with the reform of social evils and adopts a critical stance in relation to the moral values of the Haitian bourgeoisie. Like many other well-educated Haitians, he resented the American occupation, which seemed to him the embodiment of racial prejudice and materialistic values. His nationalism and his interest in social reform were both echoed, but in a much more militant form, in the political and literary career of his son. Jacques Alexis, like Jacques Roumain before him, was a dedicated Marxist who was impelled by the desire to improve the lot of the Haitian underprivileged – the 'tens of thousands of human beings gravely injured, trodden underfoot, to whom violence is done because they are black, poor, illiterate, abandoned by official justice and by their country's government'.[2] As a medical student in Port-au-Prince, he was one of the young radicals who brought about the downfall in 1946 of President Lescot, a mulatto who had openly discriminated against blacks in the civil service and the army, and who had launched an 'anti-superstition' campaign against voodoo, the religion of the masses. The same sense of commitment to the cause of the proletariat led him, in 1961, to make a quixotic, ill-equipped attempt at rallying the northern peasantry against the dictatorship of François Duvalier. Captured by Papa Doc's *tontons macoutes*, he is reported to have been blinded and stoned to death.[3] He has now entered the world of anti-Duvalier legend.

Paradise Redefined

Many influences may be seen as shaping Jacques Alexis' novels. He had an early experience of white racial prejudice as a schoolboy in Paris when his father's diplomatic career took the family to Europe.[4] Returning to Haiti at the age of 8, he lived through the last four years of the American occupation. While at school in Port-au-Prince, he spent his holidays back in the north, and his sympathetic understanding of Haitian country ways is evident in all his writing. From his adolescence he was involved in left-wing politics, and during his university years he began writing for a radical journal run by his friend Depestre. His participation in the 1946 revolution, which succeeded in getting rid of Lescot but achieved no long-term improvement in the political and economic situation of the country, seems to have been a polarizing experience which confirmed him in his commitment to the Haitian proletariat and instilled in him a bitter cynicism with regard to those in public office. From 1946 to 1954 he lived in France, completing his medical degree and specializing in neurology. In his view, his scientific work and his creative writing were mutually supportive, since both activities were 'carried on in the same sphere: that of the human'.[5] While in Paris he was a member of the French Communist Party, and moved in left-wing intellectual circles. Later, back in Port-au-Prince, where Roumain's Haitian Communist Party had been dissolved in the 1940s, Alexis was to found a new Communist party, the Party of Popular Accord.

In 1955, the year after his return to Haiti, Alexis published *Comrade General Sun*. Like his second novel, *Les Arbres musiciens* (1957), which is based on Lescot's anti-superstition campaign, *Comrade General Sun* was inspired by an event which occurred in Alexis' youth: the massacre of over 12,000 Haitian immigrant workers which took place on the Dominican frontier, at Trujillo's instigation, in October 1937.[6] In recalling these historical events, Alexis was motivated by a conviction that the novelist's goal should be not merely to describe man and society, but to 'contribute to their transformation': the novel should be 'an action in the service of mankind, a contribution to the progress of humanity'.[7] Through his writing, as through his political work, he strove to realize a patriotic and visionary ideal. Disenchanted with the Haitian authorities and the élite, he none the less remained optimistic about the nation's innate creativity and capacity for survival. Alongside his realistic depiction of working-class life, there is an idyllic perception of the 'men and women of the common people' as 'the first adherents to a way of life, a way of loving and feeling, which would be the basis of the culture of the future' (*Comrade General Sun*, p. 305). Speaking of a painting called 'The Earthly Paradise' by a fellow Haitian, Wilson Bigaud, he described it as an expression of 'the cosmic dream of abundance and fraternity'[8] which the Haitian people, while suffering from hunger and deprivation, were still capable of cherishing. His own belief was that Communism could bring such a paradise into existence and 'prevent earth from being a hell for man'.[9]

Comrade General Sun is unusual among French Caribbean novels in that it is almost entirely centred upon the urban proletariat, rather than on the peasantry or the educated middle class. Its portrayal of the slum districts of Port-au-Prince in the 1930s, beset by unemployment, malnutrition, sickness and crime, holds true for many a Caribbean capital today, as the country folk, increasingly unable to live off the land, continue to drift into the city. The novel is conceived from a Marxist perspective on class conflict, but with the added nuances that race and skin colour bring to social relationships in the West Indies. Haitian society has long been unequally divided into a tiny, mainly light-complexioned élite, comprising possibly 10 per cent of the population, and a great mass of predominantly black workers who make up the small urban proletariat and the vast ranks of the peasantry. The traditional prejudice of mulattos against blacks dates back to at least the eighteenth century, when, before the slave system was overthrown, there were already thousands of free coloured landowners – and slave-owners – in the then colony of Saint-Domingue.[10] The alliance between mulattos and blacks at the end of that century was a temporary expedient, necessary for the expulsion of the French planter class, and did not destroy the innate hostility between the two groups. This class antagonism within Haitian society lends itself to a Marxist interpretation. Alexis' analysis of the Haitian situation is very strongly influenced by Marx's critique of bourgeois society, and, like Marx, he places his faith in proletarian militancy as the force which will lead to social revolution.

The literary consequence of Alexis' political point of view is that in *Comrade General Sun*, members of the bourgeoisie (unless they are Communists) are habitually depicted as evil, and tend to be perfunctorily characterized through the technique of crude caricature. Workers and peasants, on the other hand, are sympathetically portrayed and allowed to emerge as complex individuals. Because of its Marxist stance, the novel's tone is at times openly didactic. Yet the overwhelming impression it leaves in the reader's mind is one of lyricism and poignant humanity. The author's eye is that of a poet in love with nature, who thinks in images: the sea beneath the driving rain is like an animal bristling its coat; the lightning prints phantasmagoric pictures of dead trees upon the storm-clouds; the ringed segments of a red millipede, tugged along by diligent ants, are as weighty and as colourful as a suit of samurai armour. The protagonist's political initiation is depicted in terms of a symbolic fall into darkness, followed by a slow upward movement towards the light. Simile and metaphor are the constant tools of Alexis' craft.

The hero of the novel, Hilarion Hilarius, is an epileptic, whose illness serves a twofold literary purpose. It is, in the first place, a narrative device that brings him into contact with a medical student who is a Communist, and thus sets him on the road to political awareness. This politicizing of the proletarian is represented as an act of spiritual healing, which is symbolically echoed by the physical cure that the young doctor offers his patient. In the second place, Hilarion's epilepsy, which causes others to shun and fear him, is also a metaphor for the condition of the Haitian masses, despised and repudiated by the ruling élite. His bitter isolation is the result of 'a kind of taboo' placed upon him by all the superstitious folk for whom his affliction is 'an accursed sickness of accursed men' (p. 48), 'retribution for sins or crimes' (p. 238). It has been said that Alexis' genius lies in his exploration of the fortunes of the outsider – the slum-dweller, the thief, the orphan, the prostitute.[11] Hilarion symbolizes the average Haitian, impoverished and dispossessed; the novel presents him as 'a real child of the people, a real Haitian *Toma*' (p. 97). But at the same time he feels himself to be particularly spurned, 'a disadvantaged child, bent beneath the burden of fatality' (p. 48). This sense of exclusion from society, of unique hardship, is unconsciously expressed in the dreams he has about 'a sad little black child playing far from the merry group' (p. 51). It also explains his astonished gratitude when he is befriended by the middle-class Marxist, Pierre Roumel, whose words are 'light and sunshine' to him (p. 50); by the medical student, Jean-Michel, who brings him 'light [and] hope' (p. 199); and by the pretty, self-confident Claire-Heureuse, whose name means 'bright-happy', and whose love he associates with 'the golden sun and the singing sea' (p. 79). Solar images such as these are linked in the novel with a thematic nexus which blends the ideas of social revolution, individual redemption, and an ideal fraternity that overrides the ancient divisions of class and race.

The title of the novel indicates the importance, in the narrative, of the symbolic interplay of light and darkness. The French title is *Compère Général Soleil*, a phrase which evokes both the idea of aggression (through the military *Général*) and the notion of affection and solidarity (through the term *Compère*, which is the habitual form of address used in Haiti to greet another person, meaning 'friend', 'brother', 'comrade'). The sun, the great life-giving force, is a traditional symbol of truth, justice, glory, resurrection and the divine. Paradoxically fierce yet benign, it appears in the novel as the ally of the underprivileged in their struggle against the forces of darkness – that is, the upholders of the established social order, who neglect their responsibilities towards the proletariat. Indeed, the sun is in the vanguard of this struggle, and represents a source of inspiration: 'General Sun is a great man, he is the friend of poor blacks, he's our father . . . he fights for us every minute, and shows us the way. Just as he always wins against night, just as he manages to snatch from every year one season which he controls, so we workers can change the times and snatch a season when we won't live in want' (p. 349). Night, then, is the domain of hunger, misery, ignorance and destitution; sunlight is an image of fraternity and love, and of the resistance of the poor to political oppression and economic exploitation. The solar imagery has specific Marxist ramifications, the sun being associated with the abstract idea of mental illumination, which is illustrated by the concrete case history of Hilarion, the uneducated worker who gradually emerges from his 'hopeless, lightless' condition (p. 12) as he comes to understand the concept of class struggle. This political symbolism culminates in the moment when the 'great red sun' is identified with the spreading gunshot wound in the chest of a striking canecutter (p. 284), a moment which Hilarion later looks back on (p. 350) as the real beginning of his sympathy with the aims of Communism. The sun-figures of his life are the friends – Pierre Roumel, Jean-Michel, the mechanic Ferdinand, the Dominican canecutter Paco Torres and the painter Domenica Betances – who offer him both comradeship and enlightenment, helping him to gain self-assurance as he starts to grasp the possibility of changing his exploited, submissive mode of existence. By their various origins (Roumel comes from the Haitian mulatto élite, Domenica from the wealthy Dominican bourgeoisie, while the black Jean-Michel, the mulatto Ferdinand and the 'red man', the light-skinned Paco, are from the working class), such figures illustrate Alexis' conviction that Communism is capable of transcending colour and class discord.

In the prologue to the narrative, which sets the tone of the entire work by introducing the author's main themes and preoccupations, the real and symbolic suns are both absent: a sinister, interminable night is in the ascendant, with archetypal associations of fear, uncertainty and menace. Within its intangible dimensions, a man moves stealthily, a 'shadow man', a 'Negro so dark, so black, that he seemed blue' (p. 7). This identification of the protagonist with the night itself is prolonged through further details: the gusts of the night breeze, 'coughing like a tubercular youth' (p. 14), echo the rattling of Hilarion's chest as he coughs over a cigarette stub; the dark trees swaying by the roadside, 'dancing the waltz of life', seem to participate in his own 'dance of hunger and fever, the silent dance of crime, the dance of fear and caution'

(p. 14). The notion of exposure to the elements, of vulnerability within the night, is suggested even before Hilarion leaves his shack in the small hours of the morning on his disastrous enterprise of amateur burglary. His environment is totally lacking in the qualities normally associated with the idea of a home: a haven, an enclosed, protective space within which lie sanctuary and comfort. The hovels of the slum quarter where he lives, made from old packing-cases and worm-eaten bits of wood, are too ramshackle and dilapidated to provide security; in hurricane winds they readily collapse, leaving their terrified occupants at the mercy of the elements. Their function in the narrative is not to offer refuge, but rather to emphasize the precariousness of the slum-dwellers' existence. A careless knock, and their walls may cave in; a careless step, and Hilarion's defences will crumble with equal ease. The stress laid on his literal nakedness – he is dressed in rags with 'holes like windows revealing the wretched state of his body' (p. 8) – intensifies the atmosphere of vulnerability in which he moves.

The prologue tells the story of his inept attempt to improve his situation by resorting to crime; and it relates how he is projected from the fragile shelter of his slum into the greater misery of a prison cell. The pattern of this initial episode is that of a painful upward striving, followed by a calamitous fall. Hilarion struggles to rise from the straw mat on which he sleeps, driven by a hunger so imperious that it triumphs over his state of physical weakness. Entering a garden in the rich suburb of Bois-Verna, he climbs a veranda post and gets into an upstairs bedroom where he steals a leather wallet from a bedside table. But as he climbs down he is caught in the light of a police torch and slides ignominiously to the ground, where he is beaten up by the police. Thrust eventually into jail, he suffers an epileptic fit. This icon of physical humiliation, as he loses control over his body and mind before the horrified eyes of his cellmates, symbolizes Hilarion's position in society, which is that of the outsider, the one shunned and rejected. His feelings of giddiness and heaviness, his sense of being crushed and destroyed, are the opposite of his initial, hopeful ascent towards the means of assuaging his hunger; his bruised limbs, his dirty, bleeding face and the bitter taste in his mouth are the physical equivalents of his despair, the brutal reminder of his helpless moral condition. Through the mediation of the epileptic fit, the ideas of ascent and fall are linked with those of light and darkness. In the midst of the seizure, 'his face tremendously black and distorted' (p. 22), Hilarion's eyes roll up and he can see nothing. At the end of the novel, he relates the onset of his epilepsy to an incident when he was blinded by the sun and fell down from a mango tree: 'I began to fear the sun that day . . . I thought that my sickness was an evil spell of Comrade Sun. But . . . the real truth is that the sun of Haiti shows us what we must do' (p. 349). On the symbolic plane, therefore, the novel depicts Hilarion's progress from the state of blind victim to that of clearsighted ally of the sun: a process which is accomplished by his political education.

Alexis' writing is always strongly marked by his commitment to depicting Haitian society faithfully, and striving thereby to amend its injustices. He is concerned, therefore, to explain Hilarion's milieu as one in which poverty, lack of job opportunities, inadequate food and housing, casually accepted delinquency and prostitution, weak family structures, long-standing resentment of the affluent minority – in short a combination of social and economic pressures – cause an underprivileged section of the community to drift into the habit of regarding crime as a logical means of survival. Law-breaking, in itself a disruption of the harmony of society, comes to be considered a legitimate response by the socially alienated. Haiti is the poorest country in the western hemisphere, with a population today of close on 6 million people of whom it is estimated that 75 per cent live under the absolute poverty line. Of these, 800,000 now reside in the vast urban slum of Port-au-Prince, where, for those lucky enough to find work, the minimum salary is officially fixed at about US$78 a month. Unemployment in 1981 was rated at 15 per cent, but underemployment at 72 per cent; the average per capita income was less than US$300.[12] The way of life of the mass of peasants and workers has changed little since the era which Alexis described in *Comrade General Sun*. Then, as now, it was customary for very poor parents, who could not feed their children, to place them as servants in a middle-class household. Hilarion, like his sister Zuléma, suffers this fate at an early age: 'Bad food, a poor bed, beatings, no mother and no caresses . . . Yes, he had forgotten how to play, how to let himself go; under duress he had buried his childhood deep within him' (p. 43). The wretched years he spends in the service of a wealthy mulatto family leave him with a lasting animosity towards the residents of the fashionable suburb of Bois-Verna, who 'hypocritically practise a vile form of child slavery disguised as charity and paternal concern' (p. 17). It is there that he goes to make his attempt at burglary. When he gets there, everything seems to justify his theft: the white house in its large, fragrant garden, the white sheet under which his intended victim sleeps, the orderliness and tranquillity of the middle-class bedroom, the stream of cool air from the electric fan, the luxury of the blue night-light, the casualness with which money is left lying about. All these things symbolize an unjust wealth in Hilarion's eyes and, from his viewpoint, give him 'the right to defend his existence, the right to extort money from the extortionists' (p. 19).[13]

Hilarion's class antagonism overlaps to a certain degree with racial antagonism, since the majority of the Haitian élite are light-skinned, while the masses are mainly black. But more importantly in the author's eyes, it springs from the gap between rich and poor: for Hilarion, it is chiefly money that divides the world into 'workers, dirty blacks' on the one hand, and on the other, 'rich blacks, or rich mulattos – it's the same thing' (p. 10). Later on, when he begins studying Haitian history at night classes run by Party associates of his friend Jean-Michel, he learns something of Haitian history with its 'savage struggles between conflicting castes and interests', and comes to the conclusion that it is 'not men's colour, but social categories, classes', which 'explain the miseries and misfortunes of the common people' (p. 153). One of the novel's major themes is the harm done to Haitian society by the economic inequality inherent in its class structure. In this context, it is significant that the prologue associates Hilarion with another typical Alexis outsider-figure, that of the prostitute. Alexis uses her to represent the archetypal victim, exploited and dehumanized. In his novels, he generally portrays the Haitian prostitute as foreign in origin, Cuban, Dominican or Puerto Rican (hence doubly an outsider). She drifts into her profession through lack of family, money and education, and becomes a puppet in the hands of the men who use her – the brothel-keeper, the pimp, the endless stream of clients for her mechanical favours. Alexis' third novel, *L'Espace d'un cillement* (1959), is entirely set in a brothel owned by a middle-class Haitian who enjoys stage-managing the nightly performances of his working-class tarts. His way of life is a carefully calculated balance of enjoyable slumming and bourgeois respectability. When the mood takes him, he can

The Marxist Vision of Alexis' *Comrade General Sun*

'close the box, put his dolls back in their cardboard cartons and go home' to a wife who asks no questions, and a daughter safely tucked away in her convent boarding-school awaiting the time for a suitable marriage. The only other career that tempts him is politics; and the affairs of government, Alexis suggests, are simply 'a brothel on a larger scale, a more infamous form of prostitution, more entertaining to watch and manipulate'.[14]

In keeping with this allegorical view of brothel life as a microcosm of lower-class suffering, the prologue of *Comrade General Sun* uses a recurrent image of domestic fowls – defenceless and faintly ridiculous – to link Hilarion with the girls of Port-au-Prince's red-light district. In a play on the double meaning of the French word *poule* ('hen' and 'whore'), these girls are described as 'captive hens, imprisoned in a circle marked out on the ground' (p. 15). Hilarion's hut is compared to a hen-coop (p. 10); his famished body 'trembles like a wet hen' (p. 12); and in the throes of his epileptic fit, his body struggles 'like a chicken with its throat cut' (p. 22). His route to Bois-Verna takes him past a brothel from which a Dominican girl erupts and suddenly hauls her skirt up to her waist in a drunken, defiant salute to the 'horizonless night' (p. 15). The angry desperation of this gesture reflects Hilarion's own mood of reckless bravado and underlying despair. At this point in the narrative, the negative associations of darkness are reinforced by a metaphor which turns the tropical night into a 'black-clad procuress' (p. 14).

In both of these novels, the brothel district is frequented by US Marines, who are presented in the form of stylized caricature: ugly, smelly, inebriated and full of racial prejudice. They serve to arouse bitter memories of the recent American occupation (*Comrade General Sun* is set in the late 1930s, *L'Espace d'un cillement* in 1948) and simultaneously denote Haiti's continuing economic dependence upon North America. The degrading exploitation of the prostitute is paralleled with that of the country itself by its powerful neighbour: the 'American cars which move over the body of poor Haiti like enormous toads' (*Comrade General Sun*, p. 34) are like the drunken Marines in *L'Espace d'un cillement* who crush and belabour the bodies of the whores they have bought. This kind of anti-Americanism is a characteristic motif in Alexis' work. But in *Comrade General Sun* it is specifically tied to the concepts of capitalism and class struggle: US interests are portrayed as a vital factor in the oppression of the Haitian proletariat. Political and financial exploitation are seen throughout the novel as going hand in hand. The Americans are represented as the allies of the mulatto élite, whose prejudice against the black proletariat they share. In separate vignettes, drunken Marines make a starving woman beggar walk on all fours and bark, miaow and neigh before they allow her to pick up a dollar bill with her mouth, while the small blond son of a couple of American tourists spits on the hand which a black man has extended to stroke his hair (pp. 203, 207). Although the occupation is over, Americans continue to control banks and businesses behind a Haitian front man; they can 'do what they want in the country' (p. 230). American aid effectively keeps the corrupt President Vincent in power, and sends in gunboats to help him reduce his opponents to silence. Vincent himself cuts a despicable figure as brutal oppressor of the Communists and secret accomplice of the right-wing Dominican dictator, Trujillo. The politicians in his cabinet are equally venal, and Vincent even complains that one of his ministers has pocketed three-quarters of the aid destined for flood victims. The civil service, in general, is shown as hostile to the proletariat. The police, in particular, are singled out for criticism as the most brutal embodiment of the established order (p. 20). Those policemen of humble origin have forsaken class solidarity ('gendarmes tracking down barefoot proletarians', p. 61), while their sadistic and venal superior officers feather their nests at the expense of the prisoners' food rations, and use free convict labour to dig their swimming-pools. The indifference of the rich and powerful towards the poor is neatly summed up by the newspaper report of a hurricane which has levelled the slum shacks of the city: 'Little damage was done. The only victims of the disaster were the big banana producers in the plain' (p. 87).

A final striking aspect of the prologue is the way in which notions of time and space are related to the antithetical images of darkness and sunlight. The events of the prologue unfold in a night which is 'interminably long' (p. 16). It is a 'void' like the emptiness in Hilarion's belly, a void remote from normal time-flow, where 'there is no yesterday, no tomorrow, no hope, no light' (p. 12). In spatial terms he is equally insecure, cut off from the normal experience of home as a protective enclosure, since his hut is a precarious roost which offers no real asylum. Within the shadows of his room, Hilarion's breathing is laboured, his movements are slow and effortful. As hunger forces him into the streets, his state of 'anaesthesia' wears off and the emptiness inside him becomes 'a burning, throbbing wound' (p. 15). This brief burst of energy gets him up to the balcony of the Bois-Verna house; but his slower descent is abruptly halted when he is transfixed in the light of the police torch, and he slides down the rest of the column 'as if he were coming down in a dream' (p. 20). The sudden multiplication of electric torches pinning him to the ground links his condition once more with that of the night itself, 'riddled with bright darts' (p. 21) as the coming daybreak puts it to flight. The identification of Hilarion with the night is strengthened by their shared attributes: the receding night with its heavy breathing (p. 7) is compared to 'a panic-stricken flight of bats hunted down by the dawn' (p. 21), while Hilarion's heavy breathing (p. 22)[15] arises from his plight as 'an exhausted animal, drained of strength, hunted down' (p. 11). Two particular aspects of night, the artificial light of the torches and the greyness before dawn, are associated with his beating at the hands of the police and with the epileptic fit which follows on it, hence with a state of physical abuse and spiritual degradation.

In contrast, his ensuing contact in jail with the political prisoner Pierre Roumel, who strives to give him the self-confidence he lacks, will offer Hilarion a kind of reassurance that he had been 'seeking within himself since that dreadful night' (p. 50). Roumel, a figure modelled on the politically persecuted Jacques Roumain, is the novel's first Marxist exemplar. Like Roumain, he is a member of the mulatto élite who came to prominence during the anti-American strikes and demonstrations which took place at the end of the 1920s. It is he who first explains Communism in simple terms to Hilarion: '[We ask] that the worker should be respected. That he should be paid enough to live on with his family. That he should be guaranteed work . . . That the majority of citizens should make the laws in this country; and, since the country's only worth lies in its workers, that they should be in charge of its affairs' (p. 68). He is linked with the symbolic sun of Marxism not only by his 'words of light and sunshine' (p. 50), but also by the phrase which Hilarion uses to describe him: 'a mulatto, a great man . . . had come to talk to him, descending from his rank, forgetting his own position' (p. 52). The French phrase ('un mulâtre, un grand nègre') anticipates Hilarion's description of the sun at the end of the novel ('le Général Soleil est un grand nègre', p. 349). In both cases Alexis uses the word *nègre* in the Creole sense where it does not necessarily denote race, but may simply mean 'a man'; *grand nègre* is a term of honour or affectionate regard, which may be applied to a man of any colour.[16] Roumel, whose eyes hold unfailing light (p. 60) and whose sense of comradeship overcomes the barrier of social class, sets out to restore Hilarion to the world of order, harmony and progress that he feels to be every man's birthright. Through his help and encouragement, Hilarion is enabled to envisage time once more in a normal, even optimistic perspective: 'he could raise his thoughts up now to analyse his present situation and his future prospects. He had come out of his state of sheeplike apathy' (p. 48). This temporal liberation is also, in a sense, a spatial one, for it effects a moral expansion of Hilarion's horizons and is the first step towards inner security: 'Now a new man was emerging from the sphere of hunger, exhaustion, animal impulses and dread of others' brutality' (p. 48). The opposition between the light shed by Roumel's eyes (a traditional symbol of excellent understanding and spiritual merit) and his protégé's limited vision on his entry to prison ('Hilarion saw [the cell] through a thin slit in his eyelids', p. 21) prolongs the thematic interrelationships between literal and metaphorical blindness, between darkness of perception and the radiance of political wisdom.

The themes, images, and patterns of social conflict established in the prologue are deployed in a more leisurely fashion throughout the sprawling three-part narrative, and provide a certain sense of continuity. Unity of action, however, is only loosely observed. In the first part of the novel, which takes place early in 1936, Hilarion serves his month in prison, gets a job in a sisal workshop through Roumel's mother, meets Claire-Heureuse at the beach, meets Jean-Michel through a childhood friend, attends a voodoo ceremony with his own mother and a country dance with his cousins. On the night of the dance, his cousin Josaphat kills an army officer who is attempting to rape his sister, and has to flee over the border into the Dominican Republic. The second part of the novel, covering events from June 1936 until some time in the middle of 1937, is equally episodic. Hilarion and Claire-Heureuse set up house together, and she becomes pregnant. He loses his job, but Jean-Michel helps him to find another one as a mahogany polisher. The Artibonite River floods its banks, destroying crops in the region north of Port-au-Prince on which the city depends for much of its food supply. Hilarion works one night as a waiter at a lavish party given by an unscrupulous government minister, Paturault. An elderly neighbour dies, and a wake is held for her. President Vincent is obliged to release Roumel from prison, but forces him into exile. Hilarion is virtually cured of his epilepsy. Jean-Michel gets into trouble with the police through distributing illegal Communist pamphlets. When fire destroys Hilarion's possessions and the closure of the woodware workshop puts him out of a job once more, he decides to take Claire-Heureuse to the Dominican Republic and join his cousin Josaphat as a canecutter there. Part 3, a more coherent narrative, takes place entirely in the Dominican Republic, where Claire-Heureuse's child is born and where a strike by cane workers ultimately leads to the mass killings of immigrant Haitians in October 1937. Hilarion and his family flee back towards the Haitian border, but the child is fatally mauled by army dogs on the way, and Hilarion is shot by frontier guards as he and Claire-Heureuse struggle across the swollen Massacre River. He manages to reach the Haitian bank, but dies there as the rising sun lights up his native landscape.

The episodes of this somewhat rambling plot are connected by the figure of Hilarion, but his story is part of a larger subject: the class struggle in Haitian society. With few exceptions, the members of this society are assigned to one of two groups: they are bourgeois 'puppets', frivolous, unfeeling and worthless, or·else they are of the common people, 'unpolished individuals, but human' (p. 246). Alexis sets out to place before the reader a complete panorama of the ways in which class and colour operate in both domestic and public life. It is the motif of class conflict which binds to the narrative even such flagrant digressions as the life history of Claire-Heureuse's godmother, Erica Jordan, or that of the politician Paturault, with both of whom Hilarion's contact is minimal. The background of Erica Jordan, for example, is presented by the omniscient narrator as an instance of both social and sexual injustice. She is the illegitimate granddaughter of a respectable lower-middle-class merchant, a black man who 'didn't understand class distinctions' (p. 100) and sent his daughter to a good boarding-school in the capital. Once her education was completed, the girl found she was socially unacceptable to her former school-friends, and when she was made pregnant by the son of a wealthy German businessman, marriage was quite out of the question as far as he was concerned. Her father threw her out of the house and, although he helped to support her, would never acknowledge her baby as his grandchild. This pattern of sexual exploitation by a member of the ruling class of a woman of lesser social rank is echoed at other points in the narrative. Hilarion's sister, a 14-year-old maid in a sanctimonious bourgeois household, is seduced by her employer's son and then sent home in disgrace when it is discovered that she is pregnant. His cousin in the country, Josaphat's sister, is regarded as fair game by the army officer who assaults her; and both she and her brother know that the Haitian authorities 'will never be on the side of poor people like us' (pp. 142–3), so that it is useless for them to complain to the police about the attempted rape.

In all these cases, the destructive effects of such sexual exploitation are made apparent. Josaphat, a countryman deeply attached to his land, is forced to exile himself, and his family's happiness is shattered. Hilarion's sister, sickly and prematurely aged, is unable to care for her children adequately. Erica Jordan grows up in decent, lonely spinsterhood, raised to be afraid of men and to consider other people as 'divided into two social classes: the lower class, made up of people who live together without being married, and the good class, made up of people who either marry or remain single' (p. 102). Thus she has a socially determined double standard of morality: she would not condone sex outside marriage in someone like herself, a member of the lower middle class, but she expects it for her ward Claire-Heureuse, who is the child of peasants: 'What would not have been all right for her daughter was all right for her god-daughter' (p. 102). This very permissiveness is an unperceived form of social insult, and underlines the extent to which class divisions are perpetuated by traditional differences in sexual mores. The legacy of the plantation system, in which marriage was largely the prerogative of the white plantocracy and concubinage the natural condition of the black slave, still ensures that sexual partnerships unsanctioned by church or state are considered to be one of the attributes of the socially inferior. In the same tradition, middle-class mulatto men, like their white planter forebears, take it for granted that poor black women are sexually available to them. Consequently, there is sexual as well as social resentment on the part of working-class males towards the bourgeois.

Alexis indicates this by describing the custom of popular dances which women can attend free of charge, while men have to pay for entry: poor youths cannot afford the price of a dance, so that 'young dandies from the élite' are able to 'take upon themselves the right to go there and paw working-class girls' (p. 276).

The notion of class conflict is inherent in the novel's chosen milieu of Port-au-Prince, a city which houses extremes of poverty and wealth. It is thus an intrinsic element in the daily life of Hilarion, the city-dweller, who, unlike the isolated villagers of Roumain's *Masters of the Dew*, lives within walking distance of the opulence of Bois-Verna. As the story takes him from slum to rich villa to police station, however, his own observations are continually supplemented by those of the narrator. At the police station, his tormentor, Lieutenant Martinès, appears to him simply as an arbitrary and all-powerful sadist. But the author intervenes to turn the portrait of Martinès into a caricature which combines political criticism and social satire. The police officer, a man 'of refined cruelty' and also a blatantly effeminate homosexual, is none the less much sought after as 'an excellent match for the snobbish girls from the smart districts' (p. 27) because he is a light-skinned mulatto and belongs to one of the leading families in the city. Next, the prison of Fort-Dimanche is depicted, with all its physical discomforts: mosquitoes, bedbugs, revolting food, hard and unpleasant tasks and, behind massive inner doors, the stifling horror of the coffin-like cells, 2 feet by 6, where the political prisoners are held in solitary confinement. Once again, authorial comments indicate to the reader that within this setting, the brutality of the warders towards the convicts faithfully reproduces the brutal exercise of power on the outside by the social and political élite, and their disregard of the suffering of the underdog. Later, when Hilarion and Claire-Heureuse set up house in the market quarter by the Avenue Républicaine, Alexis lingers over the description of this 'veritable theatre' where every day the passer-by may witness 'scenes bubbling with life, smells and dirt' (p. 150). Besides its picturesque liveliness and warm-hearted vulgarity, the reader is made aware of the prevailing squalor and drudgery, chiefly through selective details which highlight the women's rapid loss of youth and beauty: their teeth are missing (there is never any money to spare for a dentist), the corded muscles and veins stand out on their necks from years of carrying heavy loads on their heads, and their breasts have fallen, as 'everything falls very soon in the rotting compost of the Avenue Républicaine, as petals fall when the flowering season is over' (p. 151). Their prematurely aged appearance is in implicit contrast to the pampered look of women like Mme Paturault, the politician's wife. With rather heavy-handed satire, she is described preparing for a party by spending the entire day on her face and body: she has a massage, bathes in lavender-scented water, devotes an hour to the care of her hands, spreads beauty cream over her shoulders and breasts, and makes herself a face mask from five kinds of fresh fruit. While the women of the market quarter struggle simply to survive, Mme Paturault's 'only aim, the only meaning in her life' (p. 187) is to attract the gaze of men.

The dominant problems of the poor are conveyed through incidents that stress the gulf which separates them from the rich. Love, pride, courage, and pity for others are constantly menaced by the fear, envy and violence engendered by the unceasing battle for food and a job: 'everything [is] transformed, deformed by the belly's needs' (p. 150). They are terribly vulnerable to natural disasters. The flooding of the Artibonite valley, for example, causes an acute food shortage. Wealthy businessmen promptly stockpile all available food supplies so as to sell them later on at black-market prices which only the mulatto élite can afford to pay: 'the small people are losers on all fronts' (p. 181). When Paturault gives his party at the height of the food shortage, the hungry crowd looking through his fence is incensed by the callous display of food and drink on the laden tables in the garden. Once more, exaggeration and caricature are used to provide a social commentary: the well-dressed young bourgeois, stereotypes of self-indulgence, go off to vomit in corners so that they can continue their drunken revel; Paturault, all geniality and fat jowls, comes to the gate to throw coins at the restive crowd; huge American cars take the guests home through dawn streets where the first higglers are already shouting their wares. The crowd, attempting to stone these 'puppets on the binge', this 'bunch of thieves . . . eating up the people's money', is beaten back by policemen who 'go after the women and children with particular ferocity' (pp. 190-1). Class is again at the root of the confrontation. Paturault, a self-indulgent *arriviste*, is characterized as a 'shameless pillager of the sweat of the people' (p. 185). His beautiful, stupid, promiscuous wife, whose light complexion and indolent nature are the novel's habitual symbols for the decadence of the middle-class female, shows open contempt for Hilarion and the other servants hired for the evening, 'the common people with tough hands, the dung that one uses, but tries not to touch' (p. 188). Her attitude is presented as typical of the élite, who, beneath surface gestures of charity or cordiality, nurture a long-standing hatred of the lower classes, that will last as long as their power does. The novelist's implication is clear: social reform can only be brought about by wiping out this 'race of overlords'. In other confrontations between Hilarion and the women of the mulatto bourgeoisie – when the police captain's wife and her two friends watch the prisoners digging the hole for her swimming-pool, or when the manageress of the sisal workshop enrages him by falsely accusing one of her workers of theft – there is a recurring stereotype of such women, 'uniform in their diversity' (p. 63), as monsters of selfishness, totally incapable of sympathy or generosity towards the proletariat, who are less human to them than are their own pet animals.

The poor, for their part, live in a 'disordered world', beset by starvation, sickness and ignorance, and dreading the advent of old age, when physical weakness will turn them into 'derelicts, carriers of fear and horror, condemned to drain the muddy dregs from the bitter cup which quenches the daily thirst of an entire nation' (p. 194). This plight of the city slum-dweller is encapsulated in the life story of Hilarion, just as M'man Tine's life, in *Black Shack Alley*, was representative of the lot of the average plantation labourer. Hilarion's earliest years are one long lesson of resignation – to his parents' harsh discipline, and also to hunger, inevitable as the rain that drenches him or the sun's burning heat. He is conditioned to helplessness and apathy: 'Life was the same for all the barefoot black children like me . . . Things had always been like that, it couldn't be otherwise' (p. 344). As an unpaid child servant in Bois-Verna, he is exposed to spitefulness and mockery, forced to grovel and flatter, slapped around and overworked until he finally runs away. As a homeless adolescent, he scuffles a living round the docks, unloading freight, carrying boxes, diving for the coins that sailors throw into the harbour water, selling contraceptives and dirty postcards to tourists, touting for taxis and brothels. After leaving the dock district 'which was relentlessly stifling everything that was good in [him]' (p. 348), he can command only the casual jobs of the unskilled labourer:

baggage handler, currier in a tannery, wood turner, bellows worker at a foundry, tinsmith's assistant. What eventually distinguishes him from the other labourers in his circle is his dawning sense of perplexity concerning their common fate. His groping attempts to understand why they should be condemned to a condition of hardship and inferiority turn him, in his own estimation, into 'a stubborn Negro, a bad Negro, an argumentative Negro' (p. 349). Despite his early conditioning, he becomes the antithesis of Césaire's 'good nigger' (*Cahier*, p. 87) who never questions the assumption that he has no power over his oppressive destiny, and honestly believes in his own unworthiness. Even before meeting Roumel and Jean-Michel, Hilarion has been deeply preoccupied with the need to 'seek the reason why' (p. 348).

The various stages of Hilarion's growing socio-political awareness are carefully mapped out. His musings in prison reveal the considerable extent of his class consciousness. He despises those members of his own class who have gone into voluntary service in a bourgeois household and adopted the values of their employers: the pretentious houseboys; the maids who show open contempt for humble callers, and who use lipstick and straighten their hair in a slavish attempt to resemble their mistresses. He envies the fishermen on the small boats visible from the prison compound; they are fortunate because they have 'no boss, or rather . . . a boss like you or me. A boss who drinks his shot of cheap rum, and sings along with everybody' (p. 59). From his days as a child servant in a middle-class household, he has vivid memories of the empty, useless, sometimes vicious lives led by his employers and their friends. Thanks to his solitary questioning of the system, he is already predisposed at the start of the narrative to be receptive to Roumel's and Jean-Michel's ideas about the unjust exploitation of the Haitian working class. His innate tendency to reexamine the status quo is shown, for example, in his attitude to religion. He sees Catholicism as a bastion of racial prejudice and bigotry, and cannot understand why black men should wish to become priests; 'there were black priests, but no one had ever seen a black 'monseigneur' with a ring for people to kiss' (p. 62). He has observed that the country priest at Léogane, where his cousins live, is a corrupt individual who charges fifty centimes for confession and three chickens for a christening, and conducts a thriving side trade in holy water and prayers for the dead. After the Artibonite River floods its banks, it is common knowledge that both Catholic and Protestant priests are trying to exploit the peasants' sufferings: the former cash in on the funerals of flood victims; the latter, having 'arrived rather late in the religious market' (p. 175), offer food rations and sympathy in a veiled attempt to proselytize on behalf of their own sect. The author himself views these religions as yet another manifestation of class conflict: just as 'the State is not the State of the common people', so 'the official religion is not the religion of their class' (p. 148).

Voodoo is a more delicate issue. Here Alexis, like his predecessor Roumain, has to choose between two points of view which are mutually antagonistic. On the one hand, as an adherent of Marxism, he is inclined to see all religions as retrograde forces which encourage the faithful in their passive acceptance of social evils. On the other hand, voodoo is the religion of the oppressed masses, whom Alexis wishes to champion; it is their strongest link with the lost paradise of Africa, and the belief for which they are persecuted both by the Haitian government and by what Alexis regards as American cultural imperialism.[17] In *Masters of the Dew*, Roumain resolves these contraries by having his mouthpiece, Manuel, show respect for the religion of his elders, the 'old gods of

Guinea', but at the same time preach a vibrant message of faith in man's power to fight calamity and shape his own destiny. Like Manuel, Hilarion acquiesces in his mother's desire to make propitiatory offerings to the voodoo gods, but at heart he believes that 'the holy ones of Africa are really quite dead' (p. 112) and resents having to spend his small savings on offerings to the deaf gods of a distant continent. To him, voodoo is basically no different from other religions, all of whose deities give only in accordance with what they receive. And it is, above all, their earthly representatives who receive: the Christian priests grow fat on their gleanings in the same way that the voodoo priest of Léogane, for all his mystical powers, is also 'a quack exploiting human stupidity', a 'greedy, hypocritical witch-doctor' (p. 123).

The medical metaphors here are deliberately chosen, for it is the real doctor, Jean-Michel, who is the novel's main exemplar of truth and moral worth. The socio-political illumination shed by Jean-Michel is contrasted with the dubious illumination offered by the voodoo *houngan* when Hilarion's aunt asks him to 'give her light' on how she can best please the goddess Erzulie (p. 121), and he informs her, from signs read in the shape formed by raw egg-white in a glass of water, that she must spend extra money on a free feast for the village children, in addition to the expense of the ceremony he has contracted to provide for her. Hilarion is sharply aware that while his sickness was never cured by all his mother's prayers and sacrifices to the African gods, it has yielded to the medical science which Jean-Michel worships; and when Claire-Heureuse starts thanking the Virgin Mary for curing him, he angrily reminds her that she should thank not the Virgin, or the saints, or God – who 'doesn't give a damn about our troubles' – but 'Jean-Michel, the injections, the pink pills, medicine!' (p. 238). While voodoo is not criticized as sharply as other forms of religious belief, it is several times (for example, when Hilarion's friend Christian's child dies of typhoid) presented as a harmful phenomenon which prevents the poor from benefiting from what little medical help is available to them. The ingrained habit of blaming misfortune on supernatural intervention is, at the same time, one of the factors which militates against the acceptance by the masses of Jean-Michel's political message. Science and radical politics are, in the novel, set up in contrast to religion as the forces that offer the best hope of redressing social inequalities. Jean-Michel urges a stop to passive prayer, and a start to active revolt (p. 111). Hilarion, who never totally abandons the custom of regarding the world as a balance of comprehensible and mysterious agents, puts his learned friend in the place he had once reserved for the gods: 'Jean-Michel was the priest of this rite which had conquered his accursed sickness' (p. 234). He is fired by Jean-Michel's vision of a future struggle when the common people of Haiti will join together like the fingers of a hand united in one enormous fist – an image borrowed from Roumain's *Masters of the Dew* – and hammer away at injustice until there is 'a place for all honest folk under the great blue sky of Haiti' (p. 197).

It is evident, then, that through his early scepticism about the value of religion to the community and through his consciousness of social injustice, Hilarion is favourably biased from the start towards the Marxist analysis of what is wrong with Haiti. But the novelist takes into account the importance of the human factor in the transmission of political ideas. Hilarion does not lend an immediate ear to the preaching of the Communists. His ingrained dislike of the powerful mulatto class makes him suspicious of Roumel at first, just as his sense of an 'insurmountable barrier between the world of the educated and the common people' (p. 96) makes him ill at ease with Jean-Michel in the early days of their acquaintance, although the latter is of humble origins. Much later, in the Dominican Republic, he is equally wary of the middle-class artist Domenica Betances: 'if there was one thing clear in him, it was his awareness of class conflicts, his unconquerable distrust of a certain sort of clothes, certain refined, well-cared-for hands, or perfumes that were too delicate' (p. 293). Eventually, her evident warmth and sincerity convince him that 'despite her luxurious exterior, she [is] made of the same fibre as Pierre Roumel [and] Jean-Michel' (p. 296). But even so, he never entirely loses his social inhibitions with regard to Roumel or Domenica, despite his consciousness of a political bond; when Domenica drops in to warn him and Claire-Heureuse that some action is being secretly planned against the Haitian cane workers, his embarrassed attempts to get her out of a kitchen chair and into a more 'suitable' one are a silent commentary on the persistence of class reflexes. From all these educated friends, however, he learns that the qualities of friendship and loyalty can exist in a middle-class person of the right political colour. Their symbolic importance in his life is stressed by the continued use of solar imagery. Jean-Michel and his associates 'dream of light', and strive to give the people a glimpse of the 'faint white glimmer of freedom at the end of the tunnel' (p. 243). Roumel, going into exile, exhorts Hilarion and his other well-wishers to keep their hearts 'as pure as the bright mornings' of Haiti (p. 224). Paco Torres, the militant canecutter who is shot dead while urging a group of fellow workers to strike for better wages, continues 'even in death to be the friend who guides and enlightens' (p. 288). Domenica, placing a red flag on Paco's coffin and singing a defiant hymn to victory, is seen as accomplishing 'an act of high courage, a gesture of light' (p. 296). Their classic role as Marxist illuminators is thrown into relief by the dark night and the spreading clouds that are associated with the resignation of the common people to their lot, for example in the scene where Josaphat, an honest countryman of limited vision, walks in the dark with his cousin, seeking to convince Hilarion that 'no one can escape his destiny' and that 'man always remains what he is at his birth' (p. 132).

Although Hilarion's Communist friends play an important part in his life, very little of the novel is devoted to the actual exposition of Marxist dogma. After Roumel's simplified definition of his party's ideals, Hilarion next encounters political talk when he is drawn into a conversation with Jean-Michel and Ferdinand, and gently encouraged to overcome his conviction that he is too stupid to analyse social and historical issues. The concepts of dialectical materialism and of the unequal growth of capitalism are beyond him, but Jean-Michel's insistence on the need for Haiti to put its house in order strikes a responsive chord in him. And working-class solidarity is a phenomenon he has already gratefully observed in his new job, where he feels that 'they [are] all, men and women, bound by the same chain in that blasted factory' (p. 91). The interest aroused in him by Jean-Michel's theories is fostered at the free night school run by the Communists, where Hilarion learns reading, writing and Haitian history, and is offered a view of nineteenth-century Haitian peasant life as already being based upon the practice of an 'agrarian Communism' (p. 153), in defiance of government attempts to suppress this unofficial system of land reallocation. It is night school which introduces him not only to the facts of the Haitian past, but to a particular way of interpreting those facts: thus, for example, he is taught to see the ultimate defeat of Toussaint Louverture, hero of the slave war of independence, as a logical consequence of the fact that after leading the slaves to liberation, Toussaint became a landed proprietor in the same feudal mould as the French planters he had fought successfully to expel.

The attitude to capitalism which he absorbs at these classes is translated by him in a simple, direct way to his own life situation. Although Claire-Heureuse ekes out a very precarious living by retailing a few basic grocery items, during the economic crisis induced by the flooding of the Artibonite valley he begins to see her as an embryo capitalist and is angered by her refusal to extend credit to indigent customers. The narrative stresses the conflict between the two. Claire-Heureuse's blend of courage and passivity is portrayed as typical of the average member of the working class. She is a valiant fighter in the struggle for existence, but she accepts society as it is, with a dignified resignation, and has no idea that Hilarion is 'in anguish over the problem of how to eradicate poverty' (p. 204). Hilarion's own understanding of Marxist concepts is circumscribed by the limitations of his previous education and experience: he sees history in terms of goodies and baddies, and in his history textbook he adorns with moustaches, horns or donkey's ears the pictures of all the historical figures of whom he disapproves. However, despite this comic touch, the overwhelming, exhilarating quality of his initiation into political thought is conveyed by the vigour of the imagery attached to it: it is the tearing asunder of a veil, the cracking open of a shell that had constricted his brain, the discovery of a 'well of miraculous water of which he must drink deep in order to become a strong person' (p. 153).

But if Hilarion is set on the path to political consciousness by his mentors, he is not depicted as undergoing some unlikely instant conversion to Communism. As Alexis points out with regard to Josaphat, 'a proletarian consciousness is not created at one stroke' (p. 289). Hilarion has the natural fears of the poor and vulnerable about attracting unwelcome attention from the police. He worries in prison about having too close a relationship with Roumel, whom he sees being treated in an inhumane way by the authorities because of his Communist beliefs. He is nervous when Jean-Michel falls under police suspicion for the distribution of left-wing pamphlets, and defends him to others out of friendship and loyalty, rather than out of political conviction. His overwhelming gratitude to Jean-Michel for having brought his epilepsy under control makes him fear that he is behaving in a thankless way by not giving Jean-Michel, in return, the favour of his political support; but this would still be 'a commitment to [a] struggle whose value he did not yet admit' (p. 234). (Jean-Michel, understanding this perfectly, urges him not to join the Party just in order to please a friend: it is too grave a step to be undertaken without personal dedication to the cause.) In the Dominican Republic, although Hilarion has become much more aggressive about his rights as a worker, he is still uneasy when Domenica Betances takes him for a Party member, and reluctant even to be described as a 'sympathizer': this designation arouses in him conflicting emotions of 'perplexity, fear and pride' (p. 297). The same sort of conflict is apparent in his defensive response to Claire-Heureuse when she voices her apprehension about their friendship with Jean-Michel: 'I don't give a damn if Jean-Michel is a Communist . . . And anyway, it's not my fault if only Communists have taken notice of me and helped me!' (p. 240). It is not until he is dying that he makes an open commitment to 'the army of General Sun' (p. 349), a concept which he finally identifies with Paco's revolt and martyrdom, and with the sunlit road which Jean-Michel has tried to show him.

It is both pathetic and ironic that this moment arrives too late for him to express moral commitment by personal revolutionary action.

The last section of the novel, in which Hilarion's political ideas are finally crystallized, is set mainly on a Dominican cane plantation that provides a familiar paradigm of West Indian suffering and oppression. With a tragic inevitability, Hilarion, citizen of the first Caribbean state to end slavery, is driven by poverty and social desperation to seek a better life in a country where the 'Yankee imperialism' of American sugar interests and the 'fascist boot' of Trujillo's army and police (p. 270) combine, in the mid-1930s period which Alexis evokes, to perpetuate the old plantation ethos. Foreign overlords once more make an unscrupulous profit from the labour of their Haitian chattels. The latter live, like their slave ancestors under the French, in a state of exile, in an alien land where 'the days are hellish torment and the nights are long and bitter' (p. 156). Throughout the early twentieth century, Haitians traditionally left their economically stagnant country to seek canecutting work in the adjacent Dominican Republic or in Cuba. In 1920, for instance, there were an estimated 70,000 Haitian peasants in these two countries.[18] They were objects of contempt to the local population, stigmatized both as foreigners and as inferiors: Roumain's Manuel recalls the days when, for a Cuban policeman, 'to kill a Haitian or a dog [was] one and the same thing' (*Masters of the Dew*, p. 50). Circumstances have changed in Cuba; but the continuing scandal of Dominican exploitation of virtually unpaid Haitian labour (often child labour) is still, in the 1980s, exposed from time to time in the world press, though the Haitian government continues to condone the so-called 'green slave trade', as was the case forty or fifty years ago.[19] Alexis depicts a demoralized community of immigrant workers, grateful at first for a pitifully small wage and living in the constant expectation of hostility and rejection. But under the influence of the Dominican militant, Paco Torres, their fragile solidarity is strengthened; the shooting of Paco by a Puerto Rican overseer fuels their latent resentments and they go out on strike for a small raise of pay.

The apparent success of their strike action is soon followed by the horror of the 1937 massacre, a well-documented historical event in which Haitian cane workers were reportedly winnowed out from their Dominican fellow workers by their inability to pronounce correctly the word *perejil*, which is the Spanish for 'parsley'. According to official sources, more than 12,000 Haitian immigrants were killed by Trujillo's troops. Unofficial sources put the number slaughtered at over 20,000. The Dominican government hushed up early reports of the massacre, but was eventually forced to pay the Haitian government an indemnity in reparation, and the international scandal cost Trujillo his re-election in 1938. Lescot, Alexis' future enemy, who was the Haitian Foreign Minister at the time, was later accused of connivance with Trujillo.[20] The novel's version of this event does not attempt an omniscient authorial overview, but stresses the bewilderment, shock and chaos in the ranks of Haitian workers. In keeping with the narrative's dominant light/dark symbolism, the massacre begins on a day when the sun attempts in vain to pierce through sombre rainclouds. Under the Dominican fusillade, amongst the panic-stricken Haitians, a few voices take up the solemn chanting of the Haitian national anthem, 'bound up with so many luminous memories' (p. 311). The wounded, 'rolling, crawling, groaning, moaning, yelling' (p. 311) amidst the pale bagasse strewn on the ground, soaked with their blood, recall an ancient sorrow over the countless dead whose blood nurtured the canefields of slavery.

Hilarion, one of the few who manage to escape unscathed and hide among the tall canes, enters upon a nightmare existence where he, Claire-Heureuse and the baby must hide during the hours of daylight and attempt to cover as much ground as possible during the dark hours of the night on their frantic flight towards the border and the safety of their homeland. They find some comfort in the help they receive not only from Communist sympathizers, but from simple peasants whose natural humanity causes them to repudiate the actions of Trujillo, 'the Jackal', and his regime. But they are tenaciously pursued by military trackers, whose use of dogs arouses ancestral memories of the way in which maroon slaves were hunted down. The dreadful nature of their experiences is largely conveyed by the suffering of Claire-Heureuse – her fear of their pursuers; her overwhelming weariness as they cover the stumbling miles; her bruised, bleeding feet; her once milk-laden breasts which, after a few days of exhaustion and starvation, yield only a bloody liquid to the suckling child. The child itself, whose liveliness brought joy to their days of exile, sinks into lethargy even before the dog attack which ends its short life. Terror and pathos are the hallmarks of this final sequence.

The last hours of Hilarion's life are, in a sense, a repeat of the prologue, with its atmosphere of painful effort and tragic vulnerability. The upward striving of the prologue is here replaced by the couple's struggle to ford the raging waters of the Massacre River which marks the frontier. Once again, the scene unfolds at night, and the dancing silhouettes of the armed border patrol, 'sinister puppets' (p. 342) jerking towards the fugitives, recall the 'shadow show' of baton-waving policemen (p. 20) that descended upon the would-be thief. But the tenor of Hilarion's life has entirely altered since those early, aimless, friendless days, and here the crossing of the river, despite the fatal wound which Hilarion incurs, retains archetypal associations of successful initiation and triumphant entry into man's estate. There are biblical echoes too, of a 'calvary' patiently accomplished (p. 343); the Messianic Césairean note is sounded here, though in a muted, plaintive key. Hilarion's long dying monologue, unrealistic in literal terms, is explicable in terms of the novel's persistent solar symbolism: as the dawn approaches, he appraises all his past life and ends, at sunrise, with the fervent affirmation of his political awakening: 'Tell Jean-Michel that I saw the light on the day when, before my very eyes, a great red sun lit up the breast of a worker called Paco Torres . . . Tell him to follow faithfully the road he wanted to show me, he must follow that sun . . . General Sun! How long I've looked for him!' (p. 350).

It is significant that at this final moment of truth, Hilarion refers to his political friends not just as 'the army of General Sun' but also as 'the men of Comrade Sun' (p. 349). This gentler and more Haitian aspect of the sun, as 'compère', is as important as its militant, universal connotations. Indeed, when the phrase 'General Sun' first appears in the novel, in the aftermath of the disastrous Artibonite flood, it is indistinguishable in meaning from 'Comrade Sun', since it appears in a context of friendship, support and healing. The sun here is 'the passionate lover of the Haitian land', 'the fiery one' who pours 'the warmth of his love over the plain', making up for 'the wickedness of those in power and their hatred of the common people' (p. 171). Its heat, 'the friend of poor blacks', dries up the flood waters and destroys the germs and infections which were proliferating. All things to all men, when it shines on the children's games its 'sparkling, imperishable eye' is that of a 'good child' (p. 236). The notions of comradeship and brotherhood attached to the novel's title point to the political, allegorical level of the narrative and underscore its Marxist message, but they are of vital importance also at a human, personal level. Neighbourly friendship and support are part of the Haitian folk tradition, and find concrete expression in the custom of the *coumbite*. It is this 'great and ancient fraternity of the workers and the unfortunate' that, after the floods, 'rebuilds on all the ruins, rescues all those in distress' (p. 176). But from this universal warmth and solidarity, Hilarion is at first excluded. Perhaps the most moving aspect of the novel is its portrayal of the protagonist as a man initially without comrades, an outsider beset by desperate emotional needs, whose bleak existence is suddenly transfigured by the miraculous twin blossoming of friendship and love. Unlike Roumain's Manuel, Hilarion is no outstanding hero-figure, but a fallible, inexperienced, self-doubting individual. His moral solitude is carefully delineated in the prologue and the prison section of the story. He appears to have no friends in the slum of Nan-Palmiste. His cellmates are sly and disagreeable, and his fleeting contacts with Roumel are limited by physical barriers within the jail and by the social gulf between the two men.

It is when he is released from prison that his life is 'transformed' (p. 350), as he will recall at the moment of his death, by the marvellous accident of his meeting Claire-Heureuse. Her arrival in his life, on a day when the dazzling sunlight refracted from the surface of the sea mirrors the radiance in his heart at his new freedom and the prospect of a steady job, is an event as exhilarating as his subsequent political initiation. Claire-Heureuse offers him not only sexual love, but a comradeship as essential as that of the Communists, and one which heals the wounds of a lifetime of ostracism. Through her, he is harmoniously integrated into the mainstream of existence, and can hope for the first time to fulfil the normal human destiny of marriage and parenthood. It is interesting to observe that the solar imagery associated with the Marxist goal of an egalitarian society is equally associated with the private joys that Claire-Heureuse shares with Hilarion: her pleasure in her pregnancy (p. 215), her delight when he brings her the news that his epileptic fits will not recur (p. 238). In the same way, it is noticeable that Hilarion values Jean-Michel above all as a friend, whose affection and unquenchable optimism about the future bring him a new, positive outlook on life; as a healer, who has removed the medical obstacle to his union with Claire-Heureuse; and as a gifted intellectual, who has had the generosity of spirit to treat him as an equal. Jean-Michel's political influence is no less, but no more, important in Hilarion's life than the personal experiences which slowly shape his own social philosophy: the way his employers treat him, the gradual wearing away of Claire-Heureuse's youthful beauty and energy in the daily battle for survival, the victimization of Haitian workers in the Dominican Republic, the martyrdom of his comrade Paco. It is because they reflect the truth of his own life that his painfully acquired insights concerning the flawed structure of his native land have the power to move the reader.

Alexis' view of Haitian society is, on the whole, a dogmatic one, in which members of the élite are unfailingly assigned the villains' roles unless, like Roumel or Domenica, they have been redeemed by their adherence to Marxism. Then they fulfil, as Alexis himself aspired to do, the classic Marxist role of the renegade bourgeois intellectual bringing enlightenment to the proletariat. Apart from these clearly defined dialectical exceptions, Alexis vigorously rejects Haitian bourgeois culture, which he presents as the major stumbling-block to the establishment of his ideal Marxist state. It is indeed true that the Haitian élite has a long record of indifference to the plight of the masses, and this denial of compassion and fraternity on the part of the élite clearly justifies, in Alexis' eyes, the violence of his denunciations. At the same time, however, the author's tendency to see his bourgeois characters as symbols of oppression, rather than as individuals, causes him systematically to withhold from them the common humanity which his proletarian characters possess. This imbalance in the presentation impairs the credibility of the narrative to a certain extent, and sometimes makes it appear naive and oversimplified.

But if the bourgeoisie is lampooned with little subtlety or humour, the poor, on the other hand, are characterized with careful attention to individual particulars. The novel is full of small touches that make the details of an obscure life spring suddenly, sharply into focus. A pair of adolescent lovers sit close together in a small, dark room, with the rain beating on the roof and the wings of flying ants piling up beneath the kerosene lamp. On a long, jolting truck ride into the country, with nearly all the passengers worn out and sleeping, a man meets the clear, smiling gaze of a child and reaches out silently to caress his dusty cheek. A woman in a nightdress runs out of a yard where the rooms are catching fire, clutching a pair of sheets, an old rag doll and one large, precious photograph. A husband coughs self-consciously before he carefully reads a letter aloud to his wife. Outside in a yard on a hot evening, a young couple bend down from their small, upright wooden chairs to the straw basket at their feet and place their hands side by side on the small, gently vibrating body of their sleeping child. Powerless to comfort his sobbing, exhausted wife, a man picks up a bit of wood and pokes mindlessly at an ant-nest on the ground beside them. An old woman rocks back and forth as she waits for her god-daughter's suitor, wondering if the home-made ice-cream will be all right and thinking that soon she will have to live alone. Alexis' sense of identity with these Haitians to whose 'beauties, struggles and dramas' he bears witness, and his deep desire not merely to hold up a mirror to their reality, but also to 'transform their world',[21] instil into the novel a strength and poignancy that make it the essential urban counterpart to Roumain's peasant parable. Both novelists, in very different ways, capture the tragic dignity of a people struggling for survival against perhaps the worst odds in the Caribbean.

Notes

1 René Depestre, *Bonjour et adieu à la négritude* (Paris: Robert Laffont, 1980), p. 201. All translations from French in this chapter are my own.

2 Jacques Stéphen Alexis, open letter to Father Salgado, reprinted in Claude Souffrant, *Une Négritude socialiste: Religion et développement chez J. Roumain, J.-S. Alexis, L. Hughes* (Paris: L'Harmattan, 1978), p. 219.

3 For accounts of the circumstances of Alexis' death, see Diederich and Burt, pp. 167-8, 336; Depestre, pp. 222-4; Nicholls, p. 231; and Gérard Pierre-Charles, 'Mort et vie de Jacques Soleil', *Europe* 501 (January 1971), pp. 65-7. On Duvalier's neglect of the urban and rural proletariat, see Rémy Anselme, 'Le phénomène Duvalier', *Acoma* 4-5 (1973), pp. 130-3, 149.

4 See Souffrant, p. 65.

5 Jacques Stéphen Alexis, 'Où va le roman?', *Présence Africaine* 13 (1957), p. 96.

6 See Diederich and Burt, pp. 47-9, and Jesús de Galíndez, *The Era of Trujillo*, ed. Russell H. Fitzgibbon (1956 Spanish ed.; Tucson, Arizona: University of Arizona Press, 1973), pp. 36-8.

7 Alexis, 'Où va le roman?', p. 95.

8 Jacques Stéphen Alexis, 'Prolegomena to a manifesto on the marvellous realism of the Haitians', *Présence Africaine* (English ed.) 8/10 (1956), p. 271.

9 Alexis, letter to Salgado, in Souffrant, p. 223. On Alexis' political activities, see Depestre, pp. 208–15, 223–4; Diederich and Burt, pp. 324–7, 330, 335–6; and Michael Dash, 'Jacques Stéphen Alexis', *Black Images* 3, 4 (1974), pp. 9–16.

10 See Anselme, p. 123. Both Anselme and Nicholls give interesting accounts of the changes in Haitian class structure since the era depicted by Alexis, and in particular the growth of the black urban middle class under Duvalier.

11 On this aspect of Alexis' work, see J. Michael Dash, *Literature and Ideology in Haiti, 1915–1961* (London: Macmillan, 1981), pp. 192–3.

12 See Bertrand de la Grange, 'Haïti à la dérive', in *Le Monde* of 30 May 1981, and also *Time Magazine*, 22 June 1981, p. 41. The World Bank recently reported that 69 per cent of Haitian children were suffering from malnutrition in 1958, and 81 per cent in 1979 (*Le Monde*, 18 April 1981).

13 Dash ('Jacques Stéphen Alexis', p. 28) has an interesting discussion of this encounter as 'a confrontation between the night of the exploited and the historical whiteness of the oppressor'.

14 Jacques Stéphen Alexis, *L'Espace d'un cillement* (Paris: Gallimard, 1959), pp. 235, 236.

15 Georges Castera *fils*, on p. 74 of his article 'L'Expérience de la nuit et l'expérience du jour dans *Compère Général Soleil*', *Europe* 501 (January 1971), discusses the motif of breathing in the prologue as a device which fuses the external, objective night with the inner, subjective night which is Hilarion's moral condition.

16 Alexis explains his use of this term in *L'Espace d'un cillement*, p. 60.

17 Alexis' second novel, *Les Arbres musiciens* (Paris: Gallimard, 1957), examines the strengths and weaknesses of the voodoo religion and its place in the social and political structure of Haiti. On Alexis' own attitude to voodoo, see Dash, 'Jacques Stéphen Alexis', pp. 24–5, 31, 45, and Souffrant, pp. 73, 81, 85.

18 Marie-Denise Shelton, 'Le paysan dans le roman haïtien: *Le drame de la terre*', *Présence Francophone* 22 (1981), p. 163.

19 See, for example, *Caribbean Contact*, December 1980 and January 1981; *L'Express*, 7 March 1981; *Le Nouvel Observateur*, 23 March 1981; *The Australian*, 4 April 1981; and the recent book by Maurice Lemoine, *Sucre amer: Esclaves aujourd'hui dans les Caraïbes* (Paris: Editions Encre, 1981).

20 See Galíndez, pp. 36–8, 205–9, for a detailed account.

21 Alexis, 'Prolegomena to a manifesto on the marvellous realism of the Haitians', p. 251.

5

The Boat and the Tree: Simone Schwarz-Bart's *The Bridge of Beyond*

'Give me the obstinacy of the proud canoe'
(*Cahier*, p. 79).

The Bridge of Beyond opens and closes upon the same scene: an old woman standing in her garden, dreaming of the past and waiting tranquilly for death. The figure is that of the narrator, Telumee, who has received, late in life, the admiring nickname 'Telumee Miracle'. Her upright posture suggests dignity, strength, and a resolute will to resist adversity; these are the qualities to which the narrative continually reverts, and which serve to create its prevailing moral climate. Behind Telumee's vertical stance there is a second, latent image, that of a tree. Unexpressed at the start of the novel, this image becomes explicit as the story advances and she is successively compared to a bamboo, a poinciana or *flamboyant,* a coconut palm and an acomat. The tree, with its stable roots and promise of upward growth, is a familiar presence in the work of Césaire and Roumain: a symbol of constancy and harmonious integration, of triumphant recovery from the uprooting and alienation consequent on the Fall of slavery. Roumain, in *Masters of the Dew,* draws also upon the archetypal symbolism of the tree, representative in many mythologies of the creation of life and of all movement towards ascent and resurrection. In Simone Schwarz-Bart's *The Bridge of Beyond* the tree keeps all these connotations, but is above all associated with courage and tenacity. At the end of the novel, which tells the story of Telumee's life in early-twentieth-century Guadeloupe, the image is specifically linked to the theme of her indomitable spirit by the tribute which her neighbours pay to her: 'Mama Miracle, you are the tree our hamlet leans against' (p. 168).

The image of the tree is also implicit in the vertical metaphors which are used to convey Telumee's final assessment of her position: 'I have moved my cabin to the east and to the west; east winds and north winds, [tempests and downpours] have buffeted and soaked me; but I am still a woman standing on my own two legs, and I know a Negro is not a statue of salt to be dissolved by the rain' (p. 172).[1] The statue of salt, with its attributes of whiteness and, through the biblical story of Lot's wife (Genesis 19:26), of female self-destructiveness, is here opposed to the darkness and durability of wood: the hut withstanding the elements; Telumee herself, the upright, steadfast trunk defying the storms; and the black race with which she is constantly, intimately identified, and which has the same robust, enduring quality: 'We have struggled to be born and we have struggled to be born again, and we have called the finest tree in our forests 'resolute' – the strongest, the most sought after, the one that is cut down the most often' (p. 170). Thus the metaphorical meaning of the novel's French title (which is literally *Rain and Wind on Telumee Miracle*) is extended beyond its specific reference to Telumee's fortitude, to embrace every member of her race ('As I struggled others will struggle', p. 172) and to indicate their innate ability to survive. A further ramification of the image, in which the tree modulates into a boat, is inspired by the linking idea of physical resistance to wind and weather. The archetypal boat, found throughout the world and more particularly throughout the Caribbean, is the long, narrow canoe made from the hollowed trunk of a tree. Wood is therefore the substance of both, and both are required to suffer the onslaughts of natural forces. But the boat is also an especially fitting symbol of the unpredictable course of human experience, with its quests, setbacks and sudden changes of fortune. At the end of the novel, the two images coalesce, united by the theme of the buffeting wind: 'the days slip past and the sand blown by the wind will engulf my boat. But I shall die here, where I am, standing in my little garden. What happiness!'(p. 173). A striking and paradoxical feature of this passage is that the traditionally sombre resonance of the shipwreck metaphor is contradicted in tone by the pride and pleasure that emanate from the upright figure in the garden – attributes already present in the novel's first evocation of that solitary, yet contented figure: 'I didn't come into the world to weigh the world's woe. I prefer to dream, on and on, standing in my garden . . . till death comes and takes me as I dream, me and all my joy'(p. 2). The movement of the boat, like that of Telumee's wandering cabin, reflects the ups and downs of her life; but the movement of the tree is a transcendent one, echoing Telumee's aspiration 'to keep up my position as a Negress, to keep up the way I carry my soul'(p. 168). It is associated with other images of transcendence: the soaring kite, the rising song, the floating of the spirit above bodily pain. At the same time it is, like all plants, a reminder of the eternal, cyclical harmony of nature's rhythms, and thus a lesson in the acceptance of death as a form of renewal, when Telumee will 'become sap in the grass' (p. 172) – an image which may also be related to the survival of the black race, as Césaire so uses it in his *Cahier* (p. 76) of 'those who continue to live in the germination of grass'. Furthermore, like the real gardens which Telumee creates in the country soil of Guadeloupe, the tree evokes an earthly Eden, a place of fruitfulness and spiritual delight. Throughout *The Bridge of Beyond* , the interwoven images of boat and tree testify both to the vicissitudes of Telumee's existence and to her capacity for resistance.

The French title, *Rain and Wind on Telumee Miracle,* presents the novel's central theme of struggle and survival through the image of a conflict between Telumee and two elemental forces of nature. Underlying the narrative, and in keeping with its rural setting, there is a constant sense of man's closeness to nature and to the four elements of earth, water, air and fire. The rain and wind which metaphorically assault Telumee are hostile manifestations of water and air. Their hostility is linked with that of the fiery planet of the sun in an early description of Telumee's ageing grandmother, sitting 'proud and straight' in her rocker although her black eyes are 'faded like a garment too often exposed to sun and rain' (p. 28), 'worn out with suns and rains and tears' (p. 53). From the opening paragraph of the novel, the idea of the destructive potential of fire, air and water is present in the text through the characterization of Guadeloupe as a 'volcanic, hurricane-swept' island. Earth is the element most in harmony with the peasant farmers who make up Telumee's community. It is 'black and rich', ready to send up green shoots of hope in response to man's endeavours:

'As our sweat seeped into the soil, it became more and more ours, one with the odour of our bodies' (p. 146). And like man, it is vulnerable to drought and to the scorching sun. Water, which brings life to the fields, can also be the agent of havoc through torrential rains. It is implicitly associated with death in the recurrent motif of the boat fighting to remain afloat amidst the waves. Fire is directly linked with disaster in the novel's first chapter, when Telumee's grandparents see their child and their house destroyed by it, 'watching their sweat, their life, their joy, go up in flames' (p. 12). Sadness is thenceforth a flame that consumes the individual 'like a wood fire', turning the green of hope to 'the colour of a scorched vine' (p. 18). It is specifically associated with the canefields, which are themselves the major symbol of past slavery. When Telumee is forced to work as a canecutter, she enters 'the heart of malediction, . . . the fire of the canes . . . the fire of the sky and the prickles' (pp. 136–7). But her ultimate triumphant emergence from this ordeal is a reminder that although slavery was 'sadness [and] fire, . . . the fire is out . . . and even the embers will not last forever' (p. 38).

Critical discussions of this novel have stressed the way in which the narrator's life, like that of her female ancestors, falls into a recurrent pattern of ascent, ruin and subsequent renaissance, in seeming obedience to a cyclical view of man's progression through time.[2] The pattern is only lightly delineated in the case of Telumee's great-grandmother Minerva, the first of the Lougandor women: she is freed from a cruel master by the abolition of slavery in 1848, then is abandoned in a state of pregnancy by a transient lover, but is rescued by a tender and steadfast man who loves Minerva's child as if she were his own. It is more firmly sketched in when the narrator recounts the life of her mother, Victory, an unmarried girl struggling to bring up her first child, Regina, when she is abandoned by a faithless new lover from a neighbouring island. She is rescued from months of alcoholic despair and degeneration by the gentle, compassionate Angebert, the future father of Telumee. Then Angebert's sudden, violent death casts her back into solitude; but two years later she meets the great love of her life, and soon sets sail with him for the island of Dominica. Briefly though they appear in the narrative, both Minerva and Victory have essential virtues in common with their respective daughters, Toussine (Telumee's grandmother) and Telumee herself. Minerva, the founder of the Lougandor line, who bears the name of the goddess of wisdom, is a woman who walks with her 'head high' and has 'an unshakable faith in life' (p. 3). Victory, whose slight body perhaps reflects her moral status as the most lightweight of the Lougandor women, is none the less a valiant fighter who also 'carrie[s] her head high on a slender neck' and is moved by a 'determination to stay serene however harshly the winds might blow' (p. 17). Forever singing at her work, keeping her griefs and disappointments to herself, she survives poverty, a miscarriage, the loss of her lovers and the sole responsibility of two young children, without losing an innate knack of resilience and optimism; 'not a fallen woman', she goes through life 'with the same expectation, the same lightness she had when no man's hand had yet touched her' (p. 26). At some of the lowest moments of Telumee's life, Victory's example helps to sustain her: singing about her domestic tasks so as to distance herself from a fault-finding white employer, or mentally thanking her laundress mother for the 'steel wrists' she has inherited, which enable her to endure the heavy labour of cutting cane.

Before the story of Telumee's own life begins, it is that of her grandmother

Toussine which most clearly illustrates the cycle of ascent, fall and ultimate recovery. From the first page of the novel, Toussine is represented as 'a woman who helped you hold your head up', an object of 'veneration' to her descendants. Of all the Lougandor women, she is the most radiantly beautiful;[3] her early luck is the greatest, and so too is her fall. Rejoicing in the love of a handsome young fisherman whose skill and patience result in almost miraculous catches, she marries him (an exceptional step in a community where informal liaisons are the norm) and is granted more than ten years of happiness and prosperity before disaster overtakes her. Then her twin daughters Meranee and Eloisine, quarrelling over their homework, break an oil lamp and set the small wooden house on fire. The house and its modest treasures are consumed, and Meranee, her entire body turned into a vast, decaying, fly-plagued wound, takes seventeen days to die of her burns. Waiting for the child to expire, Toussine replies to the condolences of her neighbours with a stoical proverb: 'However heavy a woman's breasts, her chest is always strong enough to carry them'; but once Meranee is dead, she withdraws with her husband and remaining child to a ruined house 'in a desolate and inaccessible wasteland' (p. 12) beyond the village boundaries. Three years pass before she can shake off her indifference to life. During this time the pile of mouldering stone with its one habitable room, a cubbyhole with leaking roof and cardboard-covered window openings, surrounded by weeds, scrub and brushwood, is an icon of the ruin and devastation of Toussine herself, 'a body without a soul' (p. 13). When at last she finds the will to re-enter the stream of life, her first action is both practical and symbolic: she cuts down the weeds around the ruined house, and then deliberately sets about re-creating the garden which was once her 'joy and richness' (p. 10), planting Indian poppies, Congo canes, peas and vegetables to feed her family, and, in an ultimate gesture of faith in the future, the seed of a new orange tree. Victory, the child born of this moment of renaissance, is the final proof of Toussine's triumph over signal misfortune, and the reason for the nickname which the village bestows on her mother: Queen Without a Name, for no name is adequate to convey the greatness of soul which has enabled her to surmount catastrophe.

It is in the story of Toussine and her husband Jeremiah that the boat motif makes its first appearance. Initially it is introduced in a realistic, literal context: Jeremiah's boat, the *Headwind* (its very name suggestive of a joyful defiance of the elements), 'in which he used to go off [dancing] forever' (p. 4), is remarkable in the village for the abundant catches it brings back to shore. Although the narrator is at pains to eliminate any supernatural explanation of Jeremiah's fishing feats – 'Scandalmongers said he used witchcraft . . . but in fact his only secret was his enormous patience' (p. 9) – his boat is none the less endowed with a significance that soon shifts it into the plane of metaphor. When he despairs of winning Toussine's hand, he is shown 'neglecting the *Headwind,* deserting her and leaving her high and dry on the beach' (p. 4). On the night of his betrothal, he leads his friends on a fishing expedition which is so successful and so enjoyable that the prodigious catch is distributed free to the village, and goes down in its annals. The song with which Minerva teases her amorous daughter uses the image of the boat to suggest both nature's riches and sexual delight:

> I want a fisherman for a husband
> To catch me fine sea bream
> I don't know if you know

The Boat and the Tree

But I want a fisherman
O oar before, he pleases me
O oar behind, [he makes me] die.   (p. 6)

Like the first garden of Toussine and Jeremiah, which is also linked with fruitfulness and sexual pleasure (p. 9), the boat moving confidently through the
water is therefore expressive of happiness and good fortune. In accordance
with this symbolic pattern, after Meranee's death Jeremiah stops going to sea
and remains by Toussine's side in their weed-surrounded wreck of a lodging.
Only when she emerges from despair is he able to go down to the beach again
and 'fill his eyes with the sea . . . smiling . . . as in the days when the song of the
waves sounded in his head' (p. 14). By a natural association, Toussine in this
period of desolate withdrawal from life is seen by the villagers as a 'little
stranded boat, [a] woman thought to be lost forever' (p. 14). While they are
reluctant to 'desert a ship like Toussine' (p. 13), they find the sight of her silent
grief unbearable and soon begin to avoid the ruined house in which she lives. At
the time of her recovery, the image of the boat is again employed to mark her
triumph: she has become 'the ship, sail, and wind, for she [has] not made a
habit of sorrow' (p. 14).

From this moment in the narrative, the boat image becomes part of a wider
metaphoric structure in which the life of the Negro is compared to a voyage
through stormy or treacherous waters. While these waters are linked, in the
novel's context, to the 'rain and wind' of adversity that batter Telumee and her
family, they of course derive from an ancient tradition of figurative thought.
The wanderings of Homer's Ulysses, for example, have long been interpreted
as an allegorical journey through the vicissitudes of the sea of existence; the
trials and obstacles which he encountered may readily be equated with the
physical and moral hardships to which Everyman is heir.[4] In both the Old and
the New Testament, God's power over the sea is a manifestation of his power
over human destiny, as in the tempest sent to punish Jonah's defection, or the
storm on the Sea of Galilee which is calmed by Christ. The foundering of a ship
is an Old Testament metaphor of human ruin (Ezekiel 27); while the redemptive counterpart of the shipwreck image, Noah's Ark, has come to be a symbol
of the Church itself, beaten by the waves of the world yet never submerged,
bearing the faithful to salvation. The ship, then, in both pagan and Christian
tradition, has sometimes been an attribute of hope and confidence;[5] but its
fragility in the face of the ocean's power has often been likened – as in Pascal's
well-known metaphor of the human condition – to man's helplessness against
the capricious winds of fortune, which drive him hither and yon upon an ocean
where he may never cast anchor or come safely into harbour. Thus the joy of
sailing is forever tempered by the fear of sinking and drowning; and in many
folklores, the image of the boat is associated with death.[6] These various traditions relating to the voyage metaphor, minus the element of divine salvation,
are discernible in the philosophy of Queen Without a Name, who teaches her
granddaughter that 'life is a sea without a port and without a lighthouse' and
that 'men are ships without a destination' (p. 172). At the same time, the main
tenor of her remarks on life throughout Telumee's childhood also points
clearly towards her conviction that it is possible for the individual voyager to
find his own salvation. This basically optimistic view of life – tempered with
her grandmother's acceptance of the inevitability of suffering – is reflected in
Telumee's view of the black race as adept at 'forging happiness in spite of

everything', as capable of controlling its own destiny, 'at once both wind and sail' (p. 73).

The first part of the novel, entitled 'My People', consists of only two chapters, which present the lives of Minerva, Toussine and Victory. In an interview, the author has related that the publishers wanted to omit the first section and begin with the arrival of Telumee on the scene. But for Simone Schwarz-Bart, the novel would not exist without these first two chapters, for 'it is our memory. There is always a kind of seeking, of relating, always the search for a connection: "so-and-so is such-and-such a person's child". The wish to trace ancestry'.[7] This very characteristic West Indian attitude has profound implications in *The Bridge of Beyond,* where ignorance of one's ancestry is linked with the historical predicament of the slave – forever cut off from first-hand knowledge of Mother Africa – and with that of his descendants, locked into a lifestyle of precarious sexual unions and absentee parenthood. The search for the lost father, or for the father's unknown name, is a persistent theme in the folk-tales of the French Caribbean, and may be seen as an expression of uncertainty and distress about one's personal identity.[8] The absence of the father, the long-for 'centre-post' of the household, is related by Schwarz-Bart to the difficulty Guadeloupean men had in finding stable employment in the first half of this century.[9] Lack of work, and consequent lack of self-esteem – 'the bruised and shattered souls of Negroes without jobs' (p. 99) – are consistently presented in the novel as direct causes of male alienation. In a wider sense, the collective condition of orphanhood and a permanent sense of bereavement are used as metaphors for the situation of the West Indian peasantry, 'a pack of Negroes all in the same [trap], without any fathers and mothers before God' (p. 5).[10] The self-perpetuating and self-destructive aspects of West Indian sexual patterns are obliquely suggested by the defiant song of the pregnant 14-year-old school-leavers rushing 'joyously to [their] fate in the ocean':

> No mother
> No father
> Bravo!
> A woman without two men
> Isn't worth a straw.   (p. 53)

The greatest emotional havoc in Telumee's life is wreaked by her first love, Elie, a motherless boy brought up by a father who 'sometimes seems [like] a deserted child' (p. 45), and her childhood friend Letitia, 'a particularly godforsaken little girl' who 'used to go from house to house, picking up in each a piece of cod, a slice of breadfruit, some other fruit, or a scrap of meat, for the whole village was her mother' (pp. 42–3). The insecurity and consequent cruelty of this pair are contrasted with Telumee's almost unfailing tolerance, born of her confidence in her grandmother's love, which is symbolized by the protective 'fortress' of Queen Without a Name's 'great full skirt' (p. 28). And behind the figure of her grandmother, Telumee is ever conscious of 'the line of noble Negresses' (p. 139) from which she has sprung. This certainty of her own identity, the moral heritage of a race of hardy Lougandor matriarchs, is a major factor in her own ultimate survival; while on the other hand, the theme of the forsaken or parentless child is implicitly connected with 'the [fall] of the Negro . . . what had happened in ancient times and still went on now, without our knowing why or how' (p. 147).

The Boat and the Tree

The second part of the novel, 'The Story of My Life', begins when Telumee is 10 years old. Victory, passionately attached to a new lover who has the reputation of being 'a great connoisseur of feminine flesh' (p. 26), prudently decides to remove her daughters from his vicinity. Regina goes to her natural father in Basse-Terre, there to become eventually 'an elegant city lady' (p. 41). Telumee, whose father Angebert has been dead for two years, is sent to live with her maternal grandmother in the hillside village of Fond-Zombi. Like Zobel's M'man Tine, Queen Without a Name becomes the real mother of the grandchild left in her care. Too old for canefield work, she now lives off the produce of her garden and a small income from the home-made cakes and sweets which she supplies to the nearby village shop. Telumee spends the next six years at her side, helping her with her garden, her pig, rabbits and hens, fetching water, washing clothes in the river, and contributing to the household her wages from occasional work as a canefield weeder. The elementary school which she briefly attends is portrayed as almost entirely irrelevant to the realities of West Indian peasant life. It is dismissed with brief irony as a place which teaches the children 'to respect the flag of France our mother, to revere her greatness and majesty and the glory that [goes] back to the beginning of time, when we were still monkeys with their tails cut off' (p. 52). In another writer's hands, this passage might be the starting-point for a diatribe on the evils of France's colonial policy of cultural assimilation. Schwarz-Bart's interest lies rather in stressing the positive value of the moral guidance that Telumee receives from her grandmother, whose wisdom is based on personal experience and on a realistic assessment both of life's difficulties and of man's potential for self-fulfilment. The contrast in worth between the two forms of instruction offered to Telumee is suggested (p. 52) in an extension of the 'sea of life' image, in which the river or stream denotes an individual human existence. Queen Without a Name teaches Telumee that 'all rivers go down to and are drowned in the sea. And life awaits man as the sea awaits the river'. Thus, although school is ostensibly taking care of the children, who are like 'little streams . . . protected from violent suns and torrential rains', it is in fact engaged in a futile enterprise, keeping them artificially 'apart from the world . . . dammed up' until the pressure of the gathering waters forces open the sluices and casts the children into the 'current' that has always been their inevitable destiny. The inappropriate nature of their official education is underlined when the 14-year-olds find themselves riding 'a great, continuous, shuddering wave' (p. 53), with no possibility of realizing the dreams of wealth and distinction which had been born of those few reading and writing lessons, 'once the bearers of hope' (p. 54). Another of Queen Without a Name's sayings is shown as a more balanced and fitting preparation for the life that awaits these young adolescents: 'there are three paths that are bad for a man to take: to see the beauty of the world and call it ugly, to get up early to do what is impossible, and to let oneself get carried away by dreams – for whoever dreams becomes the victim of his own dream' (p. 30).

Telumee's years with her grandmother are spent in an isolated rural community. The era is the early twentieth century, a time when the members of her grandmother's generation can still recall their own acquaintance with people like Minerva, who had been slaves. Slavery, for Telumee, is at first merely an old sadness that permeates some of Queen Without a Name's songs:

> Mama where is where is where is Idahe
> She is sold and sent away Idahe . . . (p. 31)

Then it is explained to her by her grandmother's friend, Ma Cia, in a homely but brutal metaphor that relates it directly to the child's own range of experience: 'If you want to see a slave . . . you've only to go down to the market at Pointe-à-Pitre and look at the poultry in the cages, tied up, and at the terror in their eyes' (p. 37). This is the first of a chain of images throughout the novel where the helplessness of an animal in the face of human cruelty is used to evoke the wretched vulnerability of the slave, and to suggest that his descendants still occupy the same disadvantaged position in relation to the white man. As in Roumain's *Masters of the Dew,* there is sometimes the added suggestion that God is the ultimate 'white master' who has abandoned the black race. When Queen Without a Name muses upon the slave's past suffering – 'Who can blame a dog for being tied up? . . . And if he's tied up, how can you prevent him being whipped?' – Ma Cia makes an immediate connection with the present situation of the black West Indian: 'For a long time now God has lived in the sky to set us free, and lived in the white men's house . . . to flog us' (p. 38).[11] (The same attitude is implicit in the later allusion (p. 48) to the stories Queen Without a Name tells Telumee, stories which magically reverse the known order of the universe, opening up 'a world in which trees cry out, fishes fly, birds catch the fowler, and the Negro is the child of God'.) Later in the novel, Amboise (Telumee's second lover, but a man much older than herself, nearer to her grandmother's generation) defines the plight of the Negro in similar terms: 'what energy will save the tethered kid from the knife?' and his listeners accept this view of their present condition as something predetermined by the historical brutality of white against black in the Caribbean: 'we felt we were like the kid tethered in the field, and we knew the truth of our fate was not in ourselves but in the existence of the blade' (p. 152).[12] Direct references to slavery in the novel increase as Telumee grows older. Ma Cia recalls the slave markets of the past – 'the time when barrels of rotten meat were worth more than us' – when discussing with Telumee the moral condition of the peasants around them: 'We have been goods for auction, and now we are left with fractured hearts' (p. 130). In her old age, Telumee herself 'look[s] through the shadows of the past at the market', searching among the auctioned slaves for her ancestor; but all the faces are her own, for 'all of us [are] still suffering and dying silently of slavery after it is finished and forgotten' (p. 169).

This tragic consciousness of past misery and degradation is linked in the novel with a widespread tendency to self-doubt and self-depreciation. The image the black West Indian has of himself is depicted as gravely damaged by the debasing historical experience of slavery for which he himself, rather than his former masters, has assumed the shameful guilt. Even in the wisdom and serenity of old age, Telumee sometimes asks herself 'if we are men at all, because if we were, perhaps we would not have been treated like that' (p. 169). The familiar Césairean theme of racial Fall and alienation is brought in from the earliest years of Telumee's life, in the story of her father Angebert and his murderer, Germain. Germain, the first in a series of 'accursed' men that affect the course of Telumee's life, is a notorious thief and social outcast, forever prowling around the village in restless unhappiness, 'like a wild beast in a cage' (p. 21). His plight is an extreme example of the Negro's collective predicament: the symbolic connection between him and all his race is made by the application to him of one of the animal images of slavery – 'You're like a dog tied to a rope that wants to be free, but you won't get far' (p. 21). The compassionate Angebert is the only person to befriend him; but this act of charity is repaid by

treachery and death. Germain himself is dehumanized by his crime, 'already
. . . of a different species' (p. 23), and, like the dog to which he was compared,
he is led away by the police with a rope around his neck.

Germain's last despairing words to the angry crowd: 'I stabbed Angebert,
and you can kill me . . . But I swear it's not my fault' (p. 23), raise an issue
which is central to the novel: that of responsibility for misfortune. Implicit in
the definition of the black slave as an animal already tied up and helpless,
incapable of avoiding the harm that comes to him from an external and
superior force, is a desire to free the Negro from guilt or shame over his
condition – the kind of shame inculcated by the plantation system and keenly
felt, for example, by Amboise's grandmother, a former slave herself, who
teaches her grandson that 'a Negro is a well of sins, a creature of the devil'
(p. 149). The narrator attributes even Germain's murderous behaviour to 'the
madness of the West Indies', a fateful 'bird of prey' that hovers over men who
are 'incapable of offering the slightest resistance. It was on Germain's shoulder
that the bird alighted, and it put the knife in his hand, and aimed it at my
father's heart' (p. 23). This madness is elsewhere described by Schwarz-Bart as
a phenomenon observed in her childhood, 'a way of sensing our history, even
in a confused manner, when one doesn't actually know it. The fishermen, the
peasants, used to feel a sort of cloak weighing down their shoulders'.[13] It is
linked in the novel to the notion of bad luck, 'that madwoman . . . who seizes
and rends you and scatters your flesh to the crows' (p. 11). The context of this
last image, the start of the episode in which a children's squabble leads to the
fire that destroys Toussine's house and kills her daughter, seems to imply that
the responsibility of the individual for misfortune is relatively small. Good
luck, too, is sometimes like a bird that chooses arbitrarily to descend on one's
body and into one's bones (p. 88). But more often it is portrayed as a plant,
which obeys nature's cyclical rhythms and cannot be ruled by man: ' . . .
perhaps your heart will recover, and the root of your luck will grow and bloom
again' (p. 117); 'I left it [the sun] to roll through the sky and scorch the root of
my luck or make it sparkle, as it should decide' (p. 127); 'In that fine season of
my life, the root of my luck came up' (p. 146). By association with the novel's
tree symbolism and its accompanying theme of resistance to misfortune, the
image of the root of luck suggests that while no one can command either good
or bad fortune, it is possible for men to persevere through the bad times and
await the certain renewal of their luck. Certainly the moral code of Queen
Without a Name, while it implies that evil is an autonomous force which
'breeds in the heart of man' (p. 107), simultaneously preaches that the individual is responsible for perseverance through misfortune.

Apart from the Lougandor women, however, few of the characters are
depicted as holding to a calm confidence that the tide of fortune must change.
In the background of the novel there is a perpetual chorus of doom, often
placed in the mouths of the village women who resent, for instance, Toussine's
luck in finding a prosperous husband ('Toussine's more for ornament than for
use . . . They're laughing now, but after laughter comes tears', p. 7), for it
runs counter to the customary wretchedness of their lives and to their belief in
'the futility of the black man's existence' (p. 30). Behind their resentment of
Toussine there is a deep-seated conviction, another heritage of slave days, that
black people cannot expect the dignity, stability or material comforts of married life, to which the white race has exclusive rights: 'Who do they take
themselves for, these wealthy Negroes? Toussine and Jeremiah, with their

two-roomed house, their wooden veranda, their slatted shutters, and their bed with three mattresses and red borders – do they think all these things make them white?' (p. 11). In a society marked by grinding poverty and racial discrimination, the fatalistic acceptance of second-best becomes, in a twisted way, almost a source of pride: 'Madame Brindosier would flap her arms triumphantly, like wings, and declare that life was a torn garment, an old rag beyond all mending' (p. 30). Germain, the doomed outcast, uses the same metaphor: 'My life is torn apart, torn from end to end, and the stuff cannot be mended' (p. 21). This metaphor, which focuses on an aspect of alienation (the inability to control one's own destiny), is later echoed at one of the novel's moments of intense communal emotion, when the people witnessing the last moments of a dying man are 'gazing at the scene unfolding before their eyes and trying to puzzle out a story, a story with a meaning, with a beginning and an end, as you have to do here below if you want to know where you are amidst the [disconnectedness] of men's destinies' (p. 165). For 'disconnectedness' the French text uses the word *décousu*, which is a dressmaking term for a section of a garment that has come unstitched. In a typical example of the way in which Schwarz-Bart picks up and sustains a line of imagery, Queen Without a Name, who sets out to make sense of life for Telumee, is described as 'deft as a seamstress' (p. 31); Olympia, who befriends the solitary Telumee after the death of her grandmother, initiates her into the life of her new neighbourhood 'with the eagerness, delicacy, and detail of an embroideress unfolding her finest work' (p. 135); and Telumee herself, when old, thinks of the dead people she has loved as strands of coloured thread, 'faded' but 'intermingled', among which she tries 'to find the thread of [her] life too' (p. 169). A variation of this image is the metaphor of the spider's web whose interconnected threads are used by Queen Without a Name to represent the bonds of affection and solidarity that hold together the village community of Fond-Zombi (p. 85). When Telumee is rejected by her first lover, Elie, and feels herself sinking into a kind of madness, she believes that there is 'no longer any thread linking [her] cabin to the others' (p. 104). But when circumstances force her to 'untangle [her] life' from Elie's (p. 106), then her neighbours, with warm-hearted concern, set out to show her that there cannot be 'a gap in the weft', and their voices out in the street seem to be 'throwing [her] a thread in the air, throwing a light, light thread toward [her] cabin' (pp. 109–10).

Even the Lougandor women, although unique in their capacity for survival, are no more than human in the way they initially meet disaster. Queen Without a Name withdraws from the world for three years after the loss of her daughter; Victory goes through a long period of drunkenness and griefstricken divorce from reality; and Telumee, repudiated by Elie, is so numbed with pain that she falls into a state of profound depression, becoming 'dead flesh indifferent to the knife' (p. 109). The great difference between them and their neighbours is that they refuse to view their suffering as exclusively the consequence of some racial curse, and strive to accept it, even if only in retrospect, as part of the universal pattern of human life. This philosophy is put forward above all through a number of proverbial sayings by Queen Without a Name, who, with her 'lovely tired eyes that seemed to have scanned the surface of things visible and invisible' (p. 106), is the novel's supreme model of human wisdom. Perhaps for this reason, her opinions are set in a universal frame of reference, applying to all men, not only to those of her race: 'The woman who has laughed is the same one as she who will cry' (p. 104); 'Sorrow exists, and everyone has to take a bit of it on his shoulders' (p. 120); 'When you groan and despair for yourself alone, never forget that somewhere, somewhere on the earth, there's a woman glad to be alive' (p. 80); 'suffering . . . after all is only another way of existing' (p. 117); 'however tall trouble is, man must make himself taller still, even if it means making stilts' (p. 50). Telumee, while always recognizing the specific social and economic handicaps of black West Indian life which arise from the slave past, at the same time refuses the fatalistic belief that the Negro is destined to remain for ever in a condition of misery and inferiority. Like her grandmother, she believes that happiness depends not so much on external circumstances as on the individual's power to stay serene although bound to the revolving wheel of fortune: 'I think of the Negro's life and of its mystery. We have no more marks to guide us than the bird in the air or the fish in the water, and in the midst of this uncertainty we live, and some laugh and others sing' (pp. 168–9); 'They come and go, make and unmake, in the heart of uncertainty, and out of it all comes their splendour' (p. 172).

The main part of *The Bridge of Beyond* is devoted to the story of Telumee's life as a young woman. It falls into several sections which follow the recurrent pattern of rise, fall and recovery – or, to use an image more frequent in the book, the alternating rhythm of 'perfection of [ascent]' (p. 95) and descent 'into the void' (p. 102). After the happy years of her early adolescence, during which she falls deeply in love with her schoolmate and neighbour, Elie, Telumee is forced at the age of 16 to seek employment as a domestic servant in a family descended from the old white plantocracy – the very family whose 'ancestor the White of Whites' was a childhood ogre conjured up for her by Ma Cia, an ogre reputed to 'take a Negro in his arms and squeeze him till his spleen burst' (p. 38). Her fortunes swing upward when Elie, who has been taken on as an apprentice by the sawyer Amboise, manages to build a cabin for himself and Telumee, and comes to take her away from the Desaragne household. But a ferocious rainy season followed by a spell of drought brings hard times to the village of Fond-Zombi. Unable to get work, Elie turns to drink and begins to beat Telumee unmercifully. Eventually her childhood friend Letitia supplants her in his affections, and she is forced to return to her grandmother's house. She recovers from a period of almost intolerable grief only to find that Queen Without a Name has entered her last illness. Moving to the hill of La Folie, she is sustained for a while by the solid affection and the material assistance given her by Ma Cia. But Ma Cia, a 'famous witch' (p. 15), one day disappears, having apparently turned herself into a dog which haunts the clearing outside her former cabin. The market vegetables which Telumee has planted are not yet ready for harvesting, and once more she is forced to seek paid employment, this time in the canefields. She enters upon a new phase of physical and moral wretchedness, from which she is rescued by Amboise, who has loved her from a distance for many years. A long period of happiness follows, which is cut short when Amboise, now a much respected elder, is asked to head a delegation of striking caneworkers, and dies in a jet of scalding steam from the factory boilers, deliberately directed against the strikers as they threaten to tear apart the factory. During their time together, Telumee and Amboise had achieved a perfect harmony, which is described through the novel's river symbolism: 'Our waters had mingled and merged, and little warm currents ran through them all day long' (p. 152). When Amboise dies, Telumee's months of bereavement are like the draining dry of a once abundant watercourse: 'the life flowed out of my body in a continuous stream' (p. 155). But she finally picks up the threads of her existence, continuing to support herself as a small cultivator and as a wise woman or healer, for thanks to the herbal lore passed on to her by Ma Cia, she is 'raised in spite of [herself] to the rank of seer and first-class witch' (p. 156). In this penultimate phase of her life, she adopts a small girl, Sonore, who some years later is beguiled away from her by an old man she has rather reluctantly befriended, the sardonically nicknamed 'Angel Medard'. Forced, like a reincarnation of the doomed Germain, to injure further the person whose friendship he has already betrayed, Angel Medard returns to Telumee's cabin to try and kill her; but he slips and falls against the edge of her table, reopening an old head wound that this time proves fatal. Telumee finds it in her heart to offer him pity and understanding in his last hours; and for this, because 'Angel Medard lived like a dog and [she] made him die like a man' (p. 166), she is given the name of Telumee Miracle. The last chapter of the book brings us back to the old woman standing in her garden, looking back on her life and on what she has learnt from it.

The various events of Telumee's life all serve, in one way or another, to illustrate the Lougandor philosophy of resistance; and while they are all (even the episode of Ma Cia's metamorphosis) recounted in an everyday, matter-of-fact way, they are also simultaneously narrated through a series of images which continually reinforce the dominant theme of survival despite adversity. The trials of Telumee's strength are of two sorts. There are the episodes which belong to the public domain, and which symbolize the oppression of the black West Indian by the white: her work as a servant in the Desaragne household, and the time she spends as a canecutter. And there are her three private and devastating losses: of Elie, of Amboise and of Sonore. The death of her grandmother is a less crushing blow, partly because of the support of Ma Cia, always closely identified with Queen Without a Name, and partly because of the moral comfort her grandmother has given her during the final days of their very close relationship. Her grandmother, in a sense, never leaves her, for 'he who loves you has eyes for you even when his sight is extinguished' (p. 125). This consoling idea of the abiding presence of the dead is, however, evoked only in connection with the exceptional figure of Queen Without a Name – already, in her lifetime, a 'legendary', 'mythical being' (p. 2) – who 'will become a rainbow and leave her mark on the heavens' (p. 123). Telumee's other losses, by death or by desertion, are accompanied by no such consolation. Unlike Toussine, she has no husband to support her through bereavement; and without her grandmother, she sadly realizes that 'the protection of the dead can't replace the voice of the living' (p. 133).

The images of resistance which provide continuity throughout the many phases of Telumee's existence derive principally from the moral teaching of her grandmother, which is generally couched in allegorical terms. As is appropriate in a narrative of country life, these images spring from the world of nature (water, fish, birds, horses, plants) or from the simplest of artefacts (the boat, the drum, the kite). The most detailed of her grandmother's allegories is the tale of the Man Who Tried to Live on Air. Sickened by human wickedness, he refused to admit that life held any beauty at all (an attitude that recalls Queen Without a Name's early criticism of those that 'see the beauty of the world and call it ugly', p 30) and, in a reversal of normal common sense, poured out all his love and indulgence upon his horse. He eventually 'let the horse carry him where it willed', 'even ceased dismounting . . . and slept, ate, and thought' upon its back, till the day came when he wanted to get down but the horse refused to stop: 'The animal had become his master' (p. 50). This tale is told to Telumee and Elie in their childhood; significantly, Elie runs home without waiting to hear the moral, which will come into question once more at the stormy end of his relationship with Telumee: 'If ever you get on a horse, keep good hold of the reins so that it's not the horse that rides you . . . the horse mustn't ride you, you must ride it' (pp. 50-1). The horse, the archetypal phallic animal, is an ancient symbol of unbridled human passion, and has widespread associations with headlong catastrophe, darkness and death. Since Plato, in his *Phaedrus,* equated the unruly horse with lust and its driver with the noble soul, the uncontrollable steed has become a traditional image of reckless, violent behaviour, while the skilful rider is an image of wisdom and self-mastery.[14] Another of Queen Without a Name's stories concerns the clever and defiant bird whose song ('Little huntsman, don't kill me/If you kill me I'll kill you too', p. 47) charms away the menace of the hunter's gun. The bird, another traditional image, represents the human soul, and is linked with the ideas of ascent and transcendence of one's material condition. This image suggestive of the Lougandors' moral superiority is already implicit in the words of the village elder on whom Telumee eavesdrops in her childhood: 'The Lougandors have always liked to fly high, grow wings, raise themselves up' (p. 17). From the bird image springs another motif of *The Bridge of Beyond,* that of the rising song which renders the singer immune to adversity. The animal and human aspects of the motif are fused when Telumee identifies herself with 'the bird that couldn't be hit by any bullet because it invoked life with its song' (p. 48). The third image of resistance that Telumee acquires in her childhood is that of the drum. It comes from her grandmother's friend Ma Cia, who exhorts her to be 'a fine little Negress, a real drum with two sides. Let life bang and thump, but keep the underside always intact' (p. 39).[15] Within a couple of pages it is also associated with the valiant Queen Without a Name, 'a real Negress with two hearts' (p. 41). The drum, symbol of African ancestry, slave resistance, racial solidarity and rhythmic energy, is here endowed with the sound, enduring quality of the tree and of the wooden boat that defies the tempests.

Telumee's stay with the Desaragnes is the initial testing-ground of the moral apprenticeship she has served at her grandmother's side. This is suggested by the image which describes her departure from home: 'Grandmother launched me into the sky, gently, carefully, like a kite one releases, tries for the first time' (p. 58). The kite, like the bird, denotes beauty, fragility and transcendence; its astonishing ability to harness the power of the wind allies it also with the boat that masters the waves. Telumee, young and vulnerable, but with a soaring spirit and a determination to endure and succeed, finds herself cast into an alien element which assails her as slavery once assailed her ancestors. From the start of her employment, and for the first time in her life, she meets with coldness, suspicion, or an offensive condescension. In this white colonial milieu nostalgic for 'the old days, when everything was in its proper place, including the black man' (p. 63), her introductory interview with Madame Desaragne is calculated to intimidate her and to depress any pretensions she may have to personal merit:

'Can you cook?'
'Yes.'
'I mean cook, not just drop a bit of breadfruit into a pan of hot water.' . . .

'Can you iron?'
'Yes.'
'I mean iron, not just thump old rags into shape.' . . .
'. . . One thing must be clearly understood – this is a respectable
house. Have you got a husband or anything?'
'No. I live alone with my grandmother.'
'Good . . . But I warn you, you're only on trial.'   (p. 59)

Madame Desaragne is clearly meant to represent not only the middle-class
West Indian woman of a not-so-distant era, but also the rigid hierarchical
attitudes of the plantocracy and its inability to conceive of the Negro as a
human being: 'You Negroes . . . eat, you drink, you misbehave, and then you
sleep – and that's it' (p. 61). Her curt manner and cold eyes, her readiness to
find fault, her insulting speculations about the private behaviour of the peasantry, her assurances that Telumee is lucky to be having some first-hand contact with civilized white society – ironically designated as 'the only place
around here where they make béchamel sauce' (p. 64) – are all moral assaults
against which Telumee's 'one thought [is] to remain intact' (p. 63), like the
drum, leaving just 'one side to her, the mistress, for her to amuse herself, for
her to thump on' (p. 62). In a variant of the sea/river imagery, she adopts the
tactics of the 'little fish' to which her grandmother had once compared her
(p. 30) and 'glide[s] in and out between the words as if . . . swimming in the
clearest water' (p. 61). Seeing 'through the darkness' her grandmother's smile,
she takes heart anew and sings as she works: 'and when I sang I diluted my pain
. . . and it flowed into the song, and I rode my horse' (p. 60). The same resolute
courage enables her to emerge victorious from an encounter with Monsieur
Desaragne, who had assumed, like his planter ancestors, that she would be
ready to sleep with him for the price of a new dress. The river image is renewed
when she dismisses this victory calmly as 'just one of the little currents that
would ripple my waters before I was drowned in the sea' (p. 73). When she is
finally able to leave the Desaragnes, she is like a bird caught up in a breeze and
filled with 'a desire for flight and space' (p. 75). She has also shown herself to
be 'a little Negress that [is] irreducible, a real drum with two sides' (p. 61).

Her time with Elie, which dominates the central section of the novel, affords
the most memorable illustration of perfect ascent followed by ruinous fall.
Part of its resonance comes from the ways in which Telumee's ascent echoes
the exemplary rise of the young Toussine. As Telumee, rejoicing in Elie's love,
has the splendour of the red balisier or wild banana flower (translated as red
canna, p. 94), the sturdy grace of a stalk of cane (p. 94) and the shimmering
brilliance of a dragonfly (p. 96), so too once did Toussine (pp. 4, 3, 9). As
Toussine and Jeremiah, before their prosperity excited jealousy, were a symbol
of hope and happiness to their neighbours, seeming to bear witness that 'in
spite of all, the race of men is not dead' (p. 6), so the happiness of Telumee and
Elie is seen as living proof that 'a black man is something in this world, after all'
(p. 86). But this apparently promising union is in fact fated to disaster long
before it is formally recognized by Telumee's installation under Elie's roof.
Elie, the motherless child of an unhappy father, has grown up in the belief that
life is a dense forest in which man is likely to lose his way, and that woman's
capacity for sexual love inevitably brings about her ruin. Even in childhood, his
sombre expression of these views causes anguish to Telumee, who sees 'a kind
of smoke perpetually forming inside Elie' which will 'rise up one day and

The Boat and the Tree

destroy him, and [her] with him' (p. 45). He is ultimately situated in the novel's moral scheme alongside Germain and Angel Medard, men foreordained to self-destruction and impelled to lash back hurtfully through those closest to them at the intangible, malevolent fatality of which they feel themselves to be victims.

When Elie leaves school, he is seized with bitterness at the impossibility of realizing any of his early ambitions, and with a wild rage at the prospect of being reduced to canefield work 'on the land of the white men' (p. 54). Amboise, in several ways a saviour-figure in the novel, offers him work as a sawyer in the mountain forests, the old haven of the maroons and the traditional antithesis, in Caribbean history, to the servitude of the plains.[16] Thus he is able to build a home for Telumee and himself; but he approaches their union with an insecure spirit and inauspicious words. The song he sings outside the Desaragnes' house to warn Telumee that their cabin is ready is a melancholy one about a sea creature's plight:

> Why live Odilo
> Just to swim
> And always face down . . .   (p. 74)

The literal words of the French text here, 'always on your belly', echo the earlier doom-laden words of Madame Brindosier to the village women washing clothes in the river: 'Yes, we Negroes of Guadeloupe really are flat on our bellies!' (p. 30), and the washerwomen themselves appear like stranded sea creatures when Queen Without a Name urges the child Telumee away from these 'big whales left high and dry by the sea'.[17] Again, when Elie brings Telumee to her grandmother's house so as to ask formally for her hand, his words are full of self-doubt and foreboding: 'Tomorrow our water may turn into vinegar or into wine, but if it's vinegar, don't curse me, but let your maledictions sleep in the hollow of the [silk-cotton] tree. For tell me, isn't it a common sight, here in Fond-Zombi, the sight of a man being transformed into a devil?' (p. 79). The evocation of the cotton tree, the haunt of ghosts in Caribbean folklore, challenges the happiness of the moment. Queen Without a Name responds to the challenge by summoning up the image of the boat as a warning to Elie: 'If you are shipwrecked, man, she will go down with you.' At the same time, she invokes for Telumee's benefit some new images of resistance. The first of these is a Caribbean extension of the earlier bird image: 'We Lougandors are not pedigree cocks, we're fighting cocks. We know the ring, the crowd, fighting, death. We know victory and eyes gouged out. And all that has never stopped us from living, relying neither on happiness nor on sorrow for existence, like tamarind leaves that close at night and open in the day.'

The closing leaf simile here leads naturally on to a series of comparisons based on the concept of the tree's beauty and durability: 'Sway like a filao, shine like a flame tree, creak and groan like a bamboo, but find your woman's walk and change to a valiant step, my beauty' (p. 80). The *filao* or casuarina, which appears also in Césaire's *Cahier* (p. 92), is a wind-resistant evergreen symbolic of faithfulness. As a timber often used in carpentry, it is appropriate to Telumee's life which is passing into Elie's hands. The flame tree (*flamboyant,* or poinciana, in the French text), Glissant's 'symbol of glory' and 'tree of splendour'(*The Ripening,* pp. 70, 219), was earlier used as the emblem of Telumee's happy childhood friendship with Elie (pp. 44, 53) and also, by both

Simone Schwarz-Bart's *The Bridge of Beyond*

Elie and her grandmother, as a term of endearment for Telumee herself (pp. 45, 67). But it has also already been endowed with less propitious connotations. When Elie and Telumee are about to make love for the first time, she sees in his eyes the same 'gleam of apprehension' which she had noticed 'under the flame tree at school, when he spoke about the virgin forest and the ways that might one day be lost' (p. 77). Earlier, when her grandmother had reluctantly sent her off to work in the Desaragne household, she had said to Telumee, 'It happens, even to the flame tree, to tear the guts out of its belly and fill them with straw' (p. 58) - a painful reprise of a still earlier image expressive of Victory's deep distress when she has to choose between her daughters and her new lover: 'almost always you have to tear out your entrails and fill your belly with straw if you want to enjoy a little walk in the sun' (p. 27). After Elie loses his job and begins to go to pieces, he and his group of drunken, brawling cronies gather regularly at the house of Madame Brindosier, 'already old . . . but still keen on stirring up evil', who crouches nearby 'under a flame tree, her eyes fixed admiringly on the group of bold demons cursing and yelling and boxing on her handsome veranda' (p. 99). Only later in Telumee's life will the *flamboyant* recover its positive value, being opposed, as a symbol of splendour and salvation, to the poisonous manchineel tree (p. 127). The third tree cited by Queen Without a Name, the supple, evergreen bamboo, familiar in oriental art as a graceful symbol of long and happy life,[18] was earlier associated with the loving support that Telumee had brought to her solitary and ageing grandmother, who 'had found a little bamboo stick to serve as a prop to her old bones' (p. 41). In her adolescence, it is again used as an image of Telumee, this time recalling the notion of the courageous music within her and also announcing the theme of sexual love, when the villagers greet her on her days off from her job at the Desaragnes': 'What a fine bamboo in the wind you're growing and what a fine flute you'll make. Whoever plays your music will be a lucky man, eh Elie?' (p. 65). Much later in the novel, the bamboo flute will materialize in the hands of one of the mountain dwellers whom 'the wind of misfortune' has driven up to the heights above La Folie hill, who live 'right in the depths of the forest . . . impregnable, powerful, immortal', and whom the narrative identifies with Telumee herself, 'rejected, irreducible' (p. 128). The motif of transcendence is introduced when, 'standing up' (like Telumee at the end of her life), the aged flute-player greets each rising sun with music that lifts the hearers 'straight up off the earth' (p. 129). The bamboo tree, too, will appear once more in the novel, linked with the dominant motif of the tree that withstands the elements, to express the idea of human growth towards maturity: 'There is a time for carrying a child, a time for bringing it forth, a time for watching it grow and become like a bamboo in the wind' (p. 163).

Elie's fall into despair and violence is linked with the earlier motif of 'West Indian madness' which was introduced in the story of Germain, and which later recurs in the story of the literally brain-damaged Angel Medard. When drought and widespread poverty put an end to the demand for sawyers' work, he gradually stops going up to the mountain forests, the domain of independence, and admits to Telumee his fear that life is moving beyond his control: 'Telumee, we're out at sea amid the currents, and what I wonder is whether I'm going to drown outright' (p. 98). His face, which once 'looked like the prow of a ship, capable of cutting through the wind and resisting life's onslaughts' (p. 78), becomes hollow-cheeked and red-eyed, 'the veins in his temples swollen with rage and helplessness' (p. 99). When he finally forces Telumee to leave

their house, she sees him despairingly as a ship that she is compelled 'to abandon . . . and let it sink alone' (p. 117). Wood and plant symbolism also contributes to the picture of disaster. Telumee thinks of herself as a fallen tree, an
acomat dropped in the dust (p. 106). Elie derisively calls her a 'runaway [liter-
ally, maroon] Negress with no forest to go to' (p. 108). The planks which no
one can afford to buy lie faded and rotting around Elie's cabin, serving as
'nests for termites' (p. 101), symbolizing Elie's separation from the confidence
and self-respect of his working days in the woods, and heralding the time when
he will be a homeless, dying man, 'a mad ant looking for a nest' (p. 170). The
weeds growing unheeded around the cabin, like those around the ruined house
to which Toussine and Jeremiah once retreated, are a traditional symbol of the
Fall from paradise. Here they represent the desolation of spirit that afflicts not
only Elie but Telumee, who once resembled 'a fertile piece of land' (pp. 106-7)
but is now 'like a neglected garden, left to its brambles and thorns' (p. 110).
Never explicitly evoked in this part of the novel, the drum image nonetheless
comes inevitably to mind as Telumee's body is mercilessly battered by Elie,
who vents on her his own self-disgust and his rage at ill fortune. Buying a horse
with the last of their money, he rides around the neighbouring districts stirring
up trouble, the living embodiment of that legendary example of human folly
and disaster, the Man Who Tried to Live on Air. Telumee, in a shift of the
metaphor's application, sees that she has 'mounted a crazy horse, a man
ill-grafted in his mother's womb, who [is] falling to pieces limb by limb'
(p. 106). Only the loving concern of her grandmother and the rest of the
community can eventually succeed in lifting her 'back in the saddle, to hold
[her] horse's bridle with a firm grip'. Here the horse is no longer Elie but once
more life itself, 'that monster without saddle or bridle' (p. 162) whom it is
man's task to master. In a parallel movement, when Elie, the 'raft' on which
she had set out, 'starts to let in water' (pp. 110-11), Telumee is assured by her
sympathetic neighbours that 'she will come to shore' (p. 111), and her grandmother is at the heart of her recovery: 'through all her last days Grandmother
was whistling up a wind for me, to fill my sails so that I could resume my
voyage' (p. 116).

Elie's inability to withstand misfortune is never seen by him as a personal
flaw, but as an unavoidable defeat inflicted on him by an unjust fate which
oppresses the black race: 'Which of you can answer and tell me exactly what we
are hunted by – for we are hunted, aren't we?' (p. 100). This attitude to life
tallies with the theory of 'West Indian madness' as an autonomous, impersonal
agent responsible for all misfortune, but Elie's passive acceptance of the role of
victim conflicts with Queen Without a Name's doctrine of personal resistance,
and is also rejected by Amboise, who says, in reply to Elie's rhetorical question: 'Friend, nothing hunts the Negro but his own heart' (p. 100). Amboise's
answer, however, spreads 'a huge disappointment' through the crowd of
bystanders, a reaction which intimates that the drought-stricken community
needs to find some external scapegoat on which to pin its suffering. Madame
Brindosier claims that 'God's blame is on every living creature' (p. 123); Elie's
father declares that 'the gulf of the hunted ones is in [Elie's] bosom' (p. 102),
and this explanation corresponds to a general belief in the evil eye and the spells
that witches like Ma Cia are asked to raise from the Hunted Ones (p. 125). Like
Roumain's Haitian peasants, the villagers of Fond-Zombi habitually turn to a
supernatural explanation of disaster in order to make acceptable sense of what
would otherwise seem an intolerably absurd universe. Uncertainty about the

value of human existence is a strong minor counterpoint to the major theme of Lougandor courage. It is notably sounded at the wake for Queen Without a Name, in a despairing question: 'To see so much misery, be spat at so often, become helpless and die – is life on earth really right for man?' (p. 123) and in a formal obituary:

> The Queen is dead, gentlemen. Did she ever live?
> We do not know
> And if tomorrow it is my turn, shall I have lived either?
> I do not know
> Come, let's have a drink. (p. 122)

Elie's spiritual disintegration is accompanied by his belief that to be born is to suffer, without possibility of return to the state of peace and safety symbolized by the womb: 'My mother's womb brought me forth, but it will never open for me again' (p. 108). Infuriated by Telumee's strategy in the face of misfortune, which is to take a spiritual 'leap into the air and float' (p. 108), he justifies his physical cruelty to her as an endeavour to teach her 'what it means to be a woman [on earth]' (p. 112). His alienation is suggested by the 'veil . . . murky, shifting, uncertain', which absinthe hangs 'between him and the rest of the world' (p. 105). With him, as with Victory, alcoholism becomes the symptom of inconsolable despondency and of a desire to annihilate the reality of a seemingly hopeless situation. Since his despair and decadence are precipitated by lack of employment opportunities, a case may be made for seeing Elie as a representative of a disadvantaged social class, and a victim of the economic injustices of a colonial society.[19]

It is not for moral weakness that Telumee herself blames Elie in the end, but for a failure of love. In one of the novel's most memorable scenes of understated pain, Elie returns in old age to the district where Telumee is living, and wanders silently back and forth on the far side of her hedge, waiting for a word of recognition that she cannot give; for his betrayal of her, a sorrow she thought she had overcome, still has the power to wound after half a century: 'You have hauled your boat up on the beach, fixed it firmly in the sand, and yet . . . if anyone pricks this old bit of dry wood the blood still comes' (p. 170). Elie had been her partner in a love she thought eternal, the occasion of a 'first flowering' whose supreme delights were compared to the fragrant flowers of the young coconut palm, 'right up in the sky' (pp. 92, 93), and portrayed in the image of the 'two kites set[ting] off on their wanderings through the sky' (p. 78). This second image, of the two fragile man-made objects vertically conquering space, is the symbolic antithesis of the later downward plunge in which Elie's boat sinks in the sea of misfortune. During their union Telumee had depended on him not only for happiness, but for the meaning he seemed to give to her life: 'the feeling I was fulfilling my destiny as a Negress, that I was no longer a stranger on the earth [but] in my right place in life' (p. 83). Under the spell of this love she 'seemed to have entered another world . . . When Elie looked at me, then, only then, I existed, and I knew well that if ever one day he turned away from me I should disappear again into the void' (p. 95). Thus the theme of emotional rejection is tied, in the novel, to the wider theme of the individual's search for identity and for recognition of personal worth. Eyes are an important motif in this context. Telumee's early identity and self-confidence are established by the gaze of her grandmother which recognizes

The Boat and the Tree

her as a 'little crystal glass' able 'to make an old Negress's heart dance' (p. 31), and by the enveloping gaze of Ma Cia which predicts that she 'will rise over the earth like a cathedral' (p. 35). This belief in her own value is imperilled by her situation at the Desaragnes', where she is 'surrounded . . . with piercing, steely, distant eyes under whose gaze' she does not 'exist' (p. 60). She is restored to confidence when she and Elie become lovers and he drinks her up with his eyes (p. 77); but once he turns against her, he beats her 'without a word, without a look' (p. 102), and the 'only light' in his 'cloudy, sad, cold' eyes is 'a flicker of scorn' (p. 105). When he brings Letitia to his cabin and tells Telumee to leave, he does so without looking at her, 'his eyes lost in a dream' (p. 112). His refusal to acknowledge her physical presence is akin to Letitia's simultaneous denial of the 'place' Telumee felt she had found in life at Elie's side: 'Didn't you know the only place on earth that belongs to a Negress is in the graveyard?' (p. 113). Part of her 'madness' is caused by this external denial of the identity she thought she possessed, which reinforces the feelings of loss of self-esteem, isolation and uselessness that spring from her depression. Therefore a vital element in her recovery is the recognition she is accorded by the concern of her grandmother, whose 'lovely eyes' are the first thing to pierce her apathy, and by the attentions and gifts of all her neighbours, who look at her 'with screwed-up eyes, as at one who has come back from far, very far away' and gravely, with ritual, formalized exaggeration, affirm her existence and her worth: 'Here is the [valiant] one, the Negress with seven spleens, four breasts, and two navels' (p. 115).

Telumee's experience of the canefields is the other major descent into the void which imperils her sense of identity and personal integrity. Coming at a time in her life when she has lost in swift succession Elie, her grandmother and Ma Cia, it intensifies her private loneliness and dejection, which are now overlaid with the race memory of slavery, 'heavy with centuries of fear and bitterness' (p. 154). Amid 'the fire of the sky' and the 'infernal prickles' of the cane, she relives the hell known to her ancestors, and reaches the pessimistic conclusion that 'it's here, in the midst of the cane prickles, that a Negro ought to be' (p. 137). Through a brief transitional passage she ceases to 'ride her horse', and herself becomes 'a beast . . . in affliction', bearing a 'yoke', 'pull[ing] and whinn[ying]', 'occup[ying her] place in the world in the midst of the prickles' (pp. 137–9). Her slide towards drunkenness at this time, the only way in which she can escape the weight of affliction, is a sombre echo of the disintegration of Victory and Elie. But along with her awareness of degradation and her enormous physical fatigue, there is also a revelation of the stoical strength of her race and its obstinate will to survive: 'I understood at last what a Negro is: wind and sail at the same time, at once drummer and dancer' (p. 137). These images hark back not only to slavery but also to the more recent past and the strength of the Lougandors, to Toussine who showed herself to be 'the ship, sail, and wind' (p. 14), and to the younger Telumee working for the Desaragnes and learning to 'remain intact under the white man's words and gestures', in a metaphor that suggests resistance both to the torment of her time with Elie and to the bitter suffering of the slave: 'I beat a special drum in my heart, I danced, sang every part, every cry, possession, submission, domination, despair, scorn, and the longing to throw myself off the top of the mountain' (p. 63). And as the bamboo flute, a symbol of Telumee's joy in life, materialized in the hands of the 'irreducible' mountain dweller, so the drum, the emblem of Lougandor resistance, materializes under the strong hands of

Amboise, who follows Telumee into the canefields to save her from solitude and hopelessness, coming like a 'wind' to set afloat her 'ship [which] had run into the sand' (p. 139).

In this society where black men for centuries were denied the right to maintain a family, and where they still have difficulty in assuming the traditional masculine role of provider and protector, Amboise stands out as the novel's only representative of male strength, responsibility and authority. Early on he is compared to 'a tall, gaunt, gnarled tree that had already let fall its fruits' (p. 77), a metaphor in keeping with his sawyer's trade and in harmony with the narrative's persistent theme of the tree that endures and survives. His choice to work in the forests of 'the farthest hills of Guadeloupe, [far] from the canefields, far from any white face' (p. 151), links him with the figures of Queen Without a Name and Ma Cia, who have fled society (like the maroons of old) to live in the woods, and who exemplify the same maturity and courage as does Amboise. Elie, in drunken anger, calls him 'an acomat fallen among rotten timber' (p. 100) at the time when the battered Telumee, too, thinks herself an acomat fallen in the dust (p. 106). But the acomat is a tree of robust splendour: it is Elie, not Amboise, who has fallen, and Telumee survives to 'forget [she] was a fallen acomat, and . . . feel the beauty of [her] own two woman's legs again' (p. 116). The wood motif is repeated in the happy years of her life with Amboise, when the 'eternal smoke . . . from the bonfires of green acomats' (p. 146) epitomizes the quiet, enduring harmony of their relationship and their feeling of oneness with the soil they cultivate and the surrounding woods. Telumee had once seen Amboise merely as 'Elie's shadow' (p. 126); when he comes to join her in the canefields, the song he sings, which 'rise[s] into the air' in defiance of her bitter acceptance of defeat, symbolically draws a distinction between Elie's weakness, which belongs to the past, and his own energy and resolution, which belong to the present:

> In those days there lived a woman
> A woman who had a house
> Behind her house was a Blue Pool
> A Blue Whirlpool
> Many, many are the suitors
> But they must bathe in the Pool
> Bathe for the woman
> Who will win her? . . .
> The young men who bathed there
> Are in the estuary, drowned.   (pp. 139–40)

Deliberately summoning up the memory of that youthful idyll in which Telumee and Elie once bathed together in the Blue Pool, a deep basin of the river of Beyond 'where all the world's bustle died away' (p. 54), Amboise's song employs the technique of fairy-tale to transform the real pool into a whirlpool. It becomes the archetypal trial of strength for those who aspire to the hand of the princess, and, as in fairy-tales, the penalty of failure is death. The death by water links the song with the familiar theme of the boat that must survive or founder in the sea of life. Elie is the 'young man' whom Telumee has already watched 'drowning' (p. 101); the song challenges her to put his defection behind her and admit the merit of her new suitor, who for her sake is voluntarily enduring another trial in 'the fire of the canes' (p. 141). The tears that Telumee sheds are for the truth of the song and the grief of the past, but it

The Boat and the Tree

is at the same time a moment of renaissance, marked by the recurrent motif of her own rising song: 'suddenly, I don't know how, my voice escaped me and soared high above the others, piercing, lively, and gay, as in the old days' (p. 140). This renaissance is formally celebrated on the night when Amboise comes to live with her and his drumming inspires their guests to dance away the anguish of their daily existence, 'lifting [their] lives to the skies and giving them back all clear and cleansed of impurity'. The final dancer is Telumee, reluctant at first to yield to the drum's invitation, but at last feeling 'the waters of the drum flow over [her] heart and give it life again' (p. 145).

The union of Telumee and Amboise is marked by a sense of natural, joyous accord already foreshadowed by the words of Queen Without a Name, who had once set against Elie's cruelty to Telumee the promise of a better future with Amboise: 'the day will come when you'll put on your dress of life again . . . Already there's a man who . . . loves you as a sensible man loves a fertile piece of land, which will nourish and support him to beyond the grave' (pp. 106–7). As hillside cultivators, they spend most of their time together in a garden which is a small, private paradise, where everything they plant in the rich black soil flourishes, and the age-old gesture of 'setting the seeds in the womb of the earth' leads to the 'celebration [of] the continuation of life, life in all its forms, and especially those no one can buy, such as a satisfied belly visited by all the fruits of the earth' (pp. 146, 148). Amboise is entering his fifties when he comes to Telumee, and the hardships of his life have left him not embittered (like Elie) but saddened by the knowledge of his race's suffering. Picking up the theme of moral responsibility, his conversations with Telumee are imbued with a conviction that slavery has crippled the black West Indian's capacity for harmonious self-fulfilment: 'he said enemy hands had got hold of our soul and shaped it to be at war with itself' (p. 152). Yet he has faith, like Queen Without a Name, that suffering is not eternal: 'we have been beaten for a hundred years, but I tell you, girl, we have courage for a thousand' (p. 151). His consent to head the delegation of strikers marks his steadfast commitment to the destitute blacks toiling on the plain below his own small but fruitful garden. More clearly than Elie's ruin, his death in the yard of the sugar factory is an indictment of all that slavery and the canefields represent in Caribbean history. The jet of scalding steam which kills him, a combination of the elemental hostility of air, water and fire, is a symbolic reminder that although the fire of slavery is out, the black man must still 'play . . . in [its] embers' (p. 38).

The final cycle of Telumee's existence begins with her emergence from mourning, 'like a kite extricated from the topmost branches', to accept the charge of the child Sonore and feel life, 'something inaudible and long forgotten, stirring' inside herself (p. 157). Like her grandmother's planting of the orange seed, Telumee's adoption of Sonore signals a renewed willingness to be involved in the affairs of the living, and a new hope for the future, symbolized by the leaves put forth by Sonore, her 'young shoot' (p. 158). At the same time her reputation as a healer grows, and people climb up to her cabin to put in her hands 'the grief, confusion, and absurdity of their lives, bruised bodies and bruised souls' (p. 157). It is the combination of her roles as adoptive mother and village wise woman that makes her vulnerable to Angel Medard, the man 'born to evil', whose 'dancing brain' (p. 160) is the novel's ultimate illustration of the idea of 'West Indian madness'. Medard is also, in a sense, a reincarnation of Elie who plays a similar devastating part in Telumee's life: it is significant that at the moment when she meets Medard, a woman is singing in the distance the story of a deserted lover. Like Elie, he complains of the 'unpredictable assaults of life' (p. 162) and resents Telumee's apparent talent for happiness. Because Sonore pities his poverty and isolation (like Germain, he is an outcast regarded with suspicion and loathing by everyone), Telumee offers him a place of refuge, only to discover later on that he has persuaded Sonore that Telumee is a witch who has stolen her from her real mother in order to enslave her. He helps the child to flee to her native village, initiating a new phase of fall in Telumee's life and demonstrating to her that 'the door of grief is never shut' (p. 163). Then like a '[wind] of madness' (p. 164) – a comparison which recalls the novel's original French title and the earlier image of Telumee as a wind-resistant tree – he returns and threatens, as Elie had once threatened, to send her hurtling down to death. The parallel between Medard and Elie is thrown into prominence here by the reactivation of the fighting cock image, which Queen Without a Name had invoked (p. 80) in response to Elie's warning that he might make Telumee unhappy: Telumee now asserts her confidence that 'however fiercely life use[s] its spurs it [will] never pluck out [her] feathers' (p. 164). A further link is provided by the pair of scissors which she buys in her bitter desire for revenge: it recalls the advice of her grandmother's neighbours after Elie had thrown her out, 'Don't go buying a pair of scissors to stick in his heart, for that fellow's not worth a pair of scissors' (p. 115). Here her old canefield comrade Olympia makes the same type of assessment: 'Telumee, dear friend, don't soil your hands for an empty bubble. Medard is nothing, less than nothing' (p. 164).

But these figurative expressions – 'an empty bubble', 'less than nothing' – have wider implications, for, like the villagers' later declaration that 'Angel Medard lived like a dog' (p. 166), they connect the individual decline of Medard (and of Elie and Germain) to the decline of the black race in the past, when the slave was like 'a dog . . . tied up [and] bound to be whipped' (p. 38). They bring back, too, the many expressions of pessimism about the value of present-day black life which are scattered throughout the narrative: 'What is a woman? Nothing at all' (p. 14); 'A Negro is always sick' (p. 86); 'The Negro's heart is a dry land no water will improve' (p. 100); 'We are almost nothing on the earth' (p. 124); 'We [are] Negroes in the dirt' (p. 147); 'Where there's a white man, that's where the light is' (p. 149). Thus Medard, the homeless exile 'wet as a dog' (p. 161) in his leaking bamboo shelter, the man whom children stone and whose skull was laid open by his own brother, may finally be seen to represent the orphaned, alienated, godforsaken Negro whose soul has been shaped by 'enemy hands' to be 'at war with itself' (p. 152). He is the 'wounded bird' (p. 160) whose song could not charm the hunter, the 'fish' which, even under water, cannot escape from the cruelty of a world bent on destroying the bright bubbles its gills send up into the sun (p. 166). And so, when she sees him dying of his self-inflicted wound, Telumee forgives him as her murdered father had forgiven the injury inflicted on him by Germain, 'because his will was no longer his own' (p. 23). Offering Medard the tolerance that she has continually extended to all the alienated, she compares him to the crow, a bird which European tradition has generally associated with evil, death and the Devil.[20] Since it was because of its black colour, as well as its habit of scavenging, that the crow or raven was invested with these negative attributes, it may be seen here as a symbol not only of Medard, but of the black race in general as the victim of European colour prejudice. As the crow is also a symbol of solitude, it is doubly appropriate as an image for Medard the outsider, malevolent yet pitiful, whom Telumee comes to regard as having been cruelly isolated by a failure of sympathy and understanding on the part of others: men say that the crow speaks 'a foreign language', when the truth is that it speaks its own language which 'we do not understand' (p. 165).

The story of Telumee and Medard, a microcosm of the larger structure of ascent and fall, renews the tree imagery of *The Bridge of Beyond* by contrasting Medard, the fallen manchineel (p. 166), with Telumee, the *flamboyant,* trees which have earlier been proposed to the reader (p. 127) as antithetical symbols of ruin and salvation. This last cycle in the life of Telumee prepares the way for the conclusion of the book, where Telumee will finally become 'like the tree called Resolute, on which it is said the whole globe and all its calamities could lean' (p. 96) – the 'finest tree' of the forests, 'the one that is cut down the most often' but that shares with the black race the strength 'to be born again' (pp. 169–70). The dignity of her new name, Telumee Miracle, not only completes the pattern begun by her grandmother, Queen Without a Name, but also redeems and honours the forgotten women of Guadeloupe who have dreamed and suffered in the past: 'all the women lost before their time, broken, destroyed', at whose wakes the mourners tried in vain 'to think of the name, the true name they had deserved to bear' (p. 52). Built upon the paradoxical 'splendour of human uncertainty' (p. 172), *The Bridge of Beyond* promises salvation through individual courage, and celebrates the role of women in the Caribbean struggle for survival.

Notes

1 Words which occur in the French text of *Pluie et vent sur Télumée Miracle* (Paris: Editions du Seuil, 1972), but which are not literally rendered in the Barbara Bray translation, are indicated by square brackets.

2 See Roger Toumson, *'Pluie et vent sur Télumée Miracle:* Une rêverie encyclopédique: sa structure, son projet idéologique', in *Textes Etudes et Documents,* No. 2, ed. Roger Toumson (Paris: Éditions Caribéennes, 1979), pp. 30, 34, 39–40; Ernest Pépin, *'Pluie et vent sur Télumée Miracle:* le jeu des figures répétitives dans l'œuvre', in *Textes Etudes et Documents,* No. 2, pp. 76, 80–1, 97–8; Bridget Jones, introduction to *The Bridge of Beyond,* trans. by Barbara Bray (London: Heinemann, 1982), p. x; Beverley Ormerod, 'L'Aïeule: figure dominante chez Simone Schwarz-Bart', *Présence Francophone* 20 (1980), pp. 100–2.

3 See Toumson, p. 32, for comments on the solar imagery associated with Toussine's ascent.

4 Don Cameron Allen discusses early moral interpretations of the *Odyssey* in *Mysteriously Meant: The Rediscovery of pagan symbolism and allegorical interpretation in the Renaissance* (Baltimore: Johns Hopkins Press, 1970), pp. 90–8.

5 Guy de Tervarent, *Attributs et symboles dans l'art profane 1450-1600* (Geneva: Droz, 1958), cols 282-3, 'Navire'.

6 See Durand, pp. 285–6.

7 'Interview avec Simone et André Schwarz-Bart: Sur les pas de Fanotte', in *Textes Etudes et Documents,* No. 2, p. 20 (my translation).

8 See, for example, Maryse Condé, *La Civilisation du bossale* (Paris: L'Harmattan, 1978), pp. 42-3, on the Ti-Jean cycle of tales.

9 These views and the term 'centre-post' (an intriguing instance of Schwarz-Bart's use of wood imagery) occur in the interview cited above, *Textes Etudes et Documents,* No, 2, p. 17.

10 Jean Bernabé discusses the Creole origin of this phrase and its social context in 'Contribution à l'étude de la diglossie littéraire: Le cas de *Pluie et vent sur Télumée*

Miracle', in *Textes Etudes et Documents*, No. 2, pp. 116–17.

11 Bernabé (p. 126) draws a parallel between Queen Without a Name's remark and the less compassionate Guadeloupean proverb, 'A tied dog is good for beating'.

12 The image resembles another proverb, cited by Condé in *La Civilisation du bossale* (p. 30): 'In front of the knife, the chicken is never right'. Condé remarks on the tendency of many Creole proverbs to reflect the physical aggression which characterized the slave's universe.

13 Interview in *Textes Etudes et Documents*, No. 2, p. 18 (my translation). See also the discussion of the theme of madness by Toumson, pp. 58–60.

14 See, for example, Durand, pp. 78–88, and Rowland, pp. 103–12.

15 For the Creole origins of the expression see Bernabé, p. 118, where it is suggested that the drum is symbolic not only of resistance, but of 'dream and the absolute'.

16 Bridget Jones (introduction to *The Bridge of Beyond*, p. viii) points out the symbolic connection between the trade of sawyer and the 'positive values of freedom and independence' attached to wood and the forest.

17 On the use of the fish image in an earlier novel by Simone and André Schwarz-Bart, see Beverley Ormerod, '*Un plat de porc aux bananes vertes*', *Essays in French Literature* 8 (1971), pp. 86, 89–90.

18 See Garai, p. 105.

19 See Bridget Jones (p. xi), and Maryse Condé, *La Parole des femmes: Essai sur des romancières des Antilles de langue française* (Paris: L'Harmattan, 1979), p. 35, where both Elie and Amboise are considered to be victims of the social structure of a dominated country.

20 On the symbolism of the crow and raven, see Garai, pp. 68–9, and Gertrude Grace Sill, *A Handbook of Symbols in Christian Art* (London: Cassell, 1976), pp. 25, 35. The source of the image is patristic, and derives from the story of the two birds which Noah sent out of the Ark. The white dove, which returned to the Ark, was seen as a symbol of virtue; the black raven's failure to return was interpreted as symbolic of the expulsion of evil from the Ark. See for example *Patrologia Latina* 14, pp. 411–12 (St Ambrose).

Conclusion

'Who are we and what?'
(*Cahier*, p. 56).

When, in 1939, Césaire first defined the Martinican condition as one of alienation, he linked the notion of a spiritual Fall not only with the loss of Africa, but also with the present-day Martinican's estrangement from the society in which he now lives: 'In this disowning town, this strange crowd which does not gather, does not mingle . . . this desolate crowd which rejects everything expressive, affirmative or free' (*Cahier*, p. 39). And beyond the immediate predicament of Martinique, he saw the entire region as beset by the problem of establishing its national identity, the 'archipelago arched with anxiety as though to deny itself' (p. 52). The *Cahier* assumed, therefore, the existence of a West Indian public which was asking its creative writers to fulfil certain unspoken needs: tell us who we are; show us our reality; restore and explain our past; offer us your vision of our future.

Césaire's response was to diagnose a psychological wound, inflicted both during and after slavery through the imposition of an alien culture which had systematically denied the value of anything that was of African origin. By accepting this European disparagement of his own racial and cultural worth, the black West Indian had for centuries passively assented to his colonial status of social, economic and political inferiority. Spiritual healing could, however, be achieved by the establishment of an independent West Indian identity, which the *Cahier* evoked through images of death and rebirth:

> I say Hurrah! my grandfather is dying,
> Hurrah! little by little the old negritude is
> turning into a corpse.   (p. 86)

> I break open the yolk-bag
> that separates me from myself
> I force the great waters that gird me with blood.   (p. 62)

Only then would the restoration of paradise be accomplished at both the personal and the national level. Because the brutal historic separation from Africa was fundamental to Césaire's diagnosis of Caribbean alienation, he viewed the rediscovery of African roots as an essential prerequisite for the assumption of a West Indian identity. This is suggested in the *Cahier* (p. 56) when the theme of search for identity, associated with the metaphor of the deeply rooted tree, is juxtaposed with African images evocative of power and domination:

> Who are we and what? Admirable
> question!
> By looking at trees
> I have become a tree

Conclusion

and this long tree's feet
have dug great hollows of poison in the earth . . .
by thinking of the Congo
I have become a Congo noisy with forests
and rivers
where the whip cracks like a great
banner . . .
where the lightning of anger hurls a green
axe   . . .

Césaire's profound emotional attachment to Africa is reiterated in his later work through the image of the 'widowed' Caribbean island, severed from the primordial continent to which it still cries out.[1]

The six novelists who have been discussed in the present study may be seen as accepting Césaire's assertions about the causes of West Indian alienation, while differing somewhat from him in their prescriptions for its cure. The Haitian writers, Roumain and Alexis, are preoccupied with the idiosyncratic situation of a country which, despite its long independence, remains wretchedly poor and politically oppressed. Although isolated from its Caribbean neighbours, Haiti is still, like them, assailed by the class and colour divisions of the old plantation system. Actively committed to Marxism, concerned about the retrograde aspects of voodoo, and anxious to eradicate ignorance, apathy and crime, both Roumain and Alexis hold out the promise of salvation through self-education and collective revolutionary action. Involved with a society in which African cultural survivals are much more evident than in any other Caribbean territory, and a republic where independence, won through a bitterly fought war, encouraged the growth of a national consciousness many decades ago, neither Roumain nor Alexis manifest Césaire's intense yearning for an unknown ancestral continent, and neither is primarily concerned with the search for identity. Both authors, however, fully share Césaire's desire to speak on behalf of 'misfortunes which have no mouth, [and] freedoms which break down in the prison-cell of despair' (*Cahier*, p. 50).

On the other hand, the quest for a personal, social, racial or national identity is an important theme in the four novels from Martinique and Guadeloupe, and accurately reflects the anxieties and ambivalences of these islands with regard to their quasi-colonial position as Overseas Departments of France. They are culturally bombarded with French attitudes and values, yet historically and racially linked with the Third World, and in particular with the independent Caribbean states which are their immediate neighbours. Most French West Indian intellectuals view their countries' continued dependency on France as a major contributory factor to alienation, and many of them, along with political militants, press for independence and for a West Indian cultural orientation to replace the existing French one. Voting trends, however, would seem to indicate considerable resistance at grassroots level to the idea of exchanging Departmental status (with its accompanying financial advantages) for the uncertainties and material difficulties that independence would bring.[2] While the issue of their national identity remains unresolved, Martinican and Guadeloupean writers are perpetually obliged to take France into account in any attempt to define and describe the condition of their own fellow countrymen. It is significant that each of these four novelists invokes the memory of the sugar estate and uses it as a symbol of France's ongoing ascendancy over her Caribbean territories. Even today, when the Martinican and Guadeloupean sugar industries are all but dead, their

Conclusion

adverse economic effect on the majority of the population remains evident. The cane monoculture gave rise to a consumer society accustomed to live on imported French products, paid for by subsidies also originating from the metropolis. No local, self-supporting productivity has ever existed on any significant scale; no concerted creative effort has ever arisen upon which an independent identity might have been built.[3]

The plantation novels of Zobel and Lacrosil correspond closely to the fallen universe described by Césaire: 'life flat on its face, miscarried dreams and nowhere to put them, the river of life listless in its hopeless bed' (*Cahier*, p. 46). At varying social levels, the inhabitants of Lacrosil's Pâline survive by confusing dream with reality: the black labourers hope to find the legendary cache of gold, the mulatto workers aspire to whiteness, the former white master longs to turn back the clock to a time when his supremacy was unchallenged. In Black Shack Alley, in Petit-Bourg and in the servants' huts below Route Didier, the child José is always governed by the rigid class hierarchies laid down by the sugar estate, from which he will never succeed in rescuing his grandmother – the act whereby he had hoped to fulfil his 'dreams of becoming a man' (*Black Shack Alley*, p. 137). Schwarz-Bart's Telumee, though she possesses the moral strength to affirm that 'all suffering, even the prickles in the canefields, are part of the glory of man' (*The Bridge of Beyond*, p. 169), is wounded through her own men's vulnerability to the ordeals inflicted on them by a social and economic system which is heavily weighted against those who are both poor and black. The collective sense of orphanhood and bereavement which pervades Telumee's environment recalls Césaire's elegy for 'Siméon Piquine,' who had never known his father or mother; whom no town hall had ever registered, and who all his life went searching for his name' (*Cahier*, p. 81). In each of these novels, the characters are portrayed as endeavouring to set aside the unacceptable destiny which life appears to have allotted them, and to attain a more fortunate place in the world. Only Telumee, whose happiness is less dependent on exterior circumstances than are the needs of the other persons depicted, is able to define and accept her own identity and to say wholeheartedly at the end of her life, 'If I could choose it's here in Guadeloupe that I'd be born again, suffer and die' (*The Bridge of Beyond*, p. 2).

Glissant's *The Ripening* differs from these three other novels in that the protagonist's personal development is secondary to the situation of post-war Martinique, 'newly awakened to [its] own identity' (p. 18). The earliest of Glissant's novels, it is also, despite its sombre conclusion, the most optimistic in its message. Like Roumain's *Masters of the Dew*, it postulates the salvation of an endangered community through the freeing of waters, which is a metaphor for the dynamic gestures of reform that can be accomplished by the exceptional and dedicated individual. The weight it attaches, through the figure of Papa Longoué and the symbolic importance of the canefields, to the recording of black Caribbean history is akin to the *Cahier*'s affirmation that the West Indian past, far from being merely an adjunct or footnote to European history, exists in its own right and waits to be rediscovered by those to whom it belongs:

> At the end of the small hours these countries whose
> past is uninscribed on any stone, these roads without
> memory, these winds without a log.
> Does that matter?

Conclusion

> We shall speak. We shall sing. We shall shout.
> Full voice, great voice, you shall be our good and our
> guide. (*Cahier*, pp. 54–5)

Glissant, like his St Lucian contemporary Derek Walcott (whose poetry is similarly mindful of the history-orphaned islands and the ancestors lost because 'the crossing of water has erased their memories'),[4] seeks to rouse his readers to awareness of an essential yet neglected past. He believes that unless the failure of collective memory is remedied, the West Indian will be forever overcome by 'the vertigo of time' (*Le Discours antillais*, p. 435), forever unable to 'throw light on that portion of night that stir[s] within him' (*La Case du commandeur*, p. 39), forever prevented from taking root in his own country and assuming his true identity. It is towards this goal of restoring national memory that *Le Quatrième Siècle* is directed, through its attempt to re-create the daily existence of obscure ancestors who would otherwise be recalled only in an increasingly fragile and unreliable oral tradition.[5]

Because French Caribbean writers from Césaire onwards have been so profoundly concerned with definitions of alienation and prescriptions for social change, there has been a persistent tendency among literary critics to assess their work according to sociological and political criteria, rather than on purely artistic grounds. Césaire, for example, has been indicted for avoiding a direct confrontation with the concrete problems of mid-twentieth-century Martinique by taking refuge in the repeated evocation of past slavery and in a vague, romantic vision of 'future reconciliation'.[6] Roumain has been accused of writing a 'bourgeois novel' which fails to raise the issue of agrarian reform and which is more concerned with the immediate, selfish needs of an individual village than with the wider necessity of mobilizing the Haitian peasantry to take action against the oppressive landowning class.[7] The symbolical importance which he attaches to the *coumbite* has been deemed insufficient as an adaptation of the Marxist message, too mild and too limited in scope to bring about any effective reconstruction of Haitian society.[8] At the other end of the spectrum, the political stance of Alexis' *Comrade General Sun* has been deplored as 'a striking example of the unrealistic literature of socialist realism', passionate in its denunciation of injustices in Haiti, but wilfully indifferent to any similar denunciation of the Soviet Union.[9] Simone Schwarz-Bart has been dismissed as too apolitical and superficial, too much given to the use of picturesque local colour and too neglectful of the problem of alienation.[10] Lacrosil's novels have been seen as humourless attempts to settle old scores with a France from whose cultural influence the author cannot succeed in freeing herself; while Zobel, whose autobiographical hero moves away from the Creole, matriarchal society of Black Shack Alley to the male-dominated, French-oriented world of the *lycée* in Fort-de-France, has been viewed as unconsciously rejecting the peasant culture and the West Indian identity which he ostensibly celebrates.[11] The redemptive theme of Glissant's *The Ripening* and his 'utopian' figure of the irreducible maroon *Négateur* have been regarded as somehow less authentic than the hero-less world of *Malemort* which stresses the physical and moral destitution of Martinique.[12]

This type of critical appraisal, which requires the poet or novelist to toe some socio-political party line (a line which inevitably varies from critic to critic), tends to overlook the fact that there is an essential distinction between the creative writer on the one hand, and the sociologist or politician on the other.

Conclusion

All three may operate within the same social context; but while the last two are expected to deal in scientific fact and exercise practical skills, the creative writer has traditionally been free to devise fictions which are in keeping with the truth of his environment as he sees it. Each of the novelists considered in this study has devised an image or set of images which represents a particular, personal vision of the Caribbean social context. This personal vision may not correspond with that of the reader; but in every case, the novelist has endeavoured through metaphor and analogy to communicate to a disparate public the strength and validity of his or her perception of the West Indies.[13] In different ways, each may be seen as exemplifying the attitude expressed by Edouard Glissant: 'If you don't love the country in which you live, no one will love it for you . . . If you don't suffer from loving the land on which you set your foot, no one will suffer in your place.'[14]

The French Caribbean novel of recent years has continued to be concerned with the issues of dispossession and alienation. In Martinican and Guadeloupean writing, these terms denote the psychological complexes and the socio-economic deprivations which are the legacy of past slavery. In Haitian literature they also have a horrifying literal relevance to the material condition of a people currently governed by brutal intimidation. The Haitian writer, who is not at liberty to make open criticism of the Duvalier regime, may still do so indirectly through the traditional technique of political allegory. This is the case, for example, in Franketienne's *Les Affres d'un défi* (1979), where a fearful, captive population is exploited by a voodoo priest who uses his magic powers for evil purposes, turning men into zombies to work as slaves in his rice-fields. The social order established by the tyrant seems as 'immutable [and] irreversible' as once did the old plantation system: 'Nothing, nothing at all will ever change for you. You will always remain empty-handed.' But at last, in a movement of collective revolt reminiscent of the solutions offered by Roumain and Alexis, the zombies are freed and join with the local peasantry 'to follow one road only, the road to freedom for everybody'.[15]

Outside Haiti, the concepts of dispossession and alienation are still closely linked with the search for a definition of identity. In this context, some recent novels have renewed the Césairean theme of a return to ancestral Africa. Their common message, however, is ultimately that the surface resemblances of race and colour between West Indians and Africans are accompanied by profound differences in social and cultural attitudes. Rather than looking to Africa for a definition of his identity, the West Indian must look to his own country – a conclusion which was pungently expressed several decades ago in the popular verse of the Jamaican Louise Bennett:

> Go a foreign, seek yuh fortune,
> But noh tell nobody sey
> Yuh dah-go fe seek yuh homelan
> For a right deh so yuh deh![16]

The quest for historical roots takes Maryse Condé's Guadeloupean heroines to Africa 'to try and see what there was before';[17] but this pilgrimage brings only unhappiness and a deep sense of frustration. In Simone Schwarz-Bart's *Ti Jean L'horizon* (1979), an epic fiction built upon the notion of 'the precariousness of the Negro's implantation in the soil of Guadeloupe', the negative attitude of the African grandfather who stubbornly refuses to be 'grafted' upon alien soil is opposed to the optimistic attitude of his grandson who believes that West Indians, 'the branch cut from the tree', will 'one day put out roots, and then a trunk and new branches with leaves and fruit . . . fruit which [will] not resemble any other'.[18]

The problem of spiritual rootlessness has also been explored in two picaresque novels by Martinican writers, Vincent Placoly and Xavier Orville. Placoly's Marcel Gonstran leads a life characterized by sexual promiscuity and emotional sterility, unable to find contentment outside his native country, yet even there feeling himself 'a stranger to everything, a stranger everywhere'.[19] The seven successive names which Orville's protagonist adopts are a reminder of the loss of individuality sustained by the slave in the dehumanizing conditions of plantation life, and a metaphor for present-day confusion about identity: 'I was always waiting to reach myself, to find myself, to name myself at last.'[20] In a more tragic register, Edouard Glissant's latest novel, La Case du commandeur (1981), represents Martinique as an island where the loss of ancestral memories means that 'no one can find in his near or distant past any reason whatsoever for living [in harmony] with his neighbour' (p. 186), and where individual anxieties and social conflicts may never permit the forming of 'that one body whereby we might begin to enter upon our span of earth' (p. 15). The prevailing mood of this novel is one of collective helplessness, and its recurrent motif of psychiatric disturbance becomes a metaphor for the state of an alienated nation.

The French West Indian islands, however, are increasingly participating in the formation of socio-cultural links between the various Caribbean territories; and many intellectuals view these new regional affiliations as possibly the most effective remedy for national alienation. Glissant has strongly advocated the 'reinsertion of French-speaking West Indians in the West Indies' as a measure which should be taken against the destructive historical 'Balkanization' of the islands.[21] His Discours antillais (p. 179) points out that through business and leisure activities, collaboration in research or professional and university pursuits, reciprocal sporting ties, and mutual aid during natural disasters, 'Guadeloupe and Martinique are daily obliged to enter into Caribbean history'. This vision of a shared Caribbean culture, transcending linguistic and geographic barriers, was already evident in Alexis' L'Espace d'un cillement (p. 112) which looked forward to the birth of 'the great Caribbean Federation' that would some day unite the energies of 'men of the same race, the same blood, the same convictions, who have endured the same suffering, the same slavery, who have fought the same battles'. It is echoed by a younger Haitian writer, Jean Métellus, who voices through one of his fictional characters in the novel Jacmel au crépuscule (1981) the opinion that 'Haiti can no longer live alone', and must form an alliance with her Caribbean neighbours if she is ever to overcome her internal handicaps and realize her rich potential.[22] Seeking the lost ancestral Track of the Time Before, the bereaved descendant of Glissant's Négateur strives also to make contact with the islands planted in the surrounding sea, invisible, protective presences which hold the promise of a future harmony between a Martinican and a West Indian national consciousness.[23] In similar fashion, the Guadeloupean novelist Daniel Maximin links the growth of political awareness in his own island with the development of a Caribbean cultural identity: 'It is for us to invent our own future, without expecting too much of the African past or of the European present . . . Do not all West Indians form one single civilization?'[24] And so a wider, fraternal quest

Conclusion

for Caribbean salvation has emerged from Derek Walcott's 'one theme':[25]

The bowsprit, the arrow, the longing, the lunging heart –
the flight to a target whose aim we'll never know,
vain search for one island that heals with its harbour
and a guiltless horizon, where the almond's shadow
doesn't injure the sand. There are so many islands!

Notes

1 See, for example, the poem 'Dit d'errance' in Césaire's *Cadastre* (Paris: Editions du Seuil, 1961), pp. 89-92.

2 A recent survey suggests that the main reasons for popular opposition to independence are the belief that Martinique and Guadeloupe lack the capital and resources needed for self-development, and the fear of losing the job opportunities which Paris at present offers to a large number of immigrants from the Overseas Departments. See Claudie Beauvue-Fougeyrollas, *Les Femmes antillaises* (Paris: L'Harmattan, 1979).

3 The notion of Martinique as a non-productive consumer society is discussed in Edouard Glissant's *Le Discours antillais*: see, for example, pp. 174-9. A similar view of Trinidad is advanced in V.S. Naipaul's essay 'Michael X and the Black Power Killings in Trinidad', in *The Return of Eva Peron* (London: André Deutsch, 1980), pp. 55, 70.

4 Derek Walcott, *Another Life* (London: Jonathan Cape, 1973), p. 143.

5 See Maryse Condé's analysis of this novel as a 'version of the myth of origin' in 'Survivance et mort des mythes africains dans la littérature des Antilles francophones', *L'Afrique littéraire et artistique* 54-5 (1979-80), pp. 60-2. On the strengths and weaknesses of folk memory, see Michael Craton, 'Perceptions of Slavery: A Preliminary Excursion into the Possibilities of Oral History in Rural Jamaica', in *Old Roots in New Lands: Historical and Anthropological Perspectives on Black Experiences in the Americas*, ed. Ann M. Pescatello (Westport, Connecticut: Greenwood Press, 1977), 263-83.

6 Jacques André, *Caraïbales: Etudes sur la littérature antillaise* (Paris: Editions Caribéennes, 1981), p. 13.

7 Jean-Claude Fignolé, *Sur 'Gouverneurs de la rosée'* (Port-au-Prince: Editions Fardin, 1974), pp. 75-7.

8 Jean-Pierre Makouta-Mboukou, *Jacques Roumain: Essai sur la signification spirituelle et religieuse de son œuvre* (Lille: Atelier reproduction de thèses, Université de Lille III, 1978), p. 380.

9 Claude Roy, 'Clarté d'un soleil noir', *Le Nouvel Observateur* 909 (9-16 April 1982), pp. 52-3.

10 See the discussion of these criticisms in *Textes Etudes et Documents*, No. 2, ed. Toumson, pp. 21-2, 75-6; and compare Maryse Condé's early review of *The Bridge of Beyond*, 'Pluie et vent sur Télumée Miracle de Simone Schwarz-Bart', *Présence Africaine* 84 (1972), pp. 138-9, with her later assessment in 'Survivance et mort des mythes africains', pp. 62-4.

11 See André, p. 16 (Lacrosil) and pp. 55-64, 104-8 (Zobel).

12 André, pp. 17, 129, 163.

13 A problem of communication which presents itself to every French Caribbean novelist (but which lies outside the scope of the present study) is the difficulty of conveying a primarily Creole social experience to a reading public which must be addressed in French, not in Creole (since the number of literate people who can also understand French Creole is severely limited). It is for this reason that theatrical productions, and radio dramatizations of novels, have an increasingly important role in West Indian cultural life.

Conclusion

14 Glissant, *La Case du commandeur*, p. 238.

15 Franketienne, *Les Affres d'un défi* (Port-au-Prince: Henri Deschamps, 1979), pp. 5, 221.

16 Louise Bennett, 'Back to Africa' (1947), reprinted in her collected verse *Jamaica Labrish*, intro. Rex Nettleford (Jamaica: Sangster, 1966), pp. 214-15.

17 Maryse Condé, *Hérémakhonon* (Paris: Union Générale d'Editions [10/18], 1976), p. 27. See also her more recent novel *Une saison à Rihata* (Paris: Robert Laffont, 1981).

18 Simone Schwarz-Bart, *Ti Jean L'horizon* (Paris: Editions du Seuil, 1979), pp. 13, 248.

19 Vincent Placoly, *La Vie et la mort de Marcel Gonstran* (Paris: Les Lettres Nouvelles, 1971), p. 101.

20 Xavier Orville, *L'Homme aux sept noms et des poussières* (Paris: Grasset, 1981), p. 71.

21 Glissant, interview with Anne Fabre-Luce, 'Des remèdes à l'aliénation antillaise', *La Quinzaine Littéraire* 351 (1-15 July 1981), p. 7. Glissant's concept of *antillanité*, analysed at length in his *Discours antillais*, may be compared with the notion of *américanité* advanced by the Haitian writer René Depestre in *Bonjour et adieu à la négritude*.

22 Jean Métellus, *Jacmel au crépuscule* (Paris: Gallimard, 1981), p. 345.

23 Glissant, *La Case du commandeur*, p. 235.

24 Daniel Maximin, *L'Isolé soleil* (Paris: Editions du Seuil, 1981), p. 212.

25 Derek Walcott, *The Star-apple Kingdom* (London: Jonathan Cape, 1980), p. 19.

Bibliography

Alexis, Jacques Stéphen. *Compère Général Soleil*. Paris: Gallimard, 1955.

Alexis, Jacques Stéphen. 'Prolegomena to a manifesto on the marvellous realism of the Haitians'. *Présence Africaine* (English ed.) 8/10 (1956), 251–75.

Alexis, Jacques Stéphen. *Les Arbres musiciens*. Paris: Gallimard, 1957.

Alexis, Jacques Stéphen. 'Où va le roman?' *Présence Africaine* 13 (1957), 81–101.

Alexis, Jacques Stéphen. *L'Espace d'un cillement*. Paris: Gallimard, 1959.

Allen, Don Cameron. *Mysteriously Meant: The Rediscovery of pagan symbolism and allegorical interpretation in the Renaissance*. Baltimore: Johns Hopkins Press, 1970.

André, Jacques. *Caraïbales: Etudes sur la littérature antillaise*. Paris: Editions Caribéennes, 1981.

Anselme, Rémy. 'Le phénomène Duvalier'. *Acoma* 4–5 (1973), 120–49.

Augier, F.R., S.C. Gordon, D.G. Hall and M. Reckord. *The Making of the West Indies*. London: Longman, 1960.

Beauvue-Fougeyrollas, Claudie. *Les Femmes antillaises*. Paris: L'Harmattan, 1979.

Bennett, Louise. *Jamaica Labrish*, intro. Rex Nettleford. Jamaica: Sangster, 1966.

Benoist, Jean, ed. *Les Sociétés antillaises: Etudes anthropologiques*. Montreal: Département d'anthropologie de l'Université de Montréal, 1966.

Bernabé, Jean. 'Contribution à l'étude de la diglossie littéraire: Le cas de *Pluie et vent sur Télumée Miracle*', in *Textes Etudes et Documents*, No. 2, ed. Roger Toumson. Paris: Editions Caribéennes, 1979, 103–30.

Berrou, Raphaël and Pradel Pompilus. *Histoire de la littérature haïtienne*, 2 vols. Port-au-Prince: Editions Caraïbes, 1975.

Burton, Richard D.E. *Assimilation or Independence? Prospects for Martinique*. Montreal: Centre for Developing-Area Studies, 1978.

Cailler, Bernadette. *Proposition poétique: une lecture de l'œuvre d'Aimé Césaire*. Sherbrooke: Naaman, 1976.

Cailler, Bernadette. 'Un itinéraire poétique: Edouard Glissant et l'anti-*Anabase*'. *Présence Francophone* 19 (1979), 107–32.

Campbell, Joseph. *The Hero with a Thousand Faces*. 1949; rpt. London: Abacus, 1975.

Campbell, Mavis Christine. *The Dynamics of Change in a Slave Society: A Sociopolitical History of the Free Coloreds of Jamaica, 1800–1865*. New Jersey and London: Associated University Presses, 1976.

Case, F.I. 'The Novels of Edouard Glissant'. *Black Images* 2, 3/4 (1973), 3–12, 47.

Castera *fils*, Georges. 'L'Expérience de la nuit et l'expérience du jour dans *Compère Général Soleil*'. *Europe* 501 (January 1971), 71–81.

Bibliography

Césaire, Aimé. *Cahier d'un retour au pays natal*. 1939; rpt. Paris: Présence Africaine, 1971.

Césaire, Aimé. *Return to My Native Land (Cahier d'un retour au pays natal)*, trans. John Berger and Anna Bostock, intro. Mazisi Kunene. Harmondsworth: Penguin Books, 1969.

Césaire, Aimé. *Cadastre*. Paris: Editions du Seuil, 1961.

Césaire, Aimé. *Toussaint Louverture*. Paris: Présence Africaine, 1961.

Césaire, Aimé. *Une tempête*. Paris: Editions du Seuil, 1969.

Césaire, Aimé. 'La Martinique telle qu'elle est'. *French Review* 53 (1979), 183–9.

Clarke, Edith. *My Mother who fathered me*. 2nd ed., London: Allen & Unwin, 1966.

Condé, Maryse. '*Pluie et vent sur Télumée Miracle* de Simone Schwarz-Bart'. *Présence Africaine* 84 (1972), 138–9.

Condé, Maryse. *Hérémakhonon*. Paris: Union Générale d'Editions (10/18), 1976.

Condé, Maryse. *La Civilisation du bossale*. Paris: L'Harmattan, 1978.

Condé, Maryse. *La Parole des femmes: Essai sur des romancières des Antilles de langue française*. Paris: L'Harmattan, 1979.

Condé, Maryse. 'Survivance et mort des mythes africains dans la littérature des Antilles francophones'. *L'Afrique littéraire et artistique* 54–5 (1979–80), 56–65.

Condé, Maryse. *Une saison à Rihata*. Paris: Robert Laffont, 1981.

Corzani, Jean. 'La Négritude aux Antilles françaises', in *Négritude africaine, négritude caraïbe*, ed. Jeanne-Lydie Goré, Paris: Editions de la Francité, 1973, 118–28.

Corzani, Jack. *La Littérature des Antilles-Guyane Françaises*. Fort-de-France: Désormeaux, 1978, 6 vols.

Craton, Michael. 'Perceptions of Slavery: A Preliminary Excursion into the possibilities of Oral History in Rural Jamaica', in *Old Roots in New Lands: Historical and Anthropological Perspectives on Black Experiences in the Americas*, ed. Ann M. Pescatello. Westport, Connecticut: Greenwood Press, 1977, 263–83.

Craton, Michael and James Walvin. *A Jamaican Plantation: The History of Worthy Park 1670–1970*. London: W.H. Allen, 1970.

Damas, L.-G. *Pigments*. Paris: Présence Africaine, 1937.

Dash, (J.) Michael. 'Jacques Stéphen Alexis'. *Black Images* 3, 4 (1974), 1–62.

Dash, J. Michael. *Literature and Ideology in Haiti, 1915–1961*. London: Macmillan, 1981.

Davidson, Basil. *The African Slave Trade: Precolonial History 1450–1850* (originally published as *Black Mother*). Boston: Atlantic-Little, Brown, 1961.

Debien, Gabriel. *Les Esclaves aux Antilles françaises, XVIIᵉ – XVIIIᵉ siécles*. Basse-Terre: Société d'Histoire de la Guadeloupe; Fort-de-France: Société d'Histoire de la Martinique, 1974.

Depestre, René. *Bonjour et adieu à la négritude*. Paris: Robert Laffont, 1980.

Deren, Maya. *The Voodoo Gods*. 1953; new ed. St Albans: Paladin, 1975.

Diederich, Bernard and Al Burt. *Papa Doc: Haiti and its Dictator*. 1969; rpt. Harmondsworth: Penguin Books, 1972.

Durand, Gilbert. *Les Structures anthropologiques de l'imaginaire*. Paris: Bordas, 1969.

Bibliography

Fanon, Frantz. *Black Skin, White Masks* (*Peau noire, masques blancs*), trans. Charles Lam Markmann. New York: Grove Press, 1967.

Fanon, Frantz. *Toward the African Revolution* (*Pour la révolution africaine*), trans. Haakon Chevalier. Harmondsworth: Penguin Books, 1970.

Fignolé, Jean-Claude. *Sur 'Gouverneurs de la rosée'*. Port-au-Prince: Editions Fardin, 1974.

Franketienne. *Les Affres d'un défi*. Port-au-Prince: Henri Deschamps, 1979.

Frye, Northrop. *Anatomy of Criticism*. 1957; rpt. Princeton: Princeton University Press, 1971.

Galíndez, Jesús de. *The Era of Trujillo*, ed. Russell H. Fitzgibbon. 1956 Spanish ed.; Tucson, Arizona: University of Arizona Press, 1973.

Galpérina, Eugénie, ed. *Jacques Roumain, Œuvres choisies*. Moscow: Editions du Progrès, 1964.

Garai, Jana. *The Book of Symbols*. London: Lorrimer, 1973.

Garret, Naomi M. *The Renaissance of Haitian Poetry*. Paris: Présence Africaine, 1963.

Gazarian-Gautier, Marie-Lise. 'Le Symbolisme religieux dans *Gouverneurs de la rosée* de Jacques Roumain'. *Présence Francophone* 7 (1973), 19–23.

Gisler, Antoine. *L'Esclavage aux Antilles françaises, XVIIe - XIXe siècle*. Fribourg: Editions Universitaires, 1965.

Glissant, Edouard. *Soleil de la conscience*. Paris: Editions du Seuil, 1956.

Glissant, Edouard. *La Lézarde*. Paris: Editions du Seuil, 1958.

Glissant, Edouard. *The Ripening* (*La Lézarde*), trans. Frances Frenaye. New York: George Braziller, 1959.

Glissant, Edouard. *Le Sel noir*. Paris: Editions du Seuil, 1960.

Glissant, Edouard. *Monsieur Toussaint*. Paris: Editions du Seuil, 1961.

Glissant, Edouard. *Le Quatrième Siècle*. Paris: Editions du Seuil, 1964.

Glissant, Edouard. *Poèmes*. Paris: Editions du Seuil, 1965.

Glissant, Edouard. *L'Intention poétique*. Paris: Editions du Seuil, 1969.

Glissant, Edouard. 'Action culturelle et pratique politique: propositions de base'. *Acoma* 4–5 (1973), 16–20.

Glissant, Edouard. *Malemort*. Paris: Editions du Seuil, 1975.

Glissant, Edouard. *Boises*. Angers and Paris: Editions Acoma, 1979.

Glissant, Edouard. *La Case du commandeur*. Paris: Editions du Seuil, 1981.

Glissant, Edouard. *Le Discours antillais*. Paris: Editions du Seuil, 1981.

Glissant, Edouard. Interview with Anne Fabre-Luce: 'Des remèdes à l'aliénation antillaise'. *La Quinzaine Littéraire* 351 (1–15 July 1981), 7–8.

Goré, Jeanne-Lydie, ed. *Négritude africaine, négritude caraïbe*. Paris: Editions de la Francité, 1973.

Goveia, E.V. *The West Indian slave laws of the 18th century*. Kingston: Caribbean Universities Press, 1970.

Grange, Bertrand de la. 'Haïti à la dérive'. *Le Monde*, 30 May 1981.

Guérin, Daniel. *Les Antilles décolonisées*, intro. Aimé Césaire. Paris: Présence Africaine, 1956.

Hall, James. *Dictionary of Subjects and Symbols in Art*. London: John Murray, 1974.

Hazard, Samuel. *Santo Domingo, Past and Present; with a Glance at Hayti*. New York: Harper & Brothers, 1873.

Henriques, Fernando. *Family and Colour in Jamaica*. London: Eyre & Spottiswoode, 1953.

Bibliography

Hezekiah, Randolph. 'Joseph Zobel: the Mechanics of Liberation'. *Black Images* 4, 3/4 (1975), 44–55.

Higman, B.W. *Slave Population and Economy in Jamaica, 1807–1834*. Cambridge: Cambridge University Press, 1976.

Hoffmann, Léon-François. 'Complexité linguistique et rhétorique dans *Gouverneurs de la rosée* de Jacques Roumain'. *Présence Africaine* 98 (1976), 145–61.

James, C.L.R. *The Black Jacobins*. 1938; rev. ed. New York: Vintage Books, 1963.

Ki-Zerbo, Joseph. *Histoire de l'Afrique noire*. Paris: Hatier, 1978.

Knight, Vere W. 'Edouard Glissant: The Novel as History Rewritten'. *Black Images* 3, 1 (1974), 64–79.

La Bruyère. *Characters*, trans. Henri van Laun. London: Oxford University Press, 1963.

Lacrosil, Michèle. *Sapotille et le serin d'argile*. Paris: Gallimard, 1960.

Lacrosil, Michèle. *Cajou*. Paris: Gallimard, 1961.

Lacrosil, Michèle. *Demain Jab-Herma*. Paris: Gallimard, 1967.

Lara, Oruno. *La Guadeloupe dans l'histoire*. 1921; new ed. Paris: L'Harmattan, 1979.

Laurence, K.O. *Immigration into the West Indies in the 19th century*. St Lawrence, Barbados: Caribbean Universities Press, 1971.

Leiris, Michel. *Contacts de civilisations en Martinique et en Guadeloupe*. Paris: Unesco, 1955.

Lemoine, Maurice. *Sucre amer: Esclaves aujourd'hui dans les Caraïbes*. Paris: Editions Encre, 1981.

Leyburn, James. *The Haitian People*. 1941; rev. ed. intro. Sidney W. Mintz. New Haven and London: Yale University Press, 1966.

Lubin, Maurice A. *L'Afrique dans la poésie haïtienne*. Port-au-Prince: Editions Panorama, 1965.

Makouta-Mboukou, Jean-Pierre. *Jacques Roumain: Essai sur la signification spirituelle et religieuse de son œuvre*. Université de Paris IV 1975. Lille: Atelier reproduction de thèses, Université de Lille III, 1978.

Maximin, Daniel. *L'Isolé soleil*. Paris: Editions du Seuil, 1981.

Métellus, Jean. *Jacmel au crépuscule*. Paris: Gallimard, 1981.

Migne, Jacques Paul, ed. *Patrologia Latina* (= *Patrologiae cursus completus . . . Series Latina*). Petit-Montrouge: Migne, 1844–96.

Miller, Errol L. 'Body Image, Physical Beauty and Colour among Jamaican Adolescents'. *Social and Economic Studies* 18, 1 (1969), 72–89.

Milner, David. *Children and Race*. Harmondsworth: Penguin Books, 1975.

Naipaul, V.S. *The Middle Passage*. London: André Deutsch, 1962.

Naipaul, V.S. 'Michael X and the Black Power Killings in Trinidad', in *The Return of Eva Peron*. London: André Deutsch, 1980, 1–91.

Ngal, Georges. 'L'Image et l'enracinement chez Aimé Césaire'. *Présence Francophone* 6 (1973), 5–28.

Ngal, M.a M. *Aimé Césaire: un homme à la recherche d'une patrie*. Dakar: Les Nouvelles Editions Africaines, 1975.

Nicholls, David. *From Dessalines to Duvalier: Race, Colour and National Independence in Haiti*. Cambridge: Cambridge University Press, 1979.

Ormerod, Beverley. '*Un plat de porc aux bananes vertes*'. *Essays in French Literature* 8 (1971), 82–93.

Ormerod, Beverley. 'Beyond *Négritude*: Some Aspects of the Work of

Bibliography

Édouard Glissant'. *Contemporary Literature* 15 (1974), 360–9.

Ormerod, Beverley. 'Myth, Rite and Symbol in *Gouverneurs de la rosée*'. *L'Esprit Créateur* 17 (1977), 123–32.

Ormerod, Beverley. 'L'Aïeule: figure dominante chez Simone Schwarz-Bart'. *Présence Francophone* 20 (1980), 95–106.

Orville, Xavier. *L'Homme aux sept noms et des poussières*. Paris: Grasset, 1981.

Padilla, Elena. 'Les Types sociaux de la campagne antillaise', in *Les Sociétés antillaises: études anthropologiques*, ed. Jean Benoist. Montreal: Département d'anthropologie de l'Université de Montréal, 1966, 29–37.

Patterson, Orlando. *The Sociology of Slavery*. London: MacGibbon & Kee, 1967.

Pépin, Ernest. '*Pluie et vent sur Télumée Miracle*: Le jeu des figures répétitives dans l'œuvre', in *Textes Etudes et Documents*, No. 2, ed. Roger Toumson. Paris: Editions Caribéennes, 1979, 75–101.

Pierre-Charles, Gérard. 'Mort et vie de Jacques Soleil'. *Europe* 501 (January 1971), 64–70.

Placoly, Vincent. *La Vie et la mort de Marcel Gonstran*. Paris: Les Lettres Nouvelles, 1971.

Price-Mars, Jean. *Ainsi parla l'oncle*. 1928; new ed. Ottawa: Leméac, 1973.

Ramchand, Kenneth. *The West Indian Novel and its Background*. London: Faber, 1970.

Rivers of Babylon (B. Dowe and F. McNaughton), sung by The Melodians on the soundtrack of *The Harder They Come*: Island Records C34684, 1972.

Roumain, Jacques. *La Montagne ensorcelée*. 1931; new ed. Paris: Les Editeurs Français Réunis, 1972.

Roumain, Jacques. *Gouverneurs de la rosée*. 1946; rpt. Paris: Les Editeurs Français Réunis, 1964.

Roumain, Jacques. *Masters of the Dew* (*Gouverneurs de la rosée*), trans. Langston Hughes and Mercer Cook, intro. J. Michael Dash. London: Heinemann, 1978.

Rowland, Beryl. *Animals with Human Faces: A Guide to Animal Symbolism*. London: Allen & Unwin, 1974.

Roy, Claude. 'Clarté d'un soleil noir'. *Le Nouvel Observateur* 909 (9–16 April 1982), 52–3.

Rubin, Vera, 'Les Problèmes de la recherche anthropologique dans la Caraïbe', in *Les Sociétés antillaises: études anthropologiques*, ed. Jean Benoist. Montreal: Département d'anthropologie de l'Université de Montréal, 1966, 100–14.

Sartre, Jean-Paul. 'Orphée noir', introduction to Léopold Sédar Senghor's *Anthologie de la nouvelle poésie nègre et malgache*. 1948; rpt. Paris: Presses Universitaires de France, 1969.

Schwarz-Bart, Simone. *Pluie et vent sur Télumée Miracle*. Paris: Editions du Seuil, 1972.

Schwarz-Bart, Simone. *The Bridge of Beyond* (*Pluie et vent sur Télumée Miracle*), trans. Barbara Bray, intro. Bridget Jones. London: Heinemann, 1982.

Schwarz-Bart, Simone. Interview with Roger Toumson: 'Sur les pas de Fanotte', in *Textes Etudes et Documents*, No. 2, ed. Roger Toumson. Paris: Editions Caribéennes, 1979, 13–23.

Schwarz-Bart, Simone. *Ti Jean L'horizon*. Paris: Editions du Seuil, 1979.

Senghor, L.S. *Prose and Poetry*, trans. John Reed and Clive Wake. London: Oxford University Press, 1965.

Bibliography

Serres, Michel. 'Christ noir'. *Critique* 29 (1973), 3-25.

Shelton, Marie-Denise. 'Le paysan dans le roman haïtien: *Le drame de la terre*'. *Présence Francophone* 22 (1981), 157-71.

Sheridan, Richard. *The Development of the Plantations to 1750*. Kingston: Caribbean Universities Press, 1970.

Sill, Gertrude Grace. *A Handbook of Symbols in Christian Art*. London: Cassell, 1976.

Souffrant, Claude. *Une Négritude socialiste: Religion et développement chez J. Roumain, J.-S. Alexis, L. Hughes*. Paris: L'Harmattan, 1978.

Soyinka, Wole. *Myth, Literature and the African World*. Cambridge: Cambridge University Press, 1976.

Tervarent, Guy de, *Attributs et symboles dans l'art profane 1450-1600*. Geneva: Droz, 1958.

Toumson, Roger. *'Pluie et vent sur Télumée Miracle*: Une rêverie encyclopédique: sa structure, son projet idéologique', in *Textes Etudes et Documents*, No. 2, ed. Roger Toumson. Paris: Editions Caribéennes, 1979, 25-73.

Toumson, Roger, ed. *Textes Etudes et Documents*, No. 2: *Pluie et vent sur Télumée Miracle de Simone Schwarz-Bart*. Publication of GEREC, Centre Universitaire Antilles-Guyane. Paris: Editions Caribéennes, 1979.

Wagner, Jean. *Black Poets of the United States*, trans. Kenneth Douglas. Urbana: University of Illinois Press, 1973.

Walcott, Derek. *Another Life*. London: Jonathan Cape, 1973.

Walcott, Derek. *The Star-apple Kingdom*. London: Jonathan Cape, 1980.

Weston, Jessie L. *From Ritual to Romance*. Cambridge: Cambridge University Press, 1920.

Zobel, Joseph. *Diab'-là*. Paris: Nouvelles Editions Latines, 1946.

Zobel, Joseph. *Laghia de la mort*. 1946; rev. ed. Paris: Présence Africaine, 1978.

Zobel, Joseph. *La Rue Cases-Nègres*. 1950; rpt. Paris: Présence Africaine, 1974.

Zobel, Joseph. *Black Shack Alley (La Rue Cases-Nègres)*, trans. and intro. Keith Q. Warner. London: Heinemann, 1980.

Zobel, Joseph. *La Fête à Paris*. Paris: La Table Ronde, 1953.

Index

Africa, 1–5, 8–10, 44–6, 47, 132–3, 136–7; African-born slaves, 56, 58, 61; *see also* Guinea
Alexis, Jacques Stéphen, 87, 133; *Les Arbres musiciens*, 88; *Comrade General Sun (Compère Général Soleil)*, 13–14, 15, 25, 88–106, 135; *L'Espace d'un cillement*, 92–3, 137
alienation, 2–4, 8, 10–14, 37–8, 129, 132, 135–7; orphanhood as image of, 113, 134; *see also* colour and social class; Fall; sugar-cane

Bennett, Louise, 136
boat symbolism, 8, 109, 111–12, 123–4, 125, 126, 127
Brierre, Jean, 25

Césaire, Aimé, 50, 108; *Cahier d'un retour au pays natal*, 2–11, 13, 56, 73, 76, 99, 109, 122, 132–5; *Discours sur le colonialisme*, 6; *Une tempête*, 3
Cham, symbol of black race, 81
Christianity, 1, 115; rejection of, 21, 99; Christian symbolism, 7, 30, 32–3, 67, 81, 104, 129; *see also* Fall, paradise, salvation, tree
colonialism, *see* colour and social class; French presence in Caribbean; plantations
colour and social class, 13, 17–18, 56–64, 66–73, 75–9, 81–2, 87, 88–9, 90, 92–3, 96–9, 116–17, 120–1
Condé, Maryse, 136
coumbite, 20, 25–7, 32–3, 105, 135
crow, symbol of black race, 129–30

Damas, Léon, 1–2
Depestre, René, 87, 139n
dog as symbol, 51–3, 104
drum symbolism, 25–6, 120, 121, 126, 128

Fall, theme of, 1–5, 11–12, 20, 25–6, 54, 72–3, 115–16, 123–4, 132, 134; *see also* alienation
Fanon, Frantz, 9–10, 78
Franketienne, 136
French presence in Caribbean, 3, 36, 38–9, 49–50, 133–4

Glissant, Edouard, 36, 122, 137; *Boises*, 36, 37, 54; *La Case du commandeur*, 37–8, 135, 137; *Le Discours antillais*, 54n, 135, 137; *L'Intention poétique*, 37, 38, 39, 41, 45, 47; *Malemort*, 37, 38, 39, 43, 45, 47, 50, 53, 54, 135; *Monsieur Toussaint*, 36; *Le Quatrième Siècle*, 37, 38, 39, 41, 42, 44–5, 48, 52, 135; *The Ripening (La Lézarde)*, 12, 14, 37, 38, 39–54, 134, 135–6; *Soleil de la conscience*, 45
Guadeloupe, 62, 64, 133, 137; in fiction, 73–84, 108–30, 136–7; *see also* French presence in Caribbean
Guinea, 20–1, 25, 67

Haiti, 17–19, 56, 62, 87–8, 133; in fiction, 11, 13–14, 19–33, 88–106, 136; massacre on Dominican frontier, 88, 103–4; US occupation, 17, 18, 19, 87, 88, 93; *see also* colour and social class;

Marxism; voodoo
Harlem Renaissance, 4
history, attitudes to, 36-7, 45, 52, 134-5

La Bruyère, 57
Lacrosil, Michèle, 57-8, 135; *Tomorrow Jab-Herma (Demain Jab-Herma)*, 12, 13, 14, 57, 64, 73-84, 134
light/dark symbolism, 44-6, 52, 89-91, 94-5, 101, 103-5

maroons, 37, 41, 44, 46, 50, 52-3, 104, 127
Martinique, 3, 58, 62-4, 137; in fiction and poetry, 4, 10, 36-54, 64-73, 132; *see also* French presence in Caribbean
Marxism: Alexis, 14-15, 87-8, 105, 133, 135; in *Comrade General Sun*, 89-90, 94, 100-2, 104-5; Césaire, 6-7; Roumain, 14, 18, 133, 135; in *Masters of the Dew*, 24-5, 29
matriarchal households, 66, 113
Maximin, Daniel, 137
Métellus, Jean, 137

Naipaul, V. S., 2, 138n
Négritude, 2, 3, 6, 8-11, 18, 84

Orville, Xavier, 137

paradise, theme of, 1-11, 20-1, 32-3, 40, 81, 88, 109, 128, 132
Placoly, Vincent, 137
plantations, 56-84, 103, 126, 133-4; Guadeloupean sugar estate, 64, 73-84; Martinican estate village, 64-73; slave plantations, 56-63; *see also* sugar-cane
Price-Mars, Jean, 4, 18

river symbolism, 37-8, 40-1, 46-8,

51, 54, 114, 118; *see also* water
Roumain, Jacques, 17-18, 25, 28, 88, 94, 133, 135; *Masters of the Dew (Gouverneurs de la rosée)*, 11-12, 14, 18-33, 84, 99-100, 103, 108, 134; *La Montagne ensorcelée*, 19

salvation/redemption, theme of, 5-8, 11, 25, 28, 30-1, 44, 53, 90, 122, 133, 134
Sartre, Jean-Paul, 2, 78
Schwarz-Bart, Simone, 135; *The Bridge of Beyond (Pluie et vent sur Télumée Miracle)*, 12, 13, 15, 108-30, 134; *Ti Jean L'horizon*, 136-7
Senghor, Léopold Sédar, 3, 10
slavery, 1, 56-63; in fiction and poetry, 1-3, 6, 10-11, 36-7, 42, 75, 114-16, 128, 136; *see also* colour and social class; sugar-cane
Soyinka, Wole, 10
sugar-cane as symbol, 6, 12, 41-4, 50, 54, 57, 103, 110, 126-8; *see also* plantations; slavery
surrealist movement, 8-9

Toussaint Louverture, 11, 17, 101-2
tree symbolism, 7, 27-9, 46-7, 52, 108-9, 116, 122-4, 127, 128, 130, 132-3
Trujillo, 88, 93, 103

voodoo, 11, 21-3, 28-30, 33, 87, 99-100, 133, 136; *see also* witch-doctor

Walcott, Derek, 135, 138
water symbolism, 7-8, 10, 23, 25-6, 31-3, 47, 49, 54, 109-10, 127; *see also* boat; river
witch-doctor, 3, 5, 45-6, 83-4, 119, 124; *see also* voodoo

Zobel, Joseph, 58, 134; *Black Shack Alley (La Rue Cases-Nègres)*, 12, 14, 57, 64-73, 98, 134; *Diab'-là*, 66; *La Fête à Paris*, 71-2; *Laghia de la mort*, 70

Titles of related interest published by Heinemann

Black Shack Alley
Joseph Zobel
Translated and introduced by Keith Warner

José grows up on a plantation in Martinique with his grandmother, M'man Tine. Soon he moves to Lycée where he looks at the adult world with eyes of innocence and becomes aware of the realities of life for blacks. Zobel's picture of colonial society in the 1930s is vividly realistic.

1980   192pp   435 98800 X   CWS 21

Masters of the Dew
Jacques Roumain
Translated by Langston Hughes and Mercer Cook
Introduction by J. Michael Dash

The outstanding Haitian novel which tells of Manuel's struggle to keep his little community from starvation during drought. At the same time the story of his love for Annaise is told with great sensitiveness. 'A work of unusual freshness and beauty.' *New York Times*

1978   192pp   435 98745 3   CWS 12

The Bridge of Beyond
Simone Schwarz-Bart
Translated by Barbara Bray
Introduction by Bridget Jones

In this story of the proud Lougandor women, Simone Schwarz-Bart shows the survival power of the women of Guadeloupe who live in conditions of extreme poverty and deprivation and yet who are filled with dauntless courage and love for life.

1982   192pp   435 98770 4   CWS 27

The West Indian Novel and its Background
Kenneth Ramchand
Second Edition

The revised and updated edition of this well-established book has been long awaited. Novelists from the Caribbean – V.S. Naipaul, Wilson Harris, Edgar Mittelholzer, Samuel Selvon, Earl Lovelace, John Hearne and many others – have made a rich and varied contribution to contemporary literature. Dr Ramchand fills in the social and historical background essential to a full critical understanding of their achievements.

1983   320pp   435 98665 1   Studies in Caribbean Literature

West Indian Poetry
Lloyd W. Brown
Second Edition

In this well-researched study Professor Lloyd Brown traces the development of West Indian poetry from its origins in 1760 to the present day in the light of a growing Caribbean consciousness. He shows how the poetry is no simple extension of English literature.

1984   208pp   435 91830 3   Studies in Caribbean Literature

The Novels of George Lamming
Sandra Pouchet Paquet

This is the first comprehensive study of George Lamming. *In the Castle of My Skin*, first published in 1953, is established as one of the classics of Caribbean writing. The fact that this and his other works have recently become available in paperback gives value to this brisk, book-by-book study.

1982   144pp   435 91831 1   Studies in Caribbean Literature